The Poems of Goethe

Translated in the original metres
by Edgar Alfred Bowring

Contents

Original Dedication
Original Preface
Preface to the Second Edition
List of the principal Works of Goethe
Author's Dedication

SONGS
Sound, sweet Song, from some far Land
To the kind Reader
The New Amadis
When the Fox dies, his Skin counts
The Heathrose
Blindman's Buff
Christel
The Coy One
The Convert
Preservation
The Muses' Son
Found
Like and Like
Reciprocal Invitation to the Dance
Self-Deceit
Declaration of War
Lover in all Shapes
The Goldsmith's Apprentice
Answers in a Game of Questions
Different Emotions on the same Spot
Who'll buy Gods of love?
The Misanthrope
Different Threats
Maiden Wishes
Motives
True Enjoyment
The Farewell
The Beautiful Night.
Happiness and Vision
Living Remembrance
The Bliss of Absence
To Luna
The Wedding Night
Mischievous Joy
Apparent Death
November Song
To the Chosen One
First Loss
After Sensations
Proximity of the Beloved One
Presence
To the Distant One
By the River
Farewell

The Exchange
Welcome and Farewell
New Love, New Life
To Belinda
May Song
With a painted Ribbon
With a golden Necklace
On the Lake
From the Mountain
Flower-Salute
In Summer
May Song
Premature Spring
Autumn Feelings
Restless Love
The Shepherd's Lament
Comfort in Tears
Night Song
Longing
To Mignon
The Mountain Castle
The Spirit's Salute
To a Golden Heart that he wore round his neck
The Bliss of Sorrow
The Wanderer's Night-song
The Same
The Hunter's Even-Song
To the Moon
To Lina
Ever and Everywhere
Petition
To his Coy One
Night Thoughts
To Lida
Proximity
Reciprocal
Rollicking Hans
The Freebooter
Joy and Sorrow
March
April
May
June
Next Year's Spring
At Midnight Hour
To the rising full Moon
The Bridegroom
Such, such is he who pleaseth me
Sicilian Song
Swiss Song
Finnish Song

Gipsy Song
The Destruction of Magdeburg

FAMILIAR SONGS.
On the New Year
Anniversary Song
The Spring Oracle
The Happy Couple
Song of Fellowship
Constancy in Change
Table Song
Wont and Done
General Confession
Coptic Song
Another
Vanitas! vanitatum vanitas!
Fortune of War
Open Table
The Reckoning
Ergo Bibamus!
Epiphanias

BALLADS.
Mignon
The Minstrel
Ballad of the banished and returning Count
The Violet
The Faithless Boy
The Erl-King
Johanna Sebus
The Fisherman
The King of Thule
The Beauteous Flower..
Sir Curt's Wedding Journey
Wedding Song
The Treasure-digger
The Rat-catcher
The Spinner
Before a Court of Justice
The Page and the Miller's Daughter
The Youth and the Millstream
The Maid of the Mill's Treachery
The Maid of the Mill's Repentance
The Traveller and the Farm-Maiden
Effects at a distance
The Walking Bell
Faithful Eckart
The Dance of Death
The Pupil in Magic
The Bride of Corinth
The God and the Bayadere

The Pariah

I. The Pariah's Prayer.
II. Legend
III. The Pariah's Thanks
Death--lament of the noble Wife of Asan Aga

CANTATAS.
Idyll
Rinaldo
The First Walpurgis-Night

ODES.
Three Odes to my Friend
Mahomet's Song
Spirit Song over the Waters
My Goddess
Winter Journey over the Hartz Mountains
To Father Kronos. Written in a Post-chaise
The Wanderer's Storm Song
The Sea-Voyage
The Eagle and Dove
Prometheus
Ganymede
The Boundaries of Humanity
The Godlike

MISCELLANEOUS POEMS.
The German Parnassus.
Lily's Menagerie
To Charlotte
Love's Distresses
The Musagetes
Morning Lament
The Visit
The Magic Net
The Goblet
To the Grasshopper. After Anacreon
From the Sorrows of Young Werther
Trilogy of Passion :Ä

I. To Werther

II. Elegy
III. Atonement
The Remembrance of the Good
When I was still a youthful Wight
For Ever
From an Album of 1604
Lines on seeing Schiller's Skull
Royal Prayer

Human Feelings
On the Divan
Hans Sachs' Poetical Mission

SONNETS.
The Friendly Meeting
In a Word
The Maiden Speaks
Growth
Food in Travel
Departure
The Loving One Writes.
The Loving One once more
She Cannot End
Nemesis
The Christmas Box
The Warning
The Epochs
The Doubters and the Lovers
Charade

EPIGRAMS.
To Originals
The Soldier's Consolation
Genial Impulse
Neither this nor that
The way to behave
The best
As broad as it's long
The Rule of Life
The same, expanded
Calm at Sea
The Prosperous Voyage
Courage
My only Property
Admonition
Old Age
Epitaph
Rules for Monarchs
Paulo post futuri
The Fool's Epilogue

PARABLES.
Joy
Explanation of an antique Gem
Cat-Pie
Legend
Authors
The Critic
The Dilettante and the Critic
The Wrangler

The Yelpers
The Stork's Vocation
Celebrity
Playing at Priests
Songs
Poetry
A Parable
Should e'er the loveless day remain
A Plan the Muses entertained
The Death of the Fly
By the River
The Fox and Crane
The Fox and Huntsman
The Frogs
The Wedding
Burial
Threatening Signs
The Buyers
The Mountain Village
Symbols
Three Palinodias :--

I. The Smoke that from thine Altar blows.

II. Conflict of Wit and Beauty
III. Rain and Rainbow.
Valediction
The Country Schoolmaster
The Legend of the Horseshoe
A Symbol

ART.
The Drops of Nectar
The Wanderer
I Love as a Landscape Painter

GOD, SOUL, AND WORLD.
Rhymed Distichs
Prooemion
The Metamorphosis of Plants

PROVERBS
TAME XENIA

RELIGION AND CHURCH.
Thoughts on Jesus Christ's descent into Hell

ANTIQUES.
Leopold, Duke of Brunswick
To the Husbandman
Anacreon's Grave

The Brethren
Measure of Time
Warning
Solitude
The Chosen Cliff
The Consecrated Spot
The Instructors
The Unequal Marriage.
Excuse
Sakontala
The Muse's Mirror
Phoebus and Hermes
The New Amor
The Garlands
The Swiss Alps
Distichs

VENETIAN EPIGRAMS.

ELEGIES.
Roman Elegies
Alexis and Dora
Hermann and Dorothea

WEST-EASTERN DIVAN.

I. Minstrel's Book :--

Talismans
The Four Favours
Discord
Song and Structure

II. Book of Hafis :--
The Unlimited
To Hafis

III. Book of Love :--

The Types
One Pair More
Love's Torments

IV. Book of Contemplation :--

Five Things
For Woman
Firdusi

Suleika

V. Book of Gloom :--
It is a Fault

VI. Book of Proverbs

VII. Book of Timur :--

The Winter and Timur
To Suleika

VIII. Book of Suleika :--

Suleika's Love
Hatem
Suleika
Love for Love
Hatem
The Loving One speaks
The Loving One again
These tufted Branches fair
Suleika
The Sublime Type
Suleika
The Reunion
Suleika
In thousand forms

IX. The Convivial Book :--

Can the Koran from Eternity be?
Ye've often for our Drunkenness

X. Book of Parables :--

From Heaven there fell upon the foaming wave
Bulbul's Song
In the Koran with strange delight.
All kinds of Men.
It is good

XI. Book of the Parsees :--

The Bequest of the ancient Persian faith

XII. Book of Paradise:
The Privileged Men
The favoured Beasts
The Seven Sleepers

SONGS FROM VARIOUS PLAYS, ETC.
From Faust :--

Dedication

Prologue in Heaven

Chorus of Angels

Chorus of Spirits

Margaret at her Spinning Wheel

Garden Scene

Margaret's Song
From FaustÄPart II.:--

Ariel's Song and Chorus of Spirits

Scene the last
From Iphigenia in Tauris :--

Song of the Fates
From Gotz von Berlichingen :--

Liebetraut's Song
From Egmont :--

Clara and Brackenburg's Song

Clara's Song
From Wilhelm Meister's Apprenticeship :--

Who never eat with tears his bread

Who gives himself to Solitude

My Grief no Mortals know

Sing no more in mournful tones

Epilogue to Schiller's Song of the Bell

THE POEMS OF GOETHE

BY

Translated in the original metres
by Edgar Alfred Bowring

The Poems of Goethe

Translated in the original metres by Edgar Alfred Bowring

THE TRANSLATOR'S ORIGINAL DEDICATION.

TO THE COUNTESS GRANVILLE.

MY DEAR LADY GRANVILLE,--

THE reluctance which must naturally be felt by any one in venturing to give to the world a book such as the present, where the beauties of the great original must inevitably be diminished, if not destroyed, in the process of passing through the translator's hands, cannot but be felt in all its force when that translator has not penetrated beyond the outer courts of the poetic fane, and can have no hope of advancing further, or of reaching its sanctuary. But it is to me a subject of peculiar satisfaction that your kind permission to have your name inscribed upon this page serves to attain a twofold end--one direct and personal, and relating to the present day; the other reflected and historical, and belonging to times long gone by. Of the first little need now be said, for the privilege is wholly mine, in making this dedication: as to the second, one word of explanation will suffice for those who have made the greatest poet of Germany, almost of the world, their study, and to whom the story of his life is not unknown. All who have followed the career of GOETHE are familiar with the name and character of DALBERG, and also with the deep and lasting friendship that existed between them, from which SCHILLER too was not absent; recalling to the mind the days of old, when a Virgil and a Horace and a Maecenas sat side by side.

Remembering, then, the connection that, in a former century, was formed and riveted between your illustrious ancestor and him whom it is the object of these pages to represent, I deem it a happy augury that the link then established finds itself not wholly severed even now (although its strength may be immeasurably weakened in the comparison), inasmuch as this page brings them once more in contact, the one in the person of his own descendant, the other in that of the translator of his Poems.

Believe me, with great truth,
Very faithfully yours,
EDGAR A. BOWRING.
London, April, 1853.

ORIGINAL PREFACE.

I feel no small reluctance in venturing to give to the public a work of the character of that indicated by the title-page to the present volume; for, difficult as it must always be to render satisfactorily into one's own tongue the writings of the bards of other lands, the responsibility assumed by the translator is immeasurably increased when he attempts to transfer the thoughts of those great men, who have lived for all the world and for all ages, from the language in which they were originally clothed, to one to which they may as yet have been strangers. Preeminently is this the case with Goethe, the most masterly of all the master minds of modern times, whose name is already inscribed on the tablets of immortality, and whose fame already extends over the earth, although as yet only in its infancy. Scarcely have two decades passed away since he ceased to dwell among men, yet he now stands before us, not as a mere individual, like those whom the world is wont to call great, but as a type, as an emblem--the recognised emblem and representative of the human mind in its present stage of culture and advancement.

Among the infinitely varied effusions of Goethe's pen, perhaps there are none which are of as general interest as his Poems, which breathe the very spirit of Nature, and embody the real music of the feelings. In Germany, they are universally known, and are considered as the most delightful of his works. Yet in this country, this kindred country, sprung from the same stem, and so strongly resembling her sister in so many points, they are nearly unknown. Almost the only poetical work of the greatest Poet that the world has seen for ages, that is really and generally read in England, is Faust, the translations of which are almost endless; while no single person has as yet appeared to attempt to give, in an English dress, in any collective or systematic manner, those smaller productions of the genius of Goethe which it is the object of the present volume to lay before the reader, whose indulgence is requested for its many imperfections. In addition to the beauty of the language in which the Poet has given utterance to his thoughts, there is a depth of meaning in those thoughts which is not easily discoverable at first sight, and the translator incurs great risk of overlooking it, and of giving a prosaic effect to that which in the original contains the very essence of poetry. It is probably this difficulty that has deterred others from undertaking the task I have set myself, and in which I do not pretend to do more than attempt to give an idea of the minstrelsy of one so unrivalled, by as truthful an interpretation of it as lies in my power.

The principles which have guided me on the present occasion are the same as those followed in the translation of Schiller's complete Poems that was published by me in 1851, namely, as literal a rendering of the original as is consistent with good English, and also a very strict adherence to the metre of the original. Although translators usually allow themselves great license in both these points, it appears to me that by so doing they of necessity destroy the very soul of the work they profess to translate. In fact, it is not a translation, but a paraphrase that they give. It may perhaps be thought that the present translations go almost to the other extreme, and that a rendering of metre, line for line, and word for word, makes it impossible to preserve the poetry of the original both in substance and in sound. But experience has convinced me that it is not so, and that great fidelity is even the most essential element of success, whether in translating poetry or prose. It was therefore very satisfactory to me to find that the principle laid down by me to myself in translating Schiller met with the very general, if not universal, approval of the reader. At the same time, I have endeavoured to profit in the case of this, the younger born of the two attempts made by me to transplant the muse of Germany to the shores of Britain, by the criticisms, whether friendly or hostile, that have been evoked or provoked by the appearance of its elder brother.

As already mentioned, the latter contained the whole of the Poems of Schiller. It is impossible, in anything like the same compass, to give all the writings of Goethe comprised under the general title of Gedichte, or poems. They contain between 30,000 and 40,000 verses, exclusive of his plays. and similar works. Very many of these would be absolutely without interest to the English reader,--such as those having only a local application, those addressed to individuals, and so on. Others again, from their extreme length, could only be published in separate volumes. But the impossibility of giving all need form no obstacle to giving as much as possible; and it so happens that the real interest of Goethe's Poems centres in those classes of them which are not too diffuse to run any risk when translated of offending the reader by their too great number. Those by far the more generally admired are the Songs and Ballads, which are about 150 in number, and the whole of which are contained in this volume (with the exception of one or two of the former, which have been, on consideration, left out by me owing to their trifling and uninteresting nature). The same may be said of the Odes, Sonnets, Miscellaneous Poems, &c.

In addition to those portions of Goethe's poetical works which are given in this complete form, specimens of the different other classes of them, such as the Epigrams, Elegies, &c., are added, as well as a collection of the various Songs found in his Plays, making a total number of about 400 Poems, embraced in the present volume.

A sketch of the life of Goethe is prefixed, in order that the reader may have before him both the Poet himself and the Poet's offspring, and that he may see that the two are but one--that Goethe lives in his works, that his works lived in him.

The dates of the different Poems are appended throughout, that of the first publication being given, when that of the composition is unknown. The order of arrangement adopted is that of the authorized German editions. As Goethe would never arrange them himself in the chronological order of their composition, it has become impossible to do so, now that he is dead. The plan adopted in the present volume would therefore seem to be the best, as it facilitates reference to the original. The circumstances attending or giving rise to the production of any of the Poems will be found specified in those cases in which they have been ascertained by me.

Having said thus much by way of explanation, I now leave the book to speak for itself, and to testify to its own character. Whether viewed with a charitable eye by the kindly reader, who will make due allowance for the difficulties attending its execution, or received by the critic, who will judge of it only by its own merits, with the unfriendly welcome which it very probably deserves, I trust that I shall at least be pardoned for making an attempt, a failure in which does not necessarily imply disgrace, and which, by leading the way, may perhaps become the means of inducing some abler and more worthy (but not more earnest) labourer to enter upon the same field, the riches of which will remain unaltered and undiminished in value, even although they may be for the moment tarnished by the hands of the less skilful workman who first endeavours to transplant them to a foreign soil.

PREFACE TO THE SECOND EDITION.

I have taken advantage of the publication of a Second Edition of my translation of the Poems of Goethe (originally published in 1853), to add to the Collection a version of the much admired classical Poem of Hermann and Dorothea, which was previously omitted by me in consequence of its length. Its universal popularity, however, and the fact that it exhibits the versatility of Goethe's talents to a greater extent than, perhaps, any other of his poetical works, seem to call for its admission into the present volume.

On the other hand I have not thought it necessary to include the sketch of Goethe's Life that accompanied the First Edition. At the time of its publication, comparatively little was known in this country of the incidents of his career, and my sketch was avowedly written as a temporary stop-gap, as it were, pending the production of some work really deserving the tittle of a life of Goethe. Not to mention other contributions to the literature of the subject, Mr. Lewis's important volumes give the English reader all the information he is likely to require respecting Goethe's career, and my short memoir appeared to be no longer required.

I need scarcely add that I have availed myself of this opportunity to make whatever improvements have suggested themselves to me in my original version of these Poems.

E. A. B.
London, 1874.

THE POEMS OF GOETHE.

DEDICATION.

The morn arrived; his footstep quickly scared

The gentle sleep that round my senses clung,
And I, awak'ning, from my cottage fared,

And up the mountain side with light heart sprung;
At every step I felt my gaze ensnared

By new-born flow'rs that full of dew-drops hung;
The youthful day awoke with ecstacy,
And all things quicken'd were, to quicken me.

And as I mounted, from the valley rose

A streaky mist, that upward slowly spread,
Then bent, as though my form it would enclose,

Then, as on pinions, soar'd above my head:
My gaze could now on no fair view repose,

in mournful veil conceal'd, the world seem'd dead;
The clouds soon closed around me, as a tomb,
And I was left alone in twilight gloom.

At once the sun his lustre seem'd to pour,

And through the mist was seen a radiant light;
Here sank it gently to the ground once more,

There parted it, and climb'd o'er wood and height.
How did I yearn to greet him as of yore,

After the darkness waxing doubly bright!
The airy conflict ofttimes was renew'd,
Then blinded by a dazzling glow I stood.

Ere long an inward impulse prompted me

A hasty glance with boldness round to throw;
At first mine eyes had scarcely strength to see,

For all around appear'd to burn and glow.
Then saw I, on the clouds borne gracefully,

A godlike woman hov'ring to and fro.
In life I ne'er had seen a form so fair--
She gazed at me, and still she hover'd there.

"Dost thou not know me?" were the words she said

In tones where love and faith were sweetly bound;
"Knowest thou not Her who oftentimes hath shed

The purest balsam in each earthly wound?
Thou knows't me well; thy panting heart I led

To join me in a bond with rapture crown'd.
Did I not see thee, when a stripling, yearning
To welcome me with tears, heartfelt and burning?"

"Yes!" I exclaim'd, whilst, overcome with joy,

I sank to earth; "I long have worshipp'd thee;
Thou gav'st me rest, when passions rack'd the boy,

Pervading ev'ry limb unceasingly;
Thy heav'nly pinions thou didst then employ

The scorching sunbeams to ward off from me.
From thee alone Earth's fairest gifts I gain'd,
Through thee alone, true bliss can be obtain'd.

"Thy name I know not; yet I hear thee nam'd

By many a one who boasts thee as his own;
Each eye believes that tow'rd thy form 'tis aim'd,

Yet to most eyes thy rays are anguish-sown.
Ah! whilst I err'd, full many a friend I claim'd,

Now that I know thee, I am left alone;
With but myself can I my rapture share,
I needs must veil and hide thy radiance fair.

She smiled, and answering said: "Thou see'st how wise,

How prudent 'twas but little to unveil!
Scarce from the clumsiest cheat are clear'd thine eyes,

Scarce hast thou strength thy childish bars to scale,
When thou dost rank thee 'mongst the deities,

And so man's duties to perform would'st fail!
How dost thou differ from all other men?
Live with the world in peace, and know thee then!"

"Oh, pardon me," I cried, "I meant it well:

Not vainly did'st thou bless mine eyes with light;
For in my blood glad aspirations swell,

The value of thy gifts I know aright!
Those treasures in my breast for others dwell,

The buried pound no more I'll hide from sight.
Why did I seek the road so anxiously,
If hidden from my brethren 'twere to be?"

And as I answer'd, tow'rd me turn'd her face,

With kindly sympathy, that god-like one;
Within her eye full plainly could I trace

What I had fail'd in, and what rightly done.
She smiled, and cured me with that smile's sweet grace,

To new-born joys my spirit soar'd anon;
With inward confidence I now could dare
To draw yet closer, and observe her there.

Through the light cloud she then stretch'd forth her hand,

As if to bid the streaky vapour fly:
At once it seemed to yield to her command,

Contracted, and no mist then met mine eye.
My glance once more survey'd the smiling land,

Unclouded and serene appear'd the sky.
Nought but a veil of purest white she held,
And round her in a thousand folds it swell'd.

"I know thee, and I know thy wav'ring will.

I know the good that lives and glows in thee!"--
Thus spake she, and methinks I hear her still--

"The prize long destined, now receive from me;
That blest one will be safe from ev'ry ill,

Who takes this gift with soul of purity,--"
The veil of Minstrelsy from Truth's own hand,
Of sunlight and of morn's sweet fragrance plann'd.

"And when thou and thy friends at fierce noon-day

Are parched with heat, straight cast it in the air!
Then Zephyr's cooling breath will round you play,

Distilling balm and flowers' sweet incense there;
The tones of earthly woe will die away,

The grave become a bed of clouds so fair,
To sing to rest life's billows will be seen,
The day be lovely, and the night serene."--

Come, then, my friends! and whensoe'er ye find

Upon your way increase life's heavy load;
If by fresh-waken'd blessings flowers are twin'd

Around your path, and golden fruits bestow'd,
We'll seek the coming day with joyous mind!

Thus blest, we'll live, thus wander on our road
And when our grandsons sorrow o'er our tomb,
Our love, to glad their bosoms, still shall bloom.

SONGS.

Late resounds the early strain;
Weal and woe in song remain.

SOUND, SWEET SONG.

SOUND, sweet song, from some far land,
Sighing softly close at hand,

Now of joy, and now of woe!

Stars are wont to glimmer so.

Sooner thus will good unfold;
Children young and children old
Gladly hear thy numbers flow.

1820[1].

---

1   In the cases in which the date is marked thus (*), it
    signifies the original date of publication--the year of
    composition not being known. In other cases, the date given is
    that of the actual composition. All the poems are arranged in the
    order of the recognised German editions.

TO THE KIND READER.

No one talks more than a Poet;
Fain he'd have the people know it.

Praise or blame he ever loves;
None in prose confess an error,
Yet we do so, void of terror,

In the Muses' silent groves.

What I err'd in, what corrected,
What I suffer'd, what effected,

To this wreath as flow'rs belong;
For the aged, and the youthful,
And the vicious, and the truthful,

All are fair when viewed in song.

1800.*

THE NEW AMADIS.

IN my boyhood's days so drear

I was kept confined;
There I sat for many a year,

All alone I pined,
As within the womb.

Yet thou drov'st away my gloom,

Golden phantasy!
I became a hero true,

Like the Prince Pipi,
And the world roam'd through,

Many a crystal palace built,

Crush'd them with like art,
And the Dragon's life-blood spilt

With my glitt'ring dart.
Yes! I was a man!

Next I formed the knightly plan

Princess Fish to free;
She was much too complaisant,

Kindly welcomed me,--
And I was gallant.

Heav'nly bread her kisses proved,

Glowing as the wine;
Almost unto death I loved.

Sun-s appeared to shine
In her dazzling charms.

Who hath torn her from mine arms?

Could no magic band
Make her in her flight delay?

Say, where now her land?
Where, alas, the way?

    1775.*

WHEN THE FOX DIES, HIS SKIN COUNTS[2].

WE young people in the shade

Sat one sultry day;
Cupid came, and "Dies the Fox"

With us sought to play.

Each one of my friends then sat

By his mistress dear;
Cupid, blowing out the torch,

Said: "The taper's here!"

Then we quickly sent around

The expiring brand;
Each one put it hastily

In his neighbour's hand.

Dorilis then gave it me,

With a scoffing jest;
Sudden into flame it broke,

By my fingers press'd.

And it singed my eyes and face,

Set my breast on fire;
Then above my head the blaze

Mounted ever higher.

Vain I sought to put it out;

Ever burned the flame;
Stead of dying, soon the Fox

---

2 The name of a game, known in English as "Jack's alight."

Livelier still became.

1770.

THE HEATHROSE.

ONCE a boy a Rosebud spied,

Heathrose fair and tender,
All array'd in youthful pride,--
Quickly to the spot he hied,

Ravished by her splendour.
Rosebud, rosebud, rosebud red,

Heathrose fair and tender!

Said the boy, "I'll now pick thee,

Heathrose fair and tender!"
Said the rosebud, "I'll prick thee,
So that thou'lt remember me,

Ne'er will I surrender!"
Rosebud, rosebud, rosebud red,

Heathrose fair and tender!

Now the cruel boy must pick

Heathrose fair and tender;
Rosebud did her best to prick,--
Vain 'twas 'gainst her fate to kick--

She must needs surrender.
Rosebud, rosebud, rosebud red,

Heathrose fair and tender!

1779.*

BLINDMAN'S BUFF.

OH, my Theresa dear!
Thine eyes, I greatly fear,

Can through the bandage see!
Although thine eyes are bound,
By thee I'm quickly found,

And wherefore shouldst thou catch but me?

Ere long thou held'st me fast,
With arms around me cast,

Upon thy breast I fell;
Scarce was thy bandage gone,
When all my joy was flown,

Thou coldly didst the blind repel.

He groped on ev'ry side,
His limbs he sorely tried,

While scoffs arose all round;
If thou no love wilt give,
In sadness I shall live,

As if mine eyes remain'd still bound.

    1770.

CHRISTEL.

My senses ofttimes are oppress'd,

Oft stagnant is my blood;
But when by Christel's sight I'm blest,

I feel my strength renew'd.
I see her here, I see her there,

And really cannot tell

The manner how, the when, the where,

The why I love her well.

If with the merest glance I view

Her black and roguish eyes,
And gaze on her black eyebrows too,

My spirit upward flies.
Has any one a mouth so sweet,

Such love-round cheeks as she?
Ah, when the eye her beauties meet,

It ne'er content can be.

And when in airy German dance

I clasp her form divine,
So quick we whirl, so quick advance,

What rapture then like mine!
And when she's giddy, and feels warm,

I cradle her, poor thing,
Upon my breast, and in mine arm,--

I'm then a very king!

And when she looks with love on me,

Forgetting all but this,
When press'd against my bosom, she

Exchanges kiss for kiss,
All through my marrow runs a thrill,

Runs e'en my foot along!
I feel so well, I feel so ill,

I feel so weak, so strong!

Would that such moments ne'er would end!

The day ne'er long I find;
Could I the night too with her spend,

E'en that I should not mind.
If she were in mine arms but held,

To quench love's thirst I'd try;
And could my torments not be quell'd,

Upon her breast would die.

   1776.*

THE COY ONE.

ONE Spring-morning bright and fair,

Roam'd a shepherdess and sang;
Young and beauteous, free from care,

Through the fields her clear notes rang:
So, Ia, Ia! le ralla, &c.

Of his lambs some two or three

Thyrsis offer'd for a kiss;
First she eyed him roguishly,

Then for answer sang but this:
So, Ia, Ia! le ralla, &c.

Ribbons did the next one offer,

And the third, his heart so true
But, as with the lambs, the scoffer

Laugh'd at heart and ribbons too,--
Still 'twas Ia! le ralla, &c.

   1791.

THE CONVERT.

As at sunset I was straying

Silently the wood along,
Damon on his flute was playing,

And the rocks gave back the song,
So la, la! &c.

Softly tow'rds him then he drew me;

Sweet each kiss he gave me then!
And I said, "Play once more to me!"

And he kindly play'd again,
So la, la! &c.

All my peace for aye has fleeted,

All my happiness has flown;
Yet my ears are ever greeted

With that olden, blissful tone,
So la, la! &c.

    1791.

PRESERVATION.

My maiden she proved false to me;

To hate all joys I soon began,

Then to a flowing stream I ran,--
The stream ran past me hastily.

There stood I fix'd, in mute despair;

My head swam round as in a dream;

I well-nigh fell into the stream,
And earth seem'd with me whirling there.

Sudden I heard a voice that cried--

I had just turn'd my face from thence--

It was a voice to charm each sense:
"Beware, for deep is yonder tide!"

A thrill my blood pervaded now,

I look'd and saw a beauteous maid

I asked her name--twas Kate, she said--
"Oh lovely Kate! how kind art thou!

"From death I have been sav'd by thee,

'Tis through thee only that I live;

Little 'twere life alone to give,
My joy in life then deign to be!"

And then I told my sorrows o'er,

Her eyes to earth she sweetly threw;

I kiss'd her, and she kiss'd me too,
And--then I talked of death no more.

    1775.*

THE MUSES' SON.

[Goethe quotes the beginning of this song in his Autobiography, as expressing the manner in which his poetical effusions used to pour out from him.]

THROUGH field and wood to stray,

And pipe my tuneful lay,--

'Tis thus my days are pass'd;
And all keep tune with me,
And move in harmony,

And so on, to the last.

To wait I scarce have power
The garden's earliest flower,

The tree's first bloom in Spring;
They hail my joyous strain,--
When Winter comes again,

Of that sweet dream I sing.

My song sounds far and near,
O'er ice it echoes clear,

Then Winter blossoms bright;
And when his blossoms fly,
Fresh raptures meet mine eye,

Upon the well-till'd height.

When 'neath the linden tree,
Young folks I chance to see,

I set them moving soon;
His nose the dull lad curls,
The formal maiden whirls,

Obedient to my tune.

Wings to the feet ye lend,
O'er hill and vale ye send

The lover far from home;
When shall I, on your breast,.

Ye kindly muses, rest,
And cease at length to roam?

1800.*

FOUND.

ONCE through the forest

Alone I went;
To seek for nothing

My thoughts were bent.

I saw i' the shadow

A flower stand there
As stars it glisten'd,

As eyes 'twas fair.

I sought to pluck it,--

It gently said:
"Shall I be gather'd

Only to fade?"

With all its roots

I dug it with care,
And took it home

To my garden fair.

In silent corner

Soon it was set;
There grows it ever,

There blooms it yet.

1815.*

LIKE AND LIKE.

A FAIR bell-flower

Sprang tip from the ground;
And early its fragrance

It shed all around;
A bee came thither

And sipp'd from its bell;
That they for each other

Were made, we see well.

      1814.

RECIPROCAL INVITATION TO THE DANCE.

THE INDIFFERENT.

COME to the dance with me, come with me, fair one!

Dances a feast-day like this may well crown.
If thou my sweetheart art not, thou canst be so,

But if thou wilt not, we still will dance on.
Come to the dance with me, come with me, fair one!

Dances a feast-day like this may well crown.

THE TENDER.

Loved one, without thee, what then would all feast be?

Sweet one, without thee, what then were the dance?
If thou my sweetheart wert not, I would dance not.

If thou art still so, all life is one feast.

Loved one, without thee, what then would all feasts be?

Sweet one, without thee, what then were the dance?

THE INDIFFERENT.

Let them but love, then, and leave us the dancing!

Languishing love cannot bear the glad dance.
Let us whirl round in the waltz's gay measure,

And let them steal to the dim-lighted wood.
Let them but love, then, and leave us the dancing!

Languishing love cannot bear the glad dance.

THE TENDER.

Let them whirl round, then, and leave us to wander!

Wand'ring to love is a heavenly dance.
Cupid, the near one, o'erhears their deriding,

Vengeance takes suddenly, vengeance takes soon.
Let them whirl round, then, and leave us to wander!

Wand'ring to love is a heavenly dance.

        1789.*

SELF-DECEIT.

My neighbour's curtain, well I see,

Is moving to and fin.
No doubt she's list'ning eagerly,

If I'm at home or no.

And if the jealous grudge I bore

And openly confess'd,
Is nourish'd by me as before,

Within my inmost breast.

Alas! no fancies such as these

E'er cross'd the dear child's thoughts.
I see 'tis but the ev'ning breeze

That with the curtain sports.

    1803.

DECLARATION OF WAR.

OH, would I resembled

The country girls fair,
Who rosy-red ribbons

And yellow hats wear!

To believe I was pretty

I thought was allow'd;
In the town I believed it

When by the youth vow'd.

Now that Spring hath return'd,

All my joys disappear;
The girls of the country

Have lured him from here.

To change dress and figure,

Was needful I found,
My bodice is longer,

My petticoat round.

My hat now is yellow.

My bodice like snow;
The clover to sickle

With others I go.

Something pretty, e'er long

Midst the troop he explores;
The eager boy signs me

To go within doors.

I bashfully go,--

Who I am, he can't trace;
He pinches my cheeks,

And he looks in my face.

The town girl now threatens

You maidens with war;
Her twofold charms pledges .

Of victory are.

      1803.

LOVER IN ALL SHAPES.

To be like a fish,
Brisk and quick, is my wish;
If thou cam'st with thy line.

Thou wouldst soon make me thine.
To be like a fish,
Brisk and quick, is my wish.

Oh, were I a steed!
Thou wouldst love me indeed.
Oh, were I a car
Fit to bear thee afar!
Oh, were I a steed!
Thou wouldst love me indeed.

I would I were gold
That thy fingers might hold!
If thou boughtest aught then,
I'd return soon again.
I would I were gold
That thy fingers might hold!

I would I were true,
And my sweetheart still new!
To be faithful I'd swear,
And would go away ne'er.
I would I were true,
And my sweetheart still new!

I would I were old,
And wrinkled and cold,
So that if thou said'st No,
I could stand such a blow!
I would I were old,
And wrinkled and cold.

An ape I would be,
Full of mischievous glee;
If aught came to vex thee,
I'd plague and perplex thee.
An ape I would be,
Full of mischievous glee

As a lamb I'd behave,
As a lion be brave,
As a lynx clearly see,
As a fox cunning be.
As a lamb I'd behave,

As a lion be brave.

Whatever I were,
All on thee I'd confer;
With the gifts of a prince
My affection evince.
Whatever I were,
All on thee I'd confer.

As nought diff'rent can make me,
As I am thou must take me!
If I'm not good enough,
Thou must cut thine own stuff.
As nought diff'rent can make me,
As I am thou must take me!

   1815.*

THE GOLDSMITH'S APPRENTICE.

My neighbour, none can e'er deny,

Is a most beauteous maid;
Her shop is ever in mine eye,

When working at my trade.

To ring and chain I hammer then

The wire of gold assay'd,
And think the while: "For Kate, oh when

Will such a ring be made?"

And when she takes her shutters down,

Her shop at once invade,
To buy and haggle, all the town,

For all that's there displayd.

I file, and maybe overfile

The wire of gold assay'd;
My master grumbles all the while,--

Her shop the mischief made.

To ply her wheel she straight begins,

When not engaged in trade;
I know full well for what she spins,--

'Tis hope guides that dear maid.

Her leg, while her small foot treads on,

Is in my mind portray'd;
Her garter I recall anon,--

I gave it that dear maid.

Then to her lips the finest thread

Is by her hand convey'd.
Were I there only in its stead,

How I would kiss the maid!

    1808.

ANSWERS IN A GAME OF QUESTIONS.

THE LADY.

IN the small and great world too,

What most charms a woman's heart?
It is doubtless what is new,

For its blossoms joy impart;
Nobler far is what is true,

For fresh blossoms it can shoot

Even in the time of fruit.

THE YOUNG GENTLEMAN.

With the Nymphs in wood and cave

Paris was acquainted well,
Till Zeus sent, to make him rave,

Three of those in Heav'n who dwell;
And the choice more trouble gave

Than e'er fell to mortal lot,

Whether in old times or not.

THE EXPERIENCED.

Tenderly a woman view,

And thoult win her, take my word;
He who's quick and saucy too,

Will of all men be preferr'd;
Who ne'er seems as if he knew

If he pleases, if he charms,--

He 'tis injures, he 'tis harms.

THE CONTENTED.

Manifold is human strife,

Human passion, human pain;
Many a blessing yet is rife,

Many pleasures still remain.
Yet the greatest bliss in life,

And the richest prize we find,

Is a good, contented mind.

THE MERRY COUNSEL.

He by whom man's foolish will

Is each day review'd and blamed,
Who, when others fools are still,

Is himself a fool proclaim'd,--
Ne'er at mill was beast's back press'd

With a heavier load than he.
What I feel within my breast

That in truth's the thing for me!

              1789.

DIFFERENT EMOTIONS ON THE SAME SPOT.

THE MAIDEN.

I'VE seen him before me!
What rapture steals o'er me!

Oh heavenly sight!
He's coming to meet me;
Perplex'd, I retreat me,

With shame take to flight.
My mind seems to wander!
Ye rocks and trees yonder,

Conceal ye my rapture.

Conceal my delight!

THE YOUTH.

'Tis here I must find her,
'Twas here she enshrined her,

Here vanish'd from sight.
She came, as to meet me,
Then fearing to greet me,

With shame took to flight.
Is't hope? Do I wander?
Ye rocks and trees yonder,

Disclose ye the loved one,

Disclose my delight!

THE LANGUISHING.

O'er my sad, fate I sorrow,
To each dewy morrow,

Veil'd here from man's sight
By the many mistaken,
Unknown and forsaken,

Here I wing my flight!
Compassionate spirit!
Let none ever hear it,--

Conceal my affliction,

Conceal thy delight!

THE HUNTER.

To-day I'm rewarded;
Rich booty's afforded

By Fortune so bright.
My servant the pheasants,
And hares fit for presents

Takes homeward at night;
Here see I enraptured
In nets the birds captured!--

Long life to the hunter!

Long live his delight!

                    1789.

WHO'LL BUY GODS OF LOVE?

OF all the beauteous wares
Exposed for sale at fairs,
None will give more delight
Than those that to your sight
From distant lands we bring.
Oh, hark to what we sing!
These beauteous birds behold,
They're brought here to be sold.

And first the big one see,
So full of roguish glee!
With light and merry bound
He leaps upon the ground;
Then springs up on the bougd,
We will not praise him now.
The merry bird behold,--
He's brought here to be sold.

And now the small one see!
A modest look has he,
And yet he's such apother
As his big roguish brother.
'Tis chiefly when all's still
He loves to show his will.
The bird so small and bold,--
He's brought here to be sold.

Observe this little love,
This darling turtle dove!
All maidens are so neat,
So civil, so discreet
Let them their charms set loose,
And turn your love to use;
The gentle bird behold,--
She's brought here to be sold.

Their praises we won't tell;
They'll stand inspection well.
They're fond of what is new,--
And yet, to show they're true,
Nor seal nor letter's wanted;
To all have wings been granted.
The pretty birds behold,--
Such beauties ne'er were sold!

    1795.

THE MISANTHROPE.

AT first awhile sits he,

With calm, unruffled brow;
His features then I see,
Distorted hideously,--

An owl's they might be now.

What is it, askest thou?
Is't love, or is't ennui?

'Tis both at once, I vow.

    1767-9.

DIFFERENT THREATS.

I ONCE into a forest far

My maiden went to seek,
And fell upon her neck, when: "Ah!"

She threaten'd, "I will shriek!"

Then cried I haughtily: "I'll crush

The man that dares come near thee!"
"Hush!" whisper'd she: "My loved one, hush!

Or else they'll overhear thee!"

1767-9.

MAIDEN WISHES.

WHAT pleasure to me
A bridegroom would be!
When married we are,
They call us mamma.
No need then to sew,
To school we ne'er go;
Command uncontroll'd,
Have maids, whom to scold;
Choose clothes at our ease,
Of what tradesmen we please;
Walk freely about,
And go to each rout,
And unrestrained are
By papa or mamma.

1767-9.

MOTIVES.

IF to a girl who loves us truly
Her mother gives instruction duly
In virtue, duty, and what not,--
And if she hearkens ne'er a jot,
But with fresh-strengthen'd longing flies

To meet our kiss that seems to burn,--

Caprice has just as much concerned
As love in her bold enterprise.

But if her mother can succeed
In gaining for her maxims heed,
And softening the girl's heart too,
So that she coyly shuns our view,--
The heart of youth she knows but ill;

For when a maiden is thus stern,

Virtue in truth has less concern
In this, than an inconstant will.

1767-9.

TRUE ENJOYMENT.

VAINLY wouldst thou, to gain a heart,

Heap up a maiden's lap with gold;
The joys of love thou must impart,

Wouldst thou e'er see those joys unfold.
The voices of the throng gold buys,

No single heart 'twill win for thee;
Wouldst thou a maiden make thy prize,

Thyself alone the bribe must be.

If by no sacred tie thou'rt bound,

Oh youth, thou must thyself restrain!
Well may true liberty be found,

Tho' man may seem to wear a chain.
Let one alone inflame thee e'er,

And if her heart with love o'erflows,
Let tenderness unite you there,

If duty's self no fetter knows.

First feel, oh youth! A girl then find

Worthy thy choice,--let her choose thee,
In body fair, and fair in mind,

And then thou wilt be blessed, like me.
I who have made this art mine own,

A girl have chosen such as this
The blessing of the priest alone

Is wanting to complete our bliss.

Nought but my rapture is her guide,

Only for me she cares to please,--
Ne'er wanton save when by my side,

And modest when the world she sees;
That time our glow may never chill,

She yields no right through frailty;
Her favour is a favour still,

And I must ever grateful be.

Yet I'm content, and full of joy,

If she'll but grant her smile so sweet,
Or if at table she'll employ,

To pillow hers, her lover's feet,
Give me the apple that she bit,

The glass from which she drank, bestow,
And when my kiss so orders it,

Her bosom, veil'd till then, will show.

And when she wills of love to speak,

In fond and silent hours of bliss,
Words from her mouth are all I seek,

Nought else I crave,--not e'en a kiss.

With what a soul her mind is fraught,

Wreath'd round with charms unceasingly!
She's perfect,--and she fails in nought

Save in her deigning to love me.

My rev'rence throws me at her feet,

My longing throws me on her breast;
This, youth, is rapture true and sweet,

Be wise, thus seeking to be blest.
When death shall take thee from her side,

To join the angelic choir above,
In heaven's bright mansions to abide,--
No diff'rence at the change thoult prove.

    1767-8.

THE FAREWELL.

[Probably addressed to his mistress Frederica.]

LET mine eye the farewell say,

That my lips can utter ne'er;
Fain I'd be a man to-day,

Yet 'tis hard, oh, hard to bear!

Mournful in an hour like this

Is love's sweetest pledge, I ween;
Cold upon thy mouth the kiss,

Faint thy fingers' pressure e'en.

Oh what rapture to my heart

Used each stolen kiss to bring!

As the violets joy impart,

Gather'd in the early spring.

Now no garlands I entwine,

Now no roses pluck. for thee,
Though 'tis springtime, Fanny mine,

Dreary autumn 'tis to me!

    1771.

THE BEAUTIFUL NIGHT.

Now I leave this cottage lowly,

Where my love hath made her home,
And with silent footstep slowly

Through the darksome forest roam,
Luna breaks through oaks and bushes,

Zephyr hastes her steps to meet,
And the waving birch-tree blushes,

Scattering round her incense sweet.

Grateful are the cooling breezes

Of this beauteous summer night,
Here is felt the charm that pleases,

And that gives the soul delight.
Boundless is my joy; yet, Heaven,

Willingly I'd leave to thee
Thousand such nights, were one given

By my maiden loved to me!

    1767-8.

HAPPINESS AND VISION.

TOGETHER at the altar we
In vision oft were seen by thee,

Thyself as bride, as bridegroom I.
Oft from thy mouth full many a kiss
In an unguarded hour of bliss

I then would steal, while none were by.

The purest rapture we then knew,
The joy those happy hours gave too,

When tasted, fled, as time fleets on.
What now avails my joy to me?
Like dreams the warmest kisses flee,

Like kisses, soon all joys are gone.

        1767-8.

LIVING REMEMBRANCE.

HALF vex'd, half pleased, thy love will feel,
Shouldst thou her knot or ribbon steal;
To thee they're much--I won't conceal;

Such self-deceit may pardon'd be;
A veil, a kerchief, garter, rings,
In truth are no mean trifling things,

But still they're not enough for me.

She who is dearest to my heart,
Gave me, with well dissembled smart,
Of her own life, a living part,

No charm in aught beside I trace;
How do I scorn thy paltry ware!
A lock she gave me of the hair

That wantons o'er her beauteous face.

If, loved one, we must sever'd be,
Wouldst thou not wholly fly from me,
I still possess this legacy,

To look at, and to kiss in play.--
My fate is to the hair's allied,
We used to woo her with like pride,

And now we both are far away.

Her charms with equal joy we press'd,
Her swelling cheeks anon caress'd,
Lured onward by a yearning blest,

Upon her heaving bosom fell.
Oh rival, free from envy's sway,
Thou precious gift, thou beauteous prey.

Remain my joy and bliss to tell!

   1767-9.

THE BLISS OF ABSENCE.

DRINK, oh youth, joy's purest ray
From thy loved one's eyes all day,

And her image paint at night!
Better rule no lover knows,
Yet true rapture greater grows,

When far sever'd from her sight.

Powers eternal, distance, time,
Like the might of stars sublime,

Gently rock the blood to rest,
O'er my senses softness steals,
Yet my bosom lighter feels,

And I daily am more blest.

Though I can forget her ne'er,
Yet my mind is free from care,

I can calmly live and move;
Unperceived infatuation
Longing turns to adoration,

Turns to reverence my love.

Ne'er can cloud, however light,
Float in ether's regions bright,

When drawn upwards by the sun,
As my heart in rapturous calm.
Free from envy and alarm,

Ever love I her alone!

    1767-9.

TO LUNA.

SISTER of the first-born light,

Type of sorrowing gentleness!

Quivering mists in silv'ry dress
Float around thy features bright;
When thy gentle foot is heard,

From the day-closed caverns then

Wake the mournful ghosts of men,
I, too, wake, and each night-bird.

O'er a field of boundless span

Looks thy gaze both far and wide.

Raise me upwards to thy side!
Grant this to a raving man!
And to heights of rapture raised,

Let the knight so crafty peep

At his maiden while asleep,
Through her lattice-window glazed.

Soon the bliss of this sweet view,

Pangs by distance caused allays;

And I gather all thy rays,
And my look I sharpen too.
Round her unveil'd limbs I see

Brighter still become the glow,

And she draws me down below,
As Endymion once drew thee.

1767-9.

THE WEDDING NIGHT.

WITHIN the chamber, far away

From the glad feast, sits Love in dread
Lest guests disturb, in wanton play,

The silence of the bridal bed.
His torch's pale flame serves to gild

The scene with mystic sacred glow;
The room with incense-clouds is fil'd,

That ye may perfect rapture know.

How beats thy heart, when thou dost hear

The chime that warns thy guests to fly!
How glow'st thou for those lips so dear,

That soon are mute, and nought deny!
With her into the holy place

Thou hast'nest then, to perfect all;
The fire the warder's hands embrace,

Grows, like a night-light, dim and small.

How heaves her bosom, and how burns

Her face at every fervent kiss!
Her coldness now to trembling turns,

Thy daring now a duty is.
Love helps thee to undress her fast,

But thou art twice as fast as he;
And then he shuts both eye at last,

With sly and roguish modesty.

    1767.

MISCHIEVOUS JOY.

AS a butterfly renew'd,

When in life I breath'd my last,

  To the spots my flight I wing,

Scenes of heav'nly rapture past,

  Over meadows, to the spring,
Round the hill, and through the wood.

Soon a tender pair I spy,

And I look down from my seat

  On the beauteous maiden's head--

When embodied there I meet

  All I lost as soon as dead,
Happy as before am I.

Him she clasps with silent smile,

And his mouth the hour improves,

  Sent by kindly Deities;

First from breast to mouth it roves,

  Then from mouth to hands it flies,
And I round him sport the while.

And she sees me hov'ring near;

Trembling at her lovers rapture,

  Up she springs--I fly away,

"Dearest! let's the insect capture

  Come! I long to make my prey
Yonder pretty little dear!"

          1767-9.

APPARENT DEATH.

WEEP, maiden, weep here o'er the tomb of Love;

He died of nothing--by mere chance was slain.
But is he really dead?--oh, that I cannot prove:

A nothing, a mere chance, oft gives him life again.

1767-9.

NOVEMBER SONG.

To the great archer--not to him

To meet whom flies the sun,
And who is wont his features dim

With clouds to overrun--

But to the boy be vow'd these rhymes,

Who 'mongst the roses plays,
Who hear us, and at proper times

To pierce fair hearts essays.

Through him the gloomy winter night,

Of yore so cold and drear,
Brings many a loved friend to our sight,

And many a woman dear.

Henceforward shall his image fair

Stand in yon starry skies,
And, ever mild and gracious there,

Alternate set and rise.

1815.*

TO THE CHOSEN ONE.

[This sweet song is doubtless one of those addressed to Frederica.]

HAND in hand! and lip to lip!

Oh, be faithful, maiden dear!
Fare thee well! thy lover's ship

Past full many a rock must steers
But should he the haven see,

When the storm has ceased to break,
And be happy, reft of thee,--

May the Gods fierce vengeance take!

Boldly dared is well nigh won!

Half my task is solved aright;
Ev'ry star's to me a sun,

Only cowards deem it night.
Stood I idly by thy side,

Sorrow still would sadden me;
But when seas our paths divide,

Gladly toil I,--toil for thee!

Now the valley I perceive,

Where together we will go,
And the streamlet watch each eve,

Gliding peacefully below
Oh, the poplars on yon spot!

Oh, the beech trees in yon grove!
And behind we'll build a cot,

Where to taste the joys of love!

            1771.

FIRST LOSS.

AH! who'll e'er those days restore,

Those bright days of early love
Who'll one hour again concede,

Of that time so fondly cherish'd!
Silently my wounds I feed,
And with wailing evermore

Sorrow o'er each joy now perish'd.
Ah! who'll e'er the days restore

Of that time so fondly cherish'd.

    1789.*

AFTER-SENSATIONS.

WHEN the vine again is blowing,

Then the wine moves in the cask;
When the rose again is glowing,

  Wherefore should I feel oppress'd?

Down my cheeks run tears all-burning,

If I do, or leave my task;
I but feel a speechless yearning,

  That pervades my inmost breast.

But at length I see the reason,

When the question I would ask:
'Twas in such a beauteous season,

Doris glowed to make me blest!

1797.

PROXIMITY OF THE BELOVED ONE.

I THINK of thee, whene'er the sun his beams

  O'er ocean flings;
I think of thee, whene'er the moonlight gleams

  In silv'ry springs.

I see thee, when upon the distant ridge

  The dust awakes;
At midnight's hour, when on the fragile bridge

  The wanderer quakes.

I hear thee, when yon billows rise on high,

  With murmur deep.
To tread the silent grove oft wander I,

  When all's asleep.

I'm near thee, though thou far away mayst be--

  Thou, too, art near!
The sun then sets, the stars soon lighten me.

  Would thou wert here!

1795.

PRESENCE.

ALL things give token of thee!

As soon as the bright sun is shining,
Thou too wilt follow, I trust.

When in the garden thou walk'st,
Thou then art the rose of all roses,
Lily of lilies as well.

When thou dost move in the dance,
Then each constellation moves also;
With thee and round thee they move.

Night! oh, what bliss were the night!
For then thou o'ershadow'st the lustre,
Dazzling and fair, of the moon.

Dazzling and beauteous art thou,
And flowers, and moon, and the planets
Homage pay, Sun, but to thee.

Sun! to me also be thou
Creator of days bright and glorious;
Life and Eternity this!

   1813.

TO THE DISTANT ONE.

AND have I lost thee evermore?

Hast thou, oh fair one, from me flown?
Still in mine ear sounds, as of yore,

Thine ev'ry word, thine ev'ry tone.

As when at morn the wand'rer's eye

Attempts to pierce the air in vain,
When, hidden in the azure sky,

The lark high o'er him chaunts his strain:

So do I cast my troubled gaze

Through bush, through forest, o'er the lea;
Thou art invoked by all my lays;

Oh, come then, loved one, back to me!

    1789.*

BY THE RIVER.

FLOW on, ye lays so loved, so fair,

On to Oblivion's ocean flow!
May no rapt boy recall you e'er,

No maiden in her beauty's glow!

My love alone was then your theme,

But now she scorns my passion true.
Ye were but written in the stream;

As it flows on, then, flow ye too!

    1798.*

FAREWELL.

To break one's word is pleasure-fraught,

To do one's duty gives a smart;
While man, alas! will promise nought,

That is repugnant to his heart.

Using some magic strains of yore,

Thou lurest him, when scarcely calm,
On to sweet folly's fragile bark once more,

Renewing, doubling chance of harm.

Why seek to hide thyself from me?

Fly not my sight--be open then!
Known late or early it must be,

And here thou hast thy word again.

My duty is fulfill'd to-day,

No longer will I guard thee from surprise;
But, oh, forgive the friend who from thee turns away,

And to himself for refuge flies!

        1797.

THE EXCHANGE.

THE stones in the streamlet I make my bright pillow,
And open my arms to the swift-rolling billow,

That lovingly hastens to fall on my breast.
Then fickleness soon bids it onwards be flowing;
A second draws nigh, its caresses bestowing,--

And so by a twofold enjoyment I'm blest.

And yet thou art trailing in sorrow and sadness
The moments that life, as it flies, gave for gladness,

Because by thy love thou'rt remember'd no more!
Oh, call back to mind former days and their blisses!
The lips of the second will give as sweet kisses

As any the lips of the first gave before!

        1767-9.

WELCOME AND FAREWELL.

[Another of the love-songs addressed to Frederica.]

QUICK throbb'd my heart: to norse! haste, haste,

And lo! 'twas done with speed of light;
The evening soon the world embraced,

And o'er the mountains hung the night.
Soon stood, in robe of mist, the oak,

A tow'ring giant in his size,
Where darkness through the thicket broke,

And glared with hundred gloomy eyes.

From out a hill of clouds the moon

With mournful gaze began to peer:
The winds their soft wings flutter'd soon,

And murmur'd in mine awe-struck ear;
The night a thousand monsters made,

Yet fresh and joyous was my mind;
What fire within my veins then play'd!

What glow was in my bosom shrin'd!

I saw thee, and with tender pride

Felt thy sweet gaze pour joy on me;
While all my heart was at thy side.

And every breath I breath'd for thee.
The roseate hues that spring supplies

Were playing round thy features fair,
And love for me--ye Deities!

I hoped it, I deserved it ne'er!

But, when the morning sun return'd,

Departure filled with grief my heart:
Within thy kiss, what rapture burn'd!

But in thy look, what bitter smart!
I went--thy gaze to earth first roved

Thou follow'dst me with tearful eye:
And yet, what rapture to be loved!

And, Gods, to love--what ecstasy!

        1771.

NEW LOVE, NEW LIFE.

[Written at the time of Goethe's connection with Lily.]

HEART! my heart! what means this feeling?

What oppresseth thee so sore?
What strange life is o'er me stealing!

I acknowledge thee no more.
Fled is all that gave thee gladness,
Fled the cause of all thy sadness,

Fled thy peace, thine industry--

Ah, why suffer it to be?

Say, do beauty's graces youthful,

Does this form so fair and bright,
Does this gaze, so kind, so truthful,

Chain thee with unceasing might?
Would I tear me from her boldly,
Courage take, and fly her coldly,

Back to her. I'm forthwith led

By the path I seek to tread.

By a thread I ne'er can sever,

For 'tis 'twined with magic skill,
Doth the cruel maid for ever

Hold me fast against my will.
While those magic chains confine me,
To her will I must resign me.

Ah, the change in truth is great!

Love! kind love! release me straight!

    1775.

TO BELINDA.

[This song was also written for Lily. Goethe mentions, at the end of his Autobiography, that he overheard her singing it one evening after he had taken his last farewell of her.]

WHEREFORE drag me to yon glittering eddy,

  With resistless might?
Was I, then, not truly blest already

  In the silent night?

In my secret chamber refuge taking,

  'Neath the moon's soft ray,
And her awful light around me breaking,

  Musing there I lay.

And I dream'd of hours with joy o'erflowing,

Golden, truly blest,
While thine image so beloved was glowing

　　Deep within my breast.

Now to the card-table hast thou bound me,

　　'Midst the torches glare?
Whilst unhappy faces are around me,

　　Dost thou hold me there?

Spring-flow'rs are to me more rapture-giving,

　　Now conceal'd from view;
Where thou, angel, art, is Nature living,

　　Love and kindness too.

　　　　　　1775.

MAY SONG.

How fair doth Nature

Appear again!
How bright the sunbeams!

How smiles the plain!

The flow'rs are bursting

From ev'ry bough,
And thousand voices

Each bush yields now.

And joy and gladness

Fill ev'ry breast!
Oh earth!--oh sunlight!

Oh rapture blest!

Oh love! oh loved one!

As golden bright,
As clouds of morning

On yonder height!

Thou blessest gladly

The smiling field,--
The world in fragrant

Vapour conceal'd.

Oh maiden, maiden,

How love I thee!
Thine eye, how gleams it!

How lov'st thou me!

The blithe lark loveth

Sweet song and air,
The morning flow'ret

Heav'n's incense fair,

As I now love thee

With fond desire,
For thou dost give me

Youth, joy, and fire,

For new-born dances

And minstrelsy.
Be ever happy,

As thou lov'st me!

1775.*

WITH A PAINTED RIBBON.

LITTLE leaves and flow'rets too,

Scatter we with gentle hand,
Kind young spring-gods to the view,

Sporting on an airy band.

Zephyr, bear it on the wing,

Twine it round my loved one's dress;
To her glass then let her spring,

Full of eager joyousness.

Roses round her let her see,

She herself a youthful rose.
Grant, dear life, one look to me!

'Twill repay me all my woes,

What this bosom feels, feel thou.

Freely offer me thy hand;
Let the band that joins us now

Be no fragile rosy band!

1770.

WITH A GOLDEN NECKLACE.

THIS page a chain to bring thee burns,

That, train'd to suppleness of old,

On thy fair neck to nestle, yearns,

In many a hundred little fold.

To please the silly thing consent!

'Tis harmless, and from boldness free;
By day a trifling ornament,

At night 'tis cast aside by thee.

But if the chain they bring thee ever,

Heavier, more fraught with weal or woe,
I'd then, Lisette, reproach thee never

If thou shouldst greater scruples show.

    1775.*

ON THE LAKE,

[Written on the occasion of Goethe's starting with his friend Passavant on a Swiss Tour.]

I DRINK fresh nourishment, new blood

From out this world more free;
The Nature is so kind and good

That to her breast clasps me!
The billows toss our bark on high,

And with our oars keep time,
While cloudy mountains tow'rd the sky

Before our progress climb.

Say, mine eye, why sink'st thou down?
Golden visions, are ye flown?

Hence, thou dream, tho' golden-twin'd;

Here, too, love and life I find.

Over the waters are blinking

Many a thousand fair star;
Gentle mists are drinking

Round the horizon afar.
Round the shady creek lightly

Morning zephyrs awake,
And the ripen'd fruit brightly

Mirrors itself in the lake.

   1775.

FROM THE MOUNTAIN.

[Written just after the preceding one, on a mountain overlooking the Lake of Zurich.]

IF I, dearest Lily, did not love thee,

How this prospect would enchant my sight!
And yet if I, Lily, did not love thee,

Could I find, or here, or there, delight?

   1775.

FLOWER-SALUTE.

THIS nosegay,--'twas I dress'd it,--

Greets thee a thousand times!
Oft stoop'd I, and caress'd it,

Ah! full a thousand times,
And 'gainst my bosom press'd it

A hundred thousand times!

    1815.*

IN SUMMER.

How plain and height
With dewdrops are bright!
How pearls have crown'd
The plants all around!
How sighs the breeze
Thro' thicket and trees!
How loudly in the sun's clear rays
The sweet birds carol forth their lays!

But, ah! above,
Where saw I my love,
Within her room,
Small, mantled in gloom,
Enclosed around,
Where sunlight was drown'd,
How little there was earth to me,
With all its beauteous majesty!

    1776.*

MAY SONG.

BETWEEN wheatfield and corn,
Between hedgerow and thorn,
Between pasture and tree,
Where's my sweetheart
Tell it me!

Sweetheart caught I

Not at home;
She's then, thought I.

Gone to roam.
Fair and loving

Blooms sweet May;
Sweetheart's roving,

Free and gay.

By the rock near the wave,
Where her first kiss she gave,
On the greensward, to me,--
Something I see!
Is it she?

   1812.

PREMATURE SPRING.

DAYS full of rapture,

Are ye renew'd?--
Smile in the sunlight

Mountain and wood?

Streams richer laden

Flow through the dale,
Are these the meadows?

Is this the vale?

Coolness cerulean!

Heaven and height!
Fish crowd the ocean,

Golden and bright.

Birds of gay plumage

Sport in the grove,
Heavenly numbers

Singing above.

Under the verdure's

Vigorous bloom,
Bees, softly bumming,

Juices consume.

Gentle disturbance

Quivers in air,
Sleep-causing fragrance,

Motion so fair.

Soon with more power

Rises the breeze,
Then in a moment

Dies in the trees.

But to the bosom

Comes it again.
Aid me, ye Muses,

Bliss to sustain!

Say what has happen'd

Since yester e'en?
Oh, ye fair sisters,

Her I have seen!

    1802.

AUTUMN FEELINGS.

FLOURISH greener, as ye clamber,
Oh ye leaves, to seek my chamber,

Up the trellis'd vine on high!
May ye swell, twin-berries tender,
Juicier far,--and with more splendour

Ripen, and more speedily!
O'er ye broods the sun at even
As he sinks to rest, and heaven

Softly breathes into your ear
All its fertilising fullness,
While the moon's refreshing coolness,

Magic-laden, hovers near;
And, alas! ye're watered ever

By a stream of tears that rill
From mine eyes--tears ceasing never,

Tears of love that nought can still!

        1775.*

RESTLESS LOVE.

THROUGH rain, through snow,
Through tempest go!
'Mongst streaming caves,
O'er misty waves,
On, on! still on!
Peace, rest have flown!

Sooner through sadness

I'd wish to be slain,

Than all the gladness

Of life to sustain
All the fond yearning

That heart feels for heart,
Only seems burning

To make them both smart.

How shall I fly?
Forestwards hie?
Vain were all strife!
Bright crown of life.
Turbulent bliss,--
Love, thou art this!

    1789.

THE SHEPHERD'S LAMENT.

ON yonder lofty mountain

A thousand times I stand,
And on my staff reclining,

Look down on the smiling land.

My grazing flocks then I follow,

My dog protecting them well;
I find myself in the valley,

But how, I scarcely can tell.

The whole of the meadow is cover'd

With flowers of beauty rare;
I pluck them, but pluck them unknowing

To whom the offering to bear.

In rain and storm and tempest,

I tarry beneath the tree,
But closed remaineth yon portal;

'Tis all but a vision to me.

High over yonder dwelling,

There rises a rainbow gay;
But she from home hath departed

And wander'd far, far away.

Yes, far away bath she wander'd,

Perchance e'en over the sea;
Move onward, ye sheep, then, move onward!

Full sad the shepherd must be.

1803.*

COMFORT IN TEARS.

How happens it that thou art sad,

While happy all appear?
Thine eye proclaims too well that thou

Hast wept full many a tear.

"If I have wept in solitude,

None other shares my grief,
And tears to me sweet balsam are,

And give my heart relief."

Thy happy friends invite thee now,--

Oh come, then, to our breast!

And let the loss thou hast sustain'd

Be there to us confess'd!

"Ye shout, torment me, knowing not

What 'tis afflicteth me;
Ah no! I have sustained no loss,

Whate'er may wanting be."

If so it is, arise in haste!

Thou'rt young and full of life.
At years like thine, man's blest with strength.

And courage for the strife.

"Ah no! in vain 'twould be to strive,

The thing I seek is far;
It dwells as high, it gleams as fair

As yonder glitt'ring star."

The stars we never long to clasp,

We revel in their light,
And with enchantment upward gaze,

Each clear and radiant night.

"And I with rapture upward gaze,

On many a blissful day;
Then let me pass the night in tears,

Till tears are wip'd away!

    1803.*

NIGHT SONG,

WHEN on thy pillow lying,

Half listen, I implore,
And at my lute's soft sighing,

Sleep on! what wouldst thou more?

For at my lute's soft sighing

The stars their blessings pour
On feelings never-dying;

Sleep on! what wouldst thou more?

Those feelings never-dying

My spirit aid to soar
From earthly conflicts trying;

Sleep on! what wouldst thou more?

From earthly conflicts trying

Thou driv'st me to this shore;
Through thee I'm thither flying,--

Sleep on! what wouldst thou more?

Through thee I'm hither flying,

Thou wilt not list before
In slumbers thou art lying:

Sleep on! what wouldst thou more?

    1803.*

LONGING.

WHAT pulls at my heart so?

What tells me to roam?
What drags me and lures me

From chamber and home?
How round the cliffs gather

The clouds high in air!
I fain would go thither,

I fain would be there!

The sociable flight

Of the ravens comes back;
I mingle amongst them,

And follow their track.
Round wall and round mountain

Together we fly;
She tarries below there,

I after her spy.

Then onward she wanders,

My flight I wing soon
To the wood fill'd with bushes,

A bird of sweet tune.
She tarries and hearkens,

And smiling, thinks she:
"How sweetly he's singing!

He's singing to me!"

The heights are illum'd

By the fast setting sun;
The pensive fair maiden

Looks thoughtfully on;
She roams by the streamlet,

O'er meadows she goes,
And darker and darker

The pathway fast grows.

I rise on a sudden,

A glimmering star;
"What glitters above me,

So near and so far?"

And when thou with wonder

Hast gazed on the light,
I fall down before thee,

Entranced by thy sight!

    1803.

TO MIGNON.

OVER vale and torrent far
Rolls along the sun's bright car.
Ah! he wakens in his course

Mine, as thy deep-seated smart

In the heart.
Ev'ry morning with new force.

Scarce avails night aught to me;
E'en the visions that I see
Come but in a mournful guise;

And I feel this silent smart

In my heart
With creative pow'r arise.

During many a beauteous year
I have seen ships 'neath me steer,
As they seek the shelt'ring bay;

But, alas, each lasting smart

In my heart
Floats not with the stream away.

I must wear a gala dress,
Long stored up within my press,
For to-day to feasts is given;

None know with what bitter smart

Is my heart
Fearfully and madly riven.

Secretly I weep each tear,
Yet can cheerful e'en appear,
With a face of healthy red;

For if deadly were this silent smart

In my heart,
Ah, I then had long been dead!

THE MOUNTAIN CASTLE.

THERE stands on yonder high mountain

A castle built of yore,
Where once lurked horse and horseman

In rear of gate and of door.

Now door and gate are in ashes,

And all around is so still;
And over the fallen ruins

I clamber just as I will.

Below once lay a cellar,

With costly wines well stor'd;
No more the glad maid with her pitcher

Descends there to draw from the hoard.

No longer the goblet she places

Before the guests at the feast;
The flask at the meal so hallow'd

No longer she fills for the priest.

No more for the eager squire

The draught in the passage is pour'd;
No more for the flying present

Receives she the flying reward.

For all the roof and the rafters,

They all long since have been burn'd,
And stairs and passage and chapel

To rubbish and ruins are turn'd.

Yet when with lute and with flagon,

When day was smiling and bright,
I've watch'd my mistress climbing

To gain this perilous height,

Then rapture joyous and radiant

The silence so desolate brake,
And all, as in days long vanish'd,

Once more to enjoyment awoke;

As if for guests of high station

The largest rooms were prepared;
As if from those times so precious

A couple thither had fared;

As if there stood in his chapel

The priest in his sacred dress,
And ask'd: "Would ye twain be united?"

And we, with a smile, answer'd, "Yes!"

And songs that breath'd a deep feeling,

That touched the heart's innermost chord,
The music-fraught mouth of sweet echo,

Instead of the many, outpour'd.

And when at eve all was hidden

In silence unbroken and deep,
The glowing sun then look'd upwards,

And gazed on the summit so steep.

And squire and maiden then glitter'd

As bright and gay as a lord,
She seized the time for her present,

And he to give her reward.

     1803.*

THE SPIRIT'S SALUTE.

THE hero's noble shade stands high

On yonder turret grey;
And as the ship is sailing by,

He speeds it on his way.

"See with what strength these sinews thrill'd!

This heart, how firm and wild!
These bones, what knightly marrow fill'd!

This cup, how bright it smil'd!

"Half of my life I strove and fought,

And half I calmly pass'd;
And thou, oh ship with beings fraught,

Sail safely to the last!"

    1774.

TO A GOLDEN HEART THAT HE WORE ROUND HIS NECK.

[Addressed, during the Swiss tour already mentioned, to a present
Lily had given him, during the time of their happy connection,
which was then about to be terminated for ever.]

OH thou token loved of joys now perish'd

That I still wear from my neck suspended,
Art thou stronger than our spirit-bond so cherish'd?

Or canst thou prolong love's days untimely ended?

Lily, I fly from thee! I still am doom'd to range

Thro' countries strange,

Thro' distant vales and woods, link'd on to thee!
Ah, Lily's heart could surely never fall

So soon away from me!

As when a bird bath broken from his thrall,

And seeks the forest green,
Proof of imprisonment he bears behind him,
A morsel of the thread once used to bind him;

The free-born bird of old no more is seen,

For he another's prey bath been.

     1775.

THE BLISS OF SORROW.

NEVER dry, never dry,

 Tears that eternal love sheddeth!
How dreary, how dead doth the world still appear,
When only half-dried on the eye is the tear!

Never dry, never dry,

 Tears that unhappy love sheddeth!

     1789.*

THE WANDERER'S NIGHT-SONG.

THOU who comest from on high,

Who all woes and sorrows stillest,

Who, for twofold misery,

Hearts with twofold balsam fillest,
Would this constant strife would cease!

What are pain and rapture now?
Blissful Peace,

To my bosom hasten thou!

    1789.*

THE SAME.

[Written at night on the Kickelhahn, a hill in the forest of Ilmenau, on the walls of a little hermitage where Goethe composed the last act of his Iphigenia.]

HUSH'D on the hill

 Is the breeze;

Scarce by the zephyr

 The trees

Softly are press'd;
The woodbird's asleep on the bough.
Wait, then, and thou

Soon wilt find rest.

    1783.

THE HUNTER'S EVEN-SONG.

THE plain with still and wand'ring feet,

And gun full-charged, I tread,
And hov'ring see thine image sweet,

Thine image dear, o'er head.

In gentle silence thou dost fare

Through field and valley dear;
But doth my fleeting image ne'er

To thy mind's eye appear?

His image, who, by grief oppress'd,

Roams through the world forlorn,
And wanders on from east to west,

Because from thee he's torn?

When I would think of none but thee,

Mine eyes the moon survey;
A calm repose then steals o'er me,

But how, 'twere hard to say.

1776.*

TO THE MOON.

BUSH and vale thou fill'st again

With thy misty ray,
And my spirit's heavy chain

Castest far away.

Thou dost o'er my fields extend

Thy sweet soothing eye,
Watching like a gentle friend,

O'er my destiny.

Vanish'd days of bliss and woe

Haunt me with their tone,
Joy and grief in turns I know,

As I stray alone.

Stream beloved, flow on! flow on!

Ne'er can I be gay!
Thus have sport and kisses gone,

Truth thus pass'd away.

Once I seem'd the lord to be

Of that prize so fair!
Now, to our deep sorrow, we

Can forget it ne'er.

Murmur, stream, the vale along,

Never cease thy sighs;
Murmur, whisper to my song

Answering melodies!

When thou in the winter's night

Overflow'st in wrath,
Or in spring-time sparklest bright,

As the buds shoot forth.

He who from the world retires,

Void of hate, is blest;
Who a friend's true love inspires,

Leaning on his breast!

That which heedless man ne'er knew,

Or ne'er thought aright,
Roams the bosom's labyrinth through,

Boldly into night.

    1789.*

TO LINA.

SHOULD these songs, love, as they fleet,

Chance again to reach thy hand,
At the piano take thy seat,

Where thy friend was wont to stand!

Sweep with finger bold the string,

Then the book one moment see:
But read not! do nought but sing!

And each page thine own will be!

Ah, what grief the song imparts

With its letters, black on white,
That, when breath'd by thee, our hearts

Now can break and now delight!

    1800.*

EVER AND EVERYWHERE.

FAR explore the mountain hollow,
High in air the clouds then follow!

To each brook and vale the Muse

Thousand times her call renews.

Soon as a flow'ret blooms in spring,
It wakens many a strain;

And when Time spreads his fleeting wing,

The seasons come again.

        1820.*

PETITION.

OH thou sweet maiden fair,
Thou with the raven hair,

Why to the window go?

While gazing down below,
Art standing vainly there?

Oh, if thou stood'st for me,
And lett'st the latch but fly,

How happy should I be!
How soon would I leap high!

        1789.*

TO HIS COY ONE.

SEEST thou yon smiling Orange?
Upon the tree still hangs it;
Already March bath vanish'd,
And new-born flow'rs are shooting.
I draw nigh to the tree then,
And there I say: Oh Orange,

Thou ripe and juicy Orange,
Thou sweet and luscious Orange,
I shake the tree, I shake it,
Oh fall into my lap!

    1789.*

NIGHT THOUGHTS.

OH, unhappy stars! your fate I mourn,

Ye by whom the sea-toss'd sailor's lighted,
Who with radiant beams the heav'ns adorn,

But by gods and men are unrequited:
For ye love not,--ne'er have learnt to love!
Ceaselessly in endless dance ye move,
In the spacious sky your charms displaying,

What far travels ye have hasten'd through,
Since, within my loved one's arms delaying,

I've forgotten you and midnight too!

    1789.*

TO LIDA.

THE only one whom, Lida, thou canst love,

Thou claim'st, and rightly claim'st, for only thee;
He too is wholly thine; since doomed to rove

Far from thee, in life's turmoils nought I see
Save a thin veil, through which thy form I view,
As though in clouds; with kindly smile and true,

It cheers me, like the stars eterne that gleam
Across the northern-lights' far-flick'ring beam.

1789.*

PROXIMITY.

I KNOW not, wherefore, dearest love,

Thou often art so strange and coy
When 'mongst man's busy haunts we move,

Thy coldness puts to flight my joy.
But soon as night and silence round us reign,
I know thee by thy kisses sweet again!

1789.*

RECIPROCAL.

MY mistress, where sits she?

What is it that charms?
The absent she's rocking,

Held fast in her arms.

In pretty cage prison'd

She holds a bird still;
Yet lets him fly from her,

Whenever he will.

He pecks at her finger,

And pecks at her lips,
And hovers and flutters,

And round her he skips.

Then hasten thou homeward,

In fashion to be;
If thou hast the maiden,

She also hath thee.

    1816.

ROLLICKING HANS.

HALLO there! A glass!

Ha! the draught's truly sweet!
If for drink go my shoes,

I shall still have my feet.

A maiden and wine,

With sweet music and song,--
I would they were mine,

All life's journey along!

If I depart from this sad sphere,
And leave a will behind me here,
A suit at law will be preferr'd,
But as for thanks,--the deuce a word!
So ere I die, I squander all,
And that a proper will I call.

HIS COMRADE.

Hallo there! A glass!

Ha! the draught's truly sweet
If thou keepest thy shoes,

Thou wilt then spare thy feet.

A maiden and wine,

With sweet music and song,
On pavement, are thine,

All life's journey along!

THE FREEBOOTER.

No door has my house,

No house has my door;
And in and out ever

I carry my store.

No grate has my kitchen,

No kitchen my grate;
Yet roasts it and boils it

Both early and late.

My bed has no trestles,

My trestles no bed;
Yet merrier moments

No mortal e'er led.

My cellar is lofty,

My barn is full deep,
From top to the bottom,--

There lie I and sleep.

And soon as I waken,

All moves on its race;
My place has no fixture,

My fixture no place.

1827.*

JOY AND SORROW.

As a fisher-boy I fared

To the black rock in the sea,
And, while false gifts I prepared.

Listen'd and sang merrily,
Down descended the decoy,

Soon a fish attack'd the bait;
One exultant shout of joy,--

And the fish was captured straight.

Ah! on shore, and to the wood

Past the cliffs, o'er stock and stone,
One foot's traces I pursued,

And the maiden was alone.
Lips were silent, eyes downcast

As a clasp-knife snaps the bait,
With her snare she seized me fast,

And the boy was captured straight.

Heav'n knows who's the happy swain

That she rambles with anew!
I must dare the sea again,

Spite of wind and weather too.
When the great and little fish

Wail and flounder in my net,
Straight returns my eager wish

In her arms to revel yet!

1815.

MARCH.

THE snow-flakes fall in showers,

The time is absent still,
When all Spring's beauteous flowers,
When all Spring's beauteous flowers

Our hearts with joy shall fill.

With lustre false and fleeting

The sun's bright rays are thrown;
The swallow's self is cheating:
The swallow's self is cheating,

And why? He comes alone!

Can I e'er feel delighted

Alone, though Spring is near?
Yet when we are united,
Yet when we are united,

The Summer will be here.

1817.

APRIL.

TELL me, eyes, what 'tis ye're seeking;

For ye're saying something sweet,

Fit the ravish'd ear to greet,
Eloquently, softly speaking.

Yet I see now why ye're roving;

For behind those eyes so bright,

To itself abandon'd quite,
Lies a bosom, truthful, loving,--

One that it must fill with pleasure

'Mongst so many, dull and blind,

One true look at length to find,
That its worth can rightly treasure.

Whilst I'm lost in studying ever

To explain these cyphers duly,--

To unravel my looks truly
In return be your endeavour!

    1820.

MAY.

LIGHT and silv'ry cloudlets hover

In the air, as yet scarce warm;
Mild, with glimmer soft tinged over,

Peeps the sun through fragrant balm.
Gently rolls and heaves the ocean

As its waves the bank o'erflow.
And with ever restless motion

Moves the verdure to and fro,

Mirror'd brightly far below.

What is now the foliage moving?

Air is still, and hush'd the breeze,
Sultriness, this fullness loving,

Through the thicket, from the trees.
Now the eye at once gleams brightly,

See! the infant band with mirth
Moves and dances nimbly, lightly,

As the morning gave it birth,

Flutt'ring two and two o'er earth.

   *   *   *   *

1816.

JUNE.

SHE behind yon mountain lives,
Who my love's sweet guerdon gives.
Tell me, mount, how this can be!
Very glass thou seem'st to me,
And I seem to be close by,
For I see her drawing nigh;
Now, because I'm absent, sad,
Now, because she sees me, glad!

Soon between us rise to sight
Valleys cool, with bushes light,
Streams and meadows; next appear

Mills and wheels, the surest token
That a level spot is near,

Plains far-stretching and unbroken.
And so onwards, onwards roam,
To my garden and my home!

But how comes it then to pass?
All this gives no joy, alas!--
I was ravish'd by her sight,

By her eyes so fair and bright,
By her footstep soft and light.
How her peerless charms I praised,
When from head to foot I gazed!
I am here, she's far away,--
I am gone, with her to stay.

If on rugged hills she wander,

If she haste the vale along,
Pinions seem to flutter yonder,

And the air is fill'd with song;
With the glow of youth still playing,

Joyous vigour in each limb,
One in silence is delaying,

She alone 'tis blesses him.

Love, thou art too fair, I ween!
Fairer I have never seen!
From the heart full easily
Blooming flowers are cull'd by thee.
If I think: "Oh, were it so,"
Bone and marrow seen to glow!
If rewarded by her love,
Can I greater rapture prove?

And still fairer is the bride,
When in me she will confide,
When she speaks and lets me know
All her tale of joy and woe.
All her lifetime's history
Now is fully known to me.
Who in child or woman e'er
Soul and body found so fair?

              1815.

NEXT YEAR'S SPRING.

THE bed of flowers

Loosens amain,
The beauteous snowdrops

Droop o'er the plain.
The crocus opens

Its glowing bud,
Like emeralds others,

Others, like blood.
With saucy gesture

Primroses flare,
And roguish violets,

Hidden with care;
And whatsoever

There stirs and strives,
The Spring's contented,

If works and thrives.

'Mongst all the blossoms

That fairest are,
My sweetheart's sweetness

Is sweetest far;
Upon me ever

Her glances light,
My song they waken,

My words make bright,
An ever open

And blooming mind,

In sport, unsullied,

In earnest, kind.
Though roses and lilies

By Summer are brought,
Against my sweetheart

Prevails he nought.

    1816.

AT MIDNIGHT HOUR.

[Goethe relates that a remarkable situation he was in one bright moonlight night led to the composition of this sweet song, which was "the dearer to him because he could not say whence it came and whither it would."]

AT midnight hour I went, not willingly,

A little, little boy, yon churchyard past,
To Father Vicar's house; the stars on high

On all around their beauteous radiance cast,

  At midnight hour.

And when, in journeying o'er the path of life,

My love I follow'd, as she onward moved,
With stars and northern lights o'er head in strife,

 Going and coming, perfect bliss I proved

  At midnight hour.

Until at length the full moon, lustre-fraught,

Burst thro' the gloom wherein she was enshrined;
And then the willing, active, rapid thought

Around the past, as round the future twined,

    At midnight hour.

        1818.

TO THE RISING FULL MOON.

Dornburg, 25th August, 1828.

WILT thou suddenly enshroud thee,

Who this moment wert so nigh?
Heavy rising masses cloud thee,

Thou art hidden from mine eye.

Yet my sadness thou well knowest,

Gleaming sweetly as a star!
That I'm loved, 'tis thou that showest,

Though my loved one may be far.

Upward mount then! clearer, milder,

Robed in splendour far more bright!
Though my heart with grief throbs wilder,

Fraught with rapture is the night!

        1828.

THE BRIDEGROOM.*

(Not in the English sense of the word, but the German, where it has the meaning of betrothed.)

I SLEPT,--'twas midnight,--in my bosom woke,

As though 'twere day, my love-o'erflowing heart;
To me it seemed like night, when day first broke;

What is't to me, whate'er it may impart?

She was away; the world's unceasing strife

For her alone I suffer'd through the heat
Of sultry day; oh, what refreshing life

At cooling eve!--my guerdon was complete.

The sun now set, and wand'ring hand in hand,

His last and blissful look we greeted then;
While spake our eyes, as they each other scann'd:

"From the far east, let's trust, he'll come again!"

At midnight!--the bright stars, in vision blest,

Guide to the threshold where she slumbers calm:
Oh be it mine, there too at length to rest,--

Yet howsoe'er this prove, life's full of charm!

    1828.

SUCH, SUCH IS HE WHO PLEASETH ME.

FLY, dearest, fly! He is not nigh!

He who found thee one fair morn in Spring

In the wood where thou thy flight didst wing.
Fly, dearest, fly! He is not nigh!
Never rests the foot of evil spy.

Hark! flutes' sweet strains and love's refrains

Reach the loved one, borne there by the wind,

In the soft heart open doors they find.
Hark! flutes' sweet strains and love's refrains,
Hark!--yet blissful love their echo pains.

Erect his head, and firm his tread,

Raven hair around his smooth brow strays,

On his cheeks a Spring eternal plays.
Erect his head, and firm his tread,
And by grace his ev'ry step is led.

Happy his breast, with pureness bless'd,

And the dark eyes 'neath his eyebrows placed,

With full many a beauteous line are graced.
Happy his breast, with pureness bless'd,
Soon as seen, thy love must be confess'd.

His mouth is red--its power I dread,

On his lips morn's fragrant incense lies,

Round his lips the cooling Zephyr sighs.
His mouth is red--its power I dread,
With one glance from him, all sorrow's fled.

His blood is true, his heart bold too,

In his soft arms, strength, protection, dwells

And his face with noble pity swells.
His blood is true, his heart bold too,
Blest the one whom those dear arms may woo!

   1816..

SICILIAN SONG.

YE black and roguish eyes,

If ye command.
Each house in ruins lies,

No town can stand.
And shall my bosom's chain,--

This plaster wall,Ä
To think one moment, deign,--

Shall ii not fall?

          1811.

SWISS SONG,

Up in th' mountain
I was a-sitting,
With the bird there
As my guest,
Blithely singing,
Blithely springing,
And building
His nest.

In the garden
I was a-standing,
And the bee there
Saw as well,
Buzzing, humming,
Going, coming,
And building
His cell.

O'er the meadow
I was a-going,
And there saw the
Butterflies,
Sipping, dancing,
Flying, glancing,
And charming
The eyes.

And then came my
Dear Hansel,
And I show'd them
With glee,
Sipping, quaffing,
And he, laughing,
Sweet kisses
Gave me.

      1811.

FINNISH SONG.

IF the loved one, the well-known one,
Should return as he departed,
On his lips would ring my kisses,
Though the wolf's blood might have dyed them;
And a hearty grasp I'd give him,
Though his finger-ends were serpents.

Wind! Oh, if thou hadst but reason,
Word for word in turns thou'dst carry,
E'en though some perchance might perish
'Tween two lovers so far distant.

All choice morsels I'd dispense with,
Table-flesh of priests neglect too,
Sooner than renounce my lover,
Whom, in Summer having vanquish'd,
I in Winter tamed still longer.

      1810.

GIPSY SONG.

IN the drizzling mist, with the snow high-pil'd,
In the Winter night, in the forest wild,
I heard the wolves with their ravenous howl,

I heard the screaming note of the owl:

    Wille wau wau wau!

        Wille wo wo wo!

            Wito hu!

I shot, one day, a cat in a ditch--
The dear black cat of Anna the witch;
Upon me, at night, seven were-wolves came down,
Seven women they were, from out of the town.

    Wille wau wau wau!

        Wille wo wo wo!

            Wito hu!

I knew them all; ay, I knew them straight;
First, Anna, then Ursula, Eve, and Kate,
And Barbara, Lizzy, and Bet as well;
And forming a ring, they began to yell:

    Wille wau wau wau!

        Wille wo wo wo!

            Wito hu!

Then call'd I their names with angry threat:
"What wouldst thou, Anna? What wouldst thou, Bet?"
At hearing my voice, themselves they shook,
And howling and yelling, to flight they took.

    Wille wau wau wau!

        Wille wo wo wo!

            Wito hu!

                1772.

THE DESTRUCTION OF MAGDEBURG.

[For a fine account of the fearful sack of Magdeburg, by Tilly, in the year 1613, see SCHILLER's History of the Thirty Years' War.]

OH, Magdeberg the town!
Fair maids thy beauty crown,
Thy charms fair maids and matrons crown;
Oh, Magdeburg the town!

Where all so blooming stands,
Advance fierce Tilly's bands;
O'er gardens and o'er well--till'd lands
Advance fierce Tilly's bands.

Now Tilly's at the gate.
Our homes who'll liberate?
Go, loved one, hasten to the gate,
And dare the combat straight!

There is no need as yet,
However fierce his threat;
Thy rosy cheeks I'll kiss, sweet pet!
There is no need as yet.

My longing makes me pale.
Oh, what can wealth avail?
E'en now thy father may be pale.
Thou mak'st my courage fail.

Oh, mother, give me bread!
Is then my father dead?
Oh, mother, one small crust of bread!
Oh, what misfortune dread!

Thy father, dead lies he,
The trembling townsmen flee,
Adown the street the blood runs free;
Oh, whither shall we flee?

The churches ruined lie,

The houses burn on high,
The roofs they smoke, the flames out fly,
Into the street then hie!

No safety there they meet!
The soldiers fill the Street,
With fire and sword the wreck complete:
No safety there they meet!

Down falls the houses' line,
Where now is thine or mine?
That bundle yonder is not thine,
Thou flying maiden mine!

The women sorrow sore.
The maidens far, far more.
The living are no virgins more;
Thus Tilly's troops make war!

FAMILIAR SONGS.

What we sing in company
Soon from heart to heart will fly.

THE Gesellige Lieder, which I have angicisled as above, as several of them cannot be called convivial songs, are separated by Goethe from his other songs, and I have adhered to the same arrangement. The Ergo bibamus is a well-known drinking song in Germany, where it enjoys vast popularity.

ON THE NEW YEAR.

[Composed for a merry party that used to meet, in 1802, at Goethe's house.]

FATE now allows us,

'Twixt the departing

And the upstarting,
Happy to be;

And at the call of

Memory cherish'd,

Future and perish'd
Moments we see.

Seasons of anguish,--

Ah, they must ever

Truth from woe sever,
Love and joy part;
Days still more worthy

Soon will unite us,

Fairer songs light us,
Strength'ning the heart.

We, thus united,

Think of, with gladness,

Rapture and sadness,
Sorrow now flies.
Oh, how mysterious

Fortune's direction!

Old the connection,

New-born the prize!

Thank, for this, Fortune,

Wavering blindly!

Thank all that kindly
Fate may bestow!
Revel in change's

Impulses clearer,

Love far sincerer,
More heartfelt glow!

Over the old one,

Wrinkles collected,

Sad and dejected,
Others may view;
But, on us gently

Shineth a true one,

And to the new one
We, too, are new.

As a fond couple

'Midst the dance veering,

First disappearing,
Then reappear,
So let affection

Guide thro' life's mazy

Pathways so hazy
Into the year!

    1802.

ANNIVERSARY SONG.

[This little song describes the different members of the party just spoken of.]

WHY pacest thou, my neighbour fair,

The garden all alone?
If house and land thou seek'st to guard,

I'd thee as mistress own.

My brother sought the cellar-maid,

And suffered her no rest;
She gave him a refreshing draught,

A kiss, too, she impress'd.

My cousin is a prudent wight,

The cook's by him ador'd;
He turns the spit round ceaselessly,

To gain love's sweet reward.

We six together then began

A banquet to consume,
When lo! a fourth pair singing came,

And danced into the room.

Welcome were they,--and welcome too

Was a fifth jovial pair.
Brimful of news, and stored with tales

And jests both new and rare.

For riddles, spirit, raillery,

And wit, a place remain'd;
A sixth pair then our circle join'd,

And so that prize was gain'd.

And yet to make us truly blest,

One miss'd we, and full sore;
A true and tender couple came,--

We needed them no more.

The social banquet now goes on,

Unchequer'd by alloy;
The sacred double-numbers then

Let us at once enjoy!

                1802.

THE SPRING ORACLE.

OH prophetic bird so bright,
Blossom-songster, cuckoo bight!
In the fairest time of year,
Dearest bird, oh! deign to hear
What a youthful pair would pray,
Do thou call, if hope they may:
Thy cuck-oo, thy cuck-oo.
Ever more cuck-oo, cuck-oo!

Hearest thou? A loving pair
Fain would to the altar fare;
Yes! a pair in happy youth,
Full of virtue, full of truth.
Is the hour not fix'd by fate?
Say, how long must they still wait?
Hark! cuck-oo! hark! cuck-oo!
Silent yet! for shame, cuck-oo!

'Tis not our fault, certainly!
Only two years patient be!
But if we ourselves please here,
Will pa-pa-papas appear?
Know that thou'lt more kindness do us,
More thou'lt prophesy unto us.
One! cuck-oo! Two! cuck-oo!
Ever, ever, cuck-oo, cuck-oo, coo!

If we've calculated clearly,
We have half a dozen nearly.
If good promises we'll give,
Wilt thou say how long we'll live?
Truly, we'll confess to thee,

We'd prolong it willingly.
Coo cuck-oo, coo cuck-oo,
Coo, coo, coo, coo, coo, coo, coo, coo, coo!

Life is one continued feast--
(If we keep no score, at least).
If now we together dwell,
Will true love remain as well?
For if that should e'er decay,
Happiness would pass away.
Coo cuck-oo, coo cuck-oo,
Coo, coo, coo, coo, coo, coo, coo, coo, coo!

    1803.*
(Gracefully in infinitum.)

THE HAPPY COUPLE.

AFTER these vernal rains

That we so warmly sought,
Dear wife, see how our plains

With blessings sweet are fraught!
We cast our distant gaze

Far in the misty blue;
Here gentle love still strays,

Here dwells still rapture true.

Thou seest whither go

Yon pair of pigeons white,
Where swelling violets blow

Round sunny foliage bright.
'Twas there we gather'd first

A nosegay as we roved;
There into flame first burst

The passion that we proved.

Yet when, with plighted troth,

The priest beheld us fare
Home from the altar both,

With many a youthful pair,--
Then other moons had birth,

And many a beauteous sun,
Then we had gain'd the earth

Whereon life's race to run.

A hundred thousand fold

The mighty bond was seal'd;
In woods, on mountains cold,

In bushes, in the field,
Within the wall, in caves,

And on the craggy height,
And love, e'en o'er the waves,

Bore in his tube the light.

Contented we remain'd,

We deem'd ourselves a pair;
'Twas otherwise ordain'd,

For, lo! a third was there;
A fourth, fifth, sixth appear'd,

And sat around our board;
And now the plants we've rear'd

High o'er our heads have soar'd!

How fair and pleasant looks,

On yonder beauteous spot,

Embraced by poplar-brooks,

The newly-finish'd cot!
Who is it there that sits

In that glad home above?
Is't not our darling Fritz

With his own darling love?

Beside yon precipice,

Whence pent-up waters steal,
And leaving the abyss,

Fall foaming through the wheel,
Though people often tell

Of millers' wives so fair,
Yet none can e'er excel

Our dearest daughter there!

Yet where the thick-set green

Stands round yon church and sad,
Where the old fir-tree's seen

Alone tow'rd heaven to nod,--
'Tis there the ashes lie

Of our untimely dead;
From earth our gaze on high

By their blest memory's led.

See how yon hill is bright

With billowy-waving arms!
The force returns, whose might

Has vanquished war's alarms.
Who proudly hastens here

With wreath-encircled brow?
'Tis like our child so dear

Thus Charles comes homeward now.

That dearest honour'd guest

Is welcom'd by the bride;
She makes the true one blest,

At the glad festal tide.
And ev'ry one makes haste

To join the dance with glee;
While thou with wreaths hast graced

The youngest children three.

To sound of flute and horn

The time appears renew'd,
When we, in love's young morn,

In the glad dance upstood;
And perfect bliss I know

Ere the year's course is run,
For to the font we go

With grandson and with son!

1803.*

SONG OF FELLOWSHIP.

[Written and sung in honour of the birthday of the Pastor Ewald at the time of Goethe's happy connection with Lily.]

IN ev'ry hour of joy

That love and wine prolong,
The moments we'll employ

To carol forth this song!
We're gathered in His name,

Whose power hath brought us here;
He kindled first our flame,

He bids it burn more clear.

Then gladly glow to-night,

And let our hearts combine!
Up! quaff with fresh delight

This glass of sparkling wine!
Up! hail the joyous hour,

And let your kiss be true;
With each new bond of power

The old becomes the new!

Who in our circle lives,

And is not happy there?
True liberty it gives,

And brother's love so fair.
Thus heart and heart through life

With mutual love are fill'd;
And by no causeless strife

Our union e'er is chill'd.

Our hopes a God has crown'd

With life-discernment free,
And all we view around,

Renews our ecstasy.
Ne'er by caprice oppress'd,

Our bliss is ne'er destroy'd;

More freely throbs our breast,

By fancies ne'er alloy'd.

Where'er our foot we set,

The more life's path extends,
And brighter, brighter yet

Our gaze on high ascends.
We know no grief or pain,

Though all things fall and rise;
Long may we thus remain!

Eternal be our ties!

    1775.

CONSTANCY IN CHANGE.

COULD this early bliss but rest

Constant for one single hour!
But e'en now the humid West

Scatters many a vernal shower.
Should the verdure give me joy?

'Tis to it I owe the shade;
Soon will storms its bloom destroy,

Soon will Autumn bid it fade.

Eagerly thy portion seize,

If thou wouldst possess the fruit!
Fast begin to ripen these,

And the rest already shoot.
With each heavy storm of rain

Change comes o'er thy valley fair;
Once, alas! but not again

Can the same stream hold thee e'er.

And thyself, what erst at least

Firm as rocks appear'd to rise,
Walls and palaces thou seest

But with ever-changing eyes.
Fled for ever now the lip

That with kisses used to glow,
And the foot, that used to skip

O'er the mountain, like the roe.

And the hand, so true and warm,

Ever raised in charity,
And the cunning-fashion'd form,--

All are now changed utterly.
And what used to bear thy name,

When upon yon spot it stood,
Like a rolling billow came,

Hast'ning on to join the flood.

Be then the beginning found

With the end in unison,
Swifter than the forms around

Are themselves now fleeting on!
Thank the merit in thy breast,

Thank the mould within thy heart,
That the Muses' favour blest
Ne'er will perish, ne'er depart.

1803.*

TABLE SONG.

[Composed for the merry party already mentioned, on the occasion of the departure for France of the hereditary prince, who was one of the number, and who is especially alluded to in the 3rd verse.]

O'ER me--how I cannot say,--

Heav'nly rapture's growing.
Will it help to guide my way

To yon stars all-glowing?
Yet that here I'd sooner be,

To assert I'm able,
Where, with wine and harmony,

I may thump the table.

Wonder not, my dearest friends,

What 'tis gives me pleasure;
For of all that earth e'er lends,

'Tis the sweetest treasure.
Therefore solemnly I swear,

With no reservation,
That maliciously I'll ne'er

Leave my present station.

Now that here we're gather'd round,

Chasing cares and slumbers,
Let, methought, the goblet sound

To the bard's glad numbers!
Many a hundred mile away,

Go those we love dearly;
Therefore let us here to-day

Make the glass ring clearly!

Here's His health, through Whom we live!

I that faith inherit.
To our king the next toast give,

Honour is his merit,
'Gainst each in-- and outward foe

He's our rock and tower.
Of his maintenance thinks he though,

More that grows his power.

Next to her good health I drink,

Who has stirr'd my passion;
Of his mistress let each think,

Think in knightly fashion.
If the beauteous maid but see

Whom 'tis I now call so,
Let her smiling nod to me:

"Here's my love's health also!"

To those friends,--the two or three,--

Be our next toast given,
In whose presence revel we,

In the silent even,--
Who the gloomy mist so cold

Scatter gently, lightly;
To those friends, then, new or old,

Let the toast ring brightly.

Broader now the stream rolls on,

With its waves more swelling,
While in higher, nobler tone,

Comrades, we are dwelling,--
We who with collected might,

Bravely cling together,
Both in fortune's sunshine bright,

And in stormy weather.

Just as we are gather'd thus,

Others are collected;
On them, therefore, as on us,

Be Fate's smile directed!
From the springhead to the sea,

Many a mill's revolving,
And the world's prosperity

Is the task I'm solving.

    1802.

WONT AND DONE.

I HAVE loved; for the first time with passion I rave!
I then was the servant, but now am the slave;

  I then was the servant of all:
By this creature so charming I now am fast bound,
To love and love's guerdon she turns all around,

  And her my sole mistress I call.

I've had faith; for the first time my faith is now strong!
And though matters go strangely, though matters go wrong,

To the ranks of the faithful I'm true:
Though ofttimes 'twas dark and though ofttimes 'twas drear,
In the pressure of need, and when danger was near,

    Yet the dawning of light I now view.

I have eaten; but ne'er have thus relish'd my food!
For when glad are the senses, and joyous the blood,

    At table all else is effaced
As for youth, it but swallows, then whistles an air;
As for me, to a jovial resort I'd repair,

    Where to eat, and enjoy what I taste.

I have drunk; but have never thus relish'd the bowl!
For wine makes us lords, and enlivens the soul,

    And loosens the trembling slave's tongue.
Let's not seek to spare then the heart-stirring drink,
For though in the barrel the old wine may sink,

    In its place will fast mellow the young.

I have danced, and to dancing am pledged by a vow!
Though no caper or waltz may be raved about now,

    In a dance that's becoming, whirl round.
And he who a nosegay of flowers has dress'd,
And cares not for one any more than the rest,

    With a garland of mirth is aye crown'd.

Then once more be merry, and banish all woes!
For he who but gathers the blossoming rose.

    By its thorns will be tickled alone.
To-day still, as yesterday, glimmers the star;
Take care from all heads that hang down to keep far,

    And make but the future thine own.

        1813.

GENERAL CONFESSION.

In this noble ring to-day

Let my warning shame ye!
Listen to my solemn voice,--

Seldom does it name ye.
Many a thing have ye intended,

Many a thing have badly ended,
And now I must blame ye.

At some moment in our lives

We must all repent us!
So confess, with pious trust,

All your sins momentous!
Error's crooked pathways shunning.

Let us, on the straight road running,
Honestly content us!

Yes! we've oft, when waking, dream'd,

Let's confess it rightly;
Left undrain'd the brimming cup,

When it sparkled brightly;
Many a shepherd's-hour's soft blisses,

Many a dear mouth's flying kisses
We've neglected lightly.

Mute and silent have we sat,

Whilst the blockheads prated,
And above e'en song divine

Have their babblings rated;
To account we've even call'd us

For the moments that enthrall'd us,
With enjoyment freighted.

If thou'lt absolution grant

To thy true ones ever,
We, to execute thy will,

Ceaseless will endeavour,
From half-measures strive to wean us,

Wholly, fairly, well demean us,
Resting, flagging never.

At all blockheads we'll at once

Let our laugh ring clearly,
And the pearly-foaming wine

Never sip at merely.
Ne'er with eye alone give kisses,

But with boldness suck in blisses
From those lips loved dearly.

1803.*

COPTIC SONG.

LEAVE we the pedants to quarrel and strive,

Rigid and cautious the teachers to be!
All of the wisest men e'er seen alive

Smile, nod, and join in the chorus with me:
"Vain 'tis to wait till the dolt grows less silly!
Play then the fool with the fool, willy-nilly,--

Children of wisdom,--remember the word!"

Merlin the old, from his glittering grave,

When I, a stripling, once spoke to him,--gave

Just the same answer as that I've preferr'd;
"Vain 'tis to wait till the dolt grows less silly!
Play then the fool with the fool, willy-nilly,--

Children of wisdom,--remember the word!"

And on the Indian breeze as it booms,
And in the depths of Egyptian tombs,

Only the same holy saying I've heard:
"Vain 'tis to wait till the dolt grows less silly!
Play then the fool with the fool, willy-nilly,--

Children of wisdom,--remember the word!"

1789.*

ANOTHER.

Go! obedient to my call,

Turn to profit thy young days,

  Wiser make betimes thy breast

In Fate's balance as it sways,

  Seldom is the cock at rest;
Thou must either mount, or fall,

Thou must either rule and win,

Or submissively give in,
Triumph, or else yield to clamour:
Be the anvil or the hammer.

1789.

VANITAS! VANITATUM VANITAS!

MY trust in nothing now is placed,

    Hurrah!
So in the world true joy I taste,

    Hurrah!
Then he who would be a comrade of mine
Must rattle his glass, and in chorus combine,
Over these dregs of wine.

I placed my trust in gold and wealth,

    Hurrah!
But then I lost all joy and health,

    Lack-a-day!
Both here and there the money roll'd,
And when I had it here, behold,
From there had fled the gold!

I placed my trust in women next,

    Hurrah!
But there in truth was sorely vex'd,

    Lack-a-day!
The False another portion sought,
The True with tediousness were fraught,
The Best could not be bought.

My trust in travels then I placed,

    Hurrah!
And left my native land in haste.

    Lack-a-day!
But not a single thing seem'd good,
The beds were bad, and strange the food,
And I not understood.

I placed my trust in rank and fame,

    Hurrah!
Another put me straight to shame,

    Lack-a-day!
And as I had been prominent,
All scowl'd upon me as I went,
I found not one content.

I placed my trust in war and fight,

    Hurrah!
We gain'd full many a triumph bright,

    Hurrah!
Into the foeman's land we cross'd,
We put our friends to equal cost,
And there a leg I lost.

My trust is placed in nothing now,

    Hurrah!
At my command the world must bow,

    Hurrah!
And as we've ended feast and strain,
The cup we'll to the bottom drain;
No dregs must there remain!

        1806.

FORTUNE OF WAR.

NOUGHT more accursed in war I know

Than getting off scot-free;
Inured to danger, on we go

In constant victory;
We first unpack, then pack again,

With only this reward,
That when we're marching, we complain,

And when in camp, are bor'd.

The time for billeting comes next,--

The peasant curses it;
Each nobleman is sorely vex'd,

'Tis hated by the cit.
Be civil, bad though be thy food,

The clowns politely treat;
If to our hosts we're ever rude,

Jail-bread we're forced to eat.

And when the cannons growl around,

And small arms rattle clear,
And trumpet, trot, and drum resound,

We merry all appear;
And as it in the fight may chance,

We yield, then charge amain,
And now retire, and now advance,

And yet a cross ne'er gain.

At length there comes a musket-ball,

And hits the leg, please Heaven;
And then our troubles vanish all,

For to the town we're driven,
(Well cover'd by the victor's force,)

Where we in wrath first came,--
The women, frightened then, of course,

Are loving now and tame.

Cellar and heart are open'd wide,

The cook's allow'd no rest;
While beds with softest down supplied

Are by our members press'd.
The nimble lads upon us wait,

No sleep the hostess takes
Her shift is torn in pieces straight,--

What wondrous lint it makes!

If one has tended carefully

The hero's wounded limb,
Her neighbour cannot rest, for she

Has also tended him.
A third arrives in equal haste,

At length they all are there,
And in the middle he is placed

Of the whole band so fair!

On good authority the king

Hears how we love the fight,
And bids them cross and ribbon bring,

Our coat and breast to dight.
Say if a better fate can e'er

A son of Mars pursue!
'Midst tears at length we go from there,

Beloved and honour'd too.

1814.

OPEN TABLE.

MANY a guest I'd see to-day,

Met to taste my dishes!
Food in plenty is prepar'd,

Birds, and game, and fishes.
Invitations all have had,

All proposed attending.
Johnny, go and look around!

Are they hither wending?

Pretty girls I hope to see,

Dear and guileless misses,
Ignorant how sweet it is

Giving tender kisses.
Invitations all have had,

All proposed attending.
Johnny, go and look around!

Are they hither wending?

Women also I expect,

Loving tow'rd their spouses,
Whose rude grumbling in their breasts

Greater love but rouses.
Invitations they've had too,

All proposed attending!
Johnny, go and look around!

Are they hither wending?

I've too ask'd young gentlemen,

Who are far from haughty,
And whose purses are well-stock'd,

Well-behaved, not haughty.
These especially I ask'd,

All proposed attending.
Johnny, go and look around!

Are they hither wending?

Men I summon'd with respect,

Who their own wives treasure;
Who in ogling other Fair

Never take a pleasure.
To my greetings they replied,

All proposed attending.
Johnny, go and look around!

Are they hither wending?

Then to make our joy complete,

Poets I invited,
Who love other's songs far more

Than what they've indited.
All acceded to my wish,

All proposed attending.
Johnny, go and look around!

Are they hither wending?

Not a single one appears,

None seem this way posting.
All the soup boils fast away,

Joints are over-roasting.

Ah, I fear that we have been

Rather too unbending!
Johnny, tell me what you think!

None are hither wending.

Johnny, run and quickly bring

Other guests to me now!
Each arriving as he is--

That's the plan, I see now.
In the town at once 'tis known,

Every one's commending.
Johnny, open all the doors:

All are hither wending!

1815.*

THE RECKONING.

LEADER.

LET no cares now hover o'er us

Let the wine unsparing run!
Wilt thou swell our merry chorus?

Hast thou all thy duty done?

SOLO.

Two young folks--the thing is curious--

Loved each other; yesterday
Both quite mild, to-day quite furious,

Next day, quite the deuce to pay!
If her neck she there was stooping,

He must here needs pull his hair.
I revived their spirits drooping,

And they're now a happy pair.

CHORUS.

Surely we for wine may languish!

Let the bumper then go round!
For all sighs and groans of anguish

Thou to-day in joy hast drown'd.

SOLO.

Why, young orphan, all this wailing?

"Would to heaven that I were dead!
For my guardian's craft prevailing

Soon will make me beg my bread."
Knowing well the rascal genus,

Into court I dragg'd the knave;
Fair the judges were between us,

And the maiden's wealth did save.

CHORUS.

Surely we for wine may languish!

Let the bumper then go round!
For all sighs and groans of anguish

Thou to-day in joy hast drown'd.

SOLO.

To a little fellow, quiet,

Unpretending and subdued,

Has a big clown, running riot,

Been to-day extremely rude.
I bethought me of my duty,

And my courage swell'd apace,
So I spoil'd the rascal's beauty,

Slashing him across the face.

CHORUS.

Surely we for wine may languish!

Let the bumper then go round!
For all sighs and groans of anguish

Thou to-day in joy hast drown'd.

SOLO.

Brief must be my explanation,

For I really have done nought.
Free from trouble and vexation,

I a landlord's business bought.
There I've done, with all due ardour,

All that duty order'd me;
Each one ask'd me for the larder,

And there was no scarcity.

CHORUS.

Surely we for wine may languish!

Let the bumper then go round!
For all sighs and groans of anguish

Thou to-day in joy hast drown'd.

LEADER.

Each should thus make proclamation

Of what he did well to-day!
That's the match whose conflagration

Should inflame our tuneful lay.
Let it be our precept ever

To admit no waverer here!
For to act the good endeavour,

None but rascals meek appear.

CHORUS.

Surely we for wine may languish!

Let the bumper then go round!
For all sighs and groans of anguish

We have now in rapture drown'd.

TRIO.

Let each merry minstrel enter,

He's right welcome to our hall!
'Tis but with the selfÄtormentor

That we are not liberal;

For we fear that his caprices,

That his eye-brows dark and sad,
That his grief that never ceases

Hide an empty heart, or bad.

CHORUS.

No one now for wine shall languish!

Here no minstrel shall be found,

Who all sighs and groans of anguish,

Has not first in rapture drown'd!

           1810.

ERGO BIBAMUS!

FOR a praiseworthy object we're now gather'd here,

  So, brethren, sing: ERGO BIBAMUS!
Tho' talk may be hush'd, yet the glasses ring clear,

  Remember then: ERGO BIBAMUS!
In truth 'tis an old, 'tis an excellent word,
With its sound so befitting each bosom is stirr'd,
And an echo the festal hall filling is heard,

  A glorious ERGO BIBAMUS!

I saw mine own love in her beauty so rare,

  And bethought me of: ERGO BIBAMUS;
So I gently approach'd, and she let me stand there,

  While I help'd myself, thinking: BIBAMUS!
And when she's appeased, and will clasp you and kiss,
Or when those embraces and kisses ye miss,
Take refuge, till sound is some worthier bliss,

  In the comforting ERGO BIBAMUS!

I am call'd by my fate far away from each friend;

  Ye loved ones, then: ERGO BIBAMUS!
With wallet light-laden from hence I must wend.

  So double our ERGO BIBAMUS!
Whate'er to his treasures the niggard may add,
Yet regard for the joyous will ever be had,
For gladness lends over its charms to the glad,

So, brethren, sing; ERGO BIBAMUS!

And what shall we say of to-day as it flies?

I thought but of: ERGO BIBAMUS
'Tis one of those truly that seldom arise,

So again and again sing: BIBAMUS!
For joy through a wide-open portal it guides,
Bright glitter the clouds, as the curtain divides,
An a form, a divine one, to greet us in glides,

While we thunder our: ERGO BIBAMUS!

1810.

EPIPHANIAS.

THE three holy kings with their star's bright ray,--
They eat and they drink, but had rather not pay;
They like to eat and drink away,
They eat and drink, but had rather not pay.

The three holy kings have all come here,
In number not four, but three they appear;
And if a fourth join'd the other three,
Increased by one their number would be.

The first am I,--the fair and the white,
I ought to be seen when the sun shines bright!
But, alas! with all my spices and myrrh,
No girl now likes me,--I please not her.

The next am I,--the brown and the long,
Known well to women, known well to song.
Instead of spices, 'tis gold I bear,
And so I'm welcome everywhere.

The last am I,--the black and small,
And fain would be right merry withal.
I like to eat and to drink full measure,
I eat and drink, and give thanks with pleasure.

The three holy kings are friendly and mild,
They seek the Mother, and seek the Child;
The pious Joseph is sitting by,
The ox and the ass on their litter lie.

We're bringing gold, we're bringing myrrh,
The women incense always prefer;
And if we have wine of a worthy growth,
We three to drink like six are not loth.

As here we see fair lads and lasses,
But not a sign of oxen or asses,
We know that we have gone astray
And so go further on our way.

BALLADS.

Poet's art is ever able
To endow with truth mere fable.

MIGNON.
[This universally known poem is also to be found in Wilhelm Meister.]

KNOW'ST thou the land where the fair citron blows,
Where the bright orange midst the foliage glows,
Where soft winds greet us from the azure skies,
Where silent myrtles, stately laurels rise,
Know'st thou it well?

   'Tis there, 'tis there,
That I with thee, beloved one, would repair.

Know'st thou the house? On columns rests its pile,
Its halls are gleaming, and its chambers smile,
And marble statues stand and gaze on me:
"Poor child! what sorrow hath befallen thee?"
Know'st thou it well?

   'Tis there, 'tis there,
That I with thee, protector, would repair!

Know'st thou the mountain, and its cloudy bridge?
The mule can scarcely find the misty ridge;
In caverns dwells the dragon's olden brood,
The frowning crag obstructs the raging flood.
Know'st thou it well?

       'Tis there, 'tis there,
Our path lies--Father--thither, oh repair!

       1795.*

THE MINSTREL.

[This fine poem is introduced in the second book of Wilhelm Meister.]

"WHAT tuneful strains salute mine ear

Without the castle walls?
Oh, let the song re-echo here,

Within our festal halls!"
Thus spake the king, the page out-hied;
The boy return'd; the monarch cried:

"Admit the old man yonder!"

"All hail, ye noble lords to-night!

All hail, ye beauteous dames!
Star placed by star! What heavenly sight!

Whoe'er can tell their names?
Within this glittering hall sublime,
Be closed, mine eyes! 'tis not the time

For me to feast my wonder."

The minstrel straightway closed his eyes,

And woke a thrilling tone;

The knights look'd on in knightly guise,

Fair looks tow'rd earth were thrown.
The monarch, ravish'd by the strain,
Bade them bring forth a golden chain,

To be his numbers' guerdon.

"The golden chain give not to me,

But give the chain to those
In whose bold face we shiver'd see

The lances of our foes.
Or give it to thy chancellor there;
With other burdens he may bear

This one more golden burden.

"I sing, like birds of blithesome note,

That in the branches dwell;
The song that rises from the throat

Repays the minstrel well.
One boon I'd crave, if not too bold--
One bumper in a cup of gold

Be as my guerdon given."

The bowl he raised, the bowl he quaff'd:

"Oh drink, with solace fraught!
Oh, house thrice-blest, where such a draught

A trifling gift is thought!
When Fortune smiles, remember me,
And as I thank you heartily,

As warmly thank ye Heaven!"

    1795.*

BALLAD

OF THE BANISHED AND RETURNING COUNT.

[Goethe began to write an opera called Lowenstuhl, founded upon the old tradition which forms the subject of this Ballad, but he never carried out his design.]

OH, enter old minstrel, thou time-honour'd one!
We children are here in the hall all alone,

The portals we straightway will bar.
Our mother is praying, our father is gone

To the forest, on wolves to make war.
Oh sing us a ballad, the tale then repeat,

'Till brother and I learn it right;
We long have been hoping a minstrel to meet,

For children hear tales with delight.

"At midnight, when darkness its fearful veil weaves,
His lofty and stately old castle he leaves,

But first he has buried his wealth.
What figure is that in his arms one perceives,

As the Count quits the gateway by stealth?
O'er what is his mantle so hastily thrown?

What bears he along in his flight?
A daughter it is, and she gently sleeps on"--

The children they hear with delight.

"The morning soon glimmers. the world is so wide,
In valleys and forests a home is supplied,

The bard in each village is cheer'd.
Thus lives he and wanders, while years onward glide,

And longer still waxes his beard;
But the maiden so fair in his arms grows amain,

'Neath her star all-protecting and bright,
Secured in the mantle from wind and from rain--"

The children they hear with delight.

"And year upon year with swift footstep now steals,
The mantle it fades, many rents it reveals,

The maiden no more it can hold.
The father he sees her, what rapture he feels!

His joy cannot now be controll'd.
How worthy she seems of the race whence she springs,

How noble and fair to the sight!
What wealth to her dearly-loved father she brings!"--

The children they hear with delight.

"Then comes there a princely knight galloping by,
She stretches her hand out, as soon as he's nigh,

But alms he refuses to give.
He seizes her hand, with a smile in his eye:

'Thou art mine!' he exclaims, 'while I live!'
'When thou know'st,' cries the old man, 'the treasure that's there,

A princess thou'lt make her of right;
Betroth'd be she now, on this spot green and fair--'"

The children they hear with delight.

"So she's bless'd by the priest on the hallowed place,
And she goes with a smiling but sorrowful face,

From her father she fain would not part.
The old man still wanders with ne'er-changing pace,

He covers with joy his sad heart.

So I think of my daughter, as years pass away,

And my grandchildren far from my sight;
I bless them by night, and I bless them by day"--

The children they hear with delight.

He blesses the children: a knocking they hear,
The father it is! They spring forward in fear,

The old man they cannot conceal--
"Thou beggar, wouldst lure, then, my children so dear?

Straight seize him, ye vassals of steel!
To the dungeon most deep, with the fool-hardy knave!"

The mother from far hears the fight;
She hastens with flatt'ring entreaty to crave--

The children they hear with delight.

The vassals they suffer the Bard to stand there,
And mother and children implore him to spare,

The proud prince would stifle his ire,
'Till driven to fury at hearing their prayer,

His smouldering anger takes fire:
"Thou pitiful race! Oh, thou beggarly crew!

Eclipsing my star, once so bright!
Ye'll bring me destruction, ye sorely shall rue!"

The children they hear with affright.

The old man still stands there with dignified mien,
The vassals of steel quake before him, I ween,

The Count's fury increases in power;
"My wedded existence a curse long has been,

And these are the fruits from that flower!
'Tis ever denied, and the saying is true,

That to wed with the base-born is right;
The beggar has borne me a beggarly crew,--"

The children they hear with affright.

"If the husband, the father, thus treats you with scorn,
If the holiest bonds by him rashly are torn,

Then come to your father--to me!
The beggar may gladden life's pathway forlorn,

Though aged and weak he may be.
This castle is mine! thou hast made it thy prey,

Thy people 'twas put me to flight;
The tokens I bear will confirm what I say"--

The children they hear with delight.

"The king who erst govern'd returneth again,
And restores to the Faithful the goods that were ta'en,

I'll unseal all my treasures the while;
The laws shall be gentle, and peaceful the reign"--

The old man thus cries with a smile--
"Take courage, my son! all hath turned out for good,

And each hath a star that is bright,
Those the princess hath borne thee are princely in blood,"--

The children thy hear with delight.

   1816.

THE VIOLET.

UPON the mead a violet stood,
Retiring, and of modest mood,

In truth, a violet fair.
Then came a youthful shepherdess,

And roam'd with sprightly joyousness,
And blithely woo'd

With carols sweet the air

"Ah!" thought the violet, "had I been
For but the smallest moment e'en

Nature's most beauteous flower,
'Till gather'd by my love, and press'd,
When weary, 'gainst her gentle breast,
For e'en, for e'en

One quarter of an hour!"

Alas! alas! the maid drew nigh,
The violet failed to meet her eye,

She crush'd the violet sweet.
It sank and died, yet murmur'd not:
"And if I die, oh, happy lot,
For her I die,

And at her very feet!"

1775.*

THE FAITHLESS BOY.

THERE was a wooer blithe and gay,

A son of France was he,--
Who in his arms for many a day,

As though his bride were she,
A poor young maiden had caress'd,
And fondly kiss'd, and fondly press'd,

And then at length deserted.

When this was told the nut-brown maid,

Her senses straightway fled;
She laugh'd and wept, and vow'd and pray'd,

And presently was dead.
The hour her soul its farewell took,
The boy was sad, with terror shook,

Then sprang upon his charger.

He drove his spurs into his side,

And scour'd the country round;
But wheresoever he might ride,

No rest for him was found.
For seven long days and nights he rode,
It storm'd, the waters overflow'd,

It bluster'd, lighten'd, thunder'd.

On rode he through the tempest's din,

Till he a building spied;
In search of shelter crept he in,

When he his steed had tied.
And as he groped his doubtful way,
The ground began to rock and sway,--

He fell a hundred fathoms.

When he recover'd from the blow,

He saw three lights pass by;
He sought in their pursuit to go,

The lights appear'd to fly.
They led his footsteps all astray,
Up, down, through many a narrow way

Through ruin'd desert cellars.

When lo! he stood within a hall,

With hollow eyes. and grinning all;
They bade him taste the fare.

A hundred guests sat there.
He saw his sweetheart 'midst the throng,
Wrapp'd up in grave-clothes white and long;

She turn'd, and----*

1774.
(* This ballad is introduced in Act II. of Claudine of Villa
Bella, where it is suddenly broken off, as it is here.)

THE ERL-KING.

WHO rides there so late through the night dark and drear?
The father it is, with his infant so dear;
He holdeth the boy tightly clasp'd in his arm,
He holdeth him safely, he keepeth him warm.

"My son, wherefore seek'st thou thy face thus to hide?"
"Look, father, the Erl-King is close by our side!
Dost see not the Erl-King, with crown and with train?"
"My son, 'tis the mist rising over the plain."

"Oh, come, thou dear infant! oh come thou with me!
Full many a game I will play there with thee;
On my strand, lovely flowers their blossoms unfold,
My mother shall grace thee with garments of gold."

"My father, my father, and dost thou not hear
The words that the Erl-King now breathes in mine ear?"
"Be calm, dearest child, 'tis thy fancy deceives;
'Tis the sad wind that sighs through the withering leaves."

"Wilt go, then, dear infant, wilt go with me there?
My daughters shall tend thee with sisterly care
My daughters by night their glad festival keep,
They'll dance thee, and rock thee, and sing thee to sleep."

"My father, my father, and dost thou not see,
How the Erl-King his daughters has brought here for me?"

"My darling, my darling, I see it aright,
'Tis the aged grey willows deceiving thy sight."

"I love thee, I'm charm'd by thy beauty, dear boy!
And if thou'rt unwilling, then force I'll employ."
"My father, my father, he seizes me fast,
Full sorely the Erl-King has hurt me at last."

The father now gallops, with terror half wild,
He grasps in his arms the poor shuddering child;
He reaches his courtyard with toil and with dread,--
The child in his arms finds he motionless, dead.

    1782.*

JOHANNA SEBUS.

[To the memory of an excellent and beautiful girl of 17, belonging to the village of Brienen, who perished on the 13th of January, 1809, whilst giving help on the occasion of the breaking up of the ice on the Rhine, and the bursting of the dam of Cleverham.]

THE DAM BREAKS DOWN, THE ICE-PLAIN GROWLS,
THE FLOODS ARISE, THE WATER HOWLS.

"I'll bear thee, mother, across the swell,

'Tis not yet high, I can wade right well."

"Remember us too! in what danger are we!

Thy fellow-lodger, and children three!

The trembling woman!--Thou'rt going away!"

She bears the mother across the spray.

"Quick! haste to the mound, and awhile there wait,

I'll soon return, and all will be straight.

The mound's close by, and safe from the wet;

But take my goat too, my darling pet!"

THE DAM DISSOLVES, THE ICE-PLAIN GROWLS,
THE FLOODS DASH ON, THE WATER HOWLS.

She places the mother safe on the shore;

Fair Susan then turns tow'rd the flood once more.

"Oh whither? Oh whither? The breadth fast grows,

Both here and there the water o'erflows.

Wilt venture, thou rash one, the billows to brave?"
"THEY SHALL, AND THEY MUST BE PRESERVED FROM THE WAVE!"

THE DAM DISAPPEARS, THE WATER GROWLS,
LIKE OCEAN BILLOWS IT HEAVES AND HOWLS.

Fair Susan returns by the way she had tried,

The waves roar around, but she turns not aside;

She reaches the mound, and the neighbour straight,

But for her and the children, alas, too late!

THE DAM DISAPPEAR'D,--LIKE A SEA IT GROWLS,
ROUND THE HILLOCK IN CIRCLING EDDIES IT HOWLS.

The foaming abyss gapes wide, and whirls round,

The women and children are borne to the ground;

The horn of the goat by one is seized fast,

But, ah, they all must perish at last!

Fair Susan still stands-there, untouch'd by the wave;

The youngest, the noblest, oh, who now will save?

Fair Susan still stands there, as bright as a star,

But, alas! all hope, all assistance is far.

The foaming waters around her roar,

To save her, no bark pushes off from the shore.

Her gaze once again she lifts up to Heaven,

Then gently away by the flood she is driven.

NO DAM, NO PLAIN! TO MARK THE PLACE
SOME STRAGGLING TREES ARE THE ONLY TRACE.

The rushing water the wilderness covers,

Yet Susan's image still o'er it hovers.--

The water sinks, the plains re-appear.

Fair Susan's lamented with many a tear,--

May he who refuses her story to tell,

Be neglected in life and in death as well!

        1809.

THE FISHERMAN.

THE waters rush'd, the waters rose,

A fisherman sat by,
While on his line in calm repose

He cast his patient eye.
And as he sat, and hearken'd there,

The flood was cleft in twain,
And, lo! a dripping mermaid fair

Sprang from the troubled main.

She sang to him, and spake the while:

"Why lurest thou my brood,
With human wit and human guile

From out their native flood?
Oh, couldst thou know how gladly dart

The fish across the sea,
Thou wouldst descend, e'en as thou art,

And truly happy be!

"Do not the sun and moon with grace

Their forms in ocean lave?
Shines not with twofold charms their face,

When rising from the wave?
The deep, deep heavens, then lure thee not,--

The moist yet radiant blue,--
Not thine own form,--to tempt thy lot

'Midst this eternal dew?"

The waters rush'd, the waters rose,

Wetting his naked feet;
As if his true love's words were those,

His heart with longing beat.
She sang to him, to him spake she,

His doom was fix'd, I ween;
Half drew she him, and half sank he,

And ne'er again was seen.

1779.*

THE KING OF THULE.*

(* This ballad is also introduced in Faust, where it is sung by Margaret.)

IN Thule lived a monarch,

Still faithful to the grave,
To whom his dying mistress

A golden goblet gave.

Beyond all price he deem'd it,

He quaff'd it at each feast;
And, when he drain'd that goblet,

His tears to flow ne'er ceas'd.

And when he felt death near him,

His cities o'er he told,
And to his heir left all things,

But not that cup of gold.

A regal banquet held he

In his ancestral hall,
In yonder sea-wash'd castle,

'Mongst his great nobles all.

There stood the aged reveller,

And drank his last life's-glow,--
Then hurl'd the holy goblet

Into the flood below.

He saw it falling, filling,

And sinking 'neath the main,
His eyes then closed for ever,

He never drank again.

                1774.

THE BEAUTEOUS FLOWER.

SONG OF THE IMPRISONED COUNT.

COUNT.

I KNOW a flower of beauty rare,

Ah, how I hold it dear!
To seek it I would fain repair,

Were I not prison'd here.
My sorrow sore oppresses me,
For when I was at liberty,

I had it close beside me.

Though from this castle's walls so steep

I cast mine eyes around,
And gaze oft from the lofty keep,

The flower can not be found.
Whoe'er would bring it to my sight,
Whether a vassal he, or knight,

My dearest friend I'd deem him.

THE ROSE.

I blossom fair,--thy tale of woes

I hear from 'neath thy grate.
Thou doubtless meanest me, the rose.

Poor knight of high estate!
Thou hast in truth a lofty mind;
The queen of flowers is then enshrin'd,

I doubt not, in thy bosom.

COUNT.

Thy red, in dress of green array'd,

As worth all praise I hold;
And so thou'rt treasured by each maid

Like precious stones or gold.
Thy wreath adorns the fairest face
But still thou'rt not the flower whose grace

I honour here in silence.

THE LILY.

The rose is wont with pride to swell,

And ever seeks to rise;
But gentle sweethearts love full well

The lily's charms to prize,
The heart that fills a bosom true,
That is, like me, unsullied too,

My merit values duly.

COUNT.

In truth, I hope myself unstain'd,

And free from grievous crime;
Yet I am here a prisoner chain'd,

And pass in grief my time,
To me thou art an image sure
Of many a maiden, mild and pure,

And yet I know a dearer.

THE PINK.

That must be me, the pink, who scent

The warder's garden here;
Or wherefore is he so intent

My charms with care to rear?
My petals stand in beauteous ring,
Sweet incense all around I fling,

And boast a thousand colours.

COUNT.

The pink in truth we should not slight,

It is the gardener's pride
It now must stand exposed to light,

Now in the shade abide.
Yet what can make the Count's heart glow
Is no mere pomp of outward show;

It is a silent flower.

THE VIOLET.

Here stand I, modestly half hid,

And fain would silence keep;
Yet since to speak I now am bid,

I'll break my silence deep.
If, worthy Knight, I am that flower,
It grieves me that I have not power

To breathe forth all my sweetness.

COUNT.

The violet's charms I prize indeed,

So modest 'tis, and fair,
And smells so sweet; yet more I need

To ease my heavy care.
The truth I'll whisper in thine ear:
Upon these rocky heights so drear,

I cannot find the loved one.

The truest maiden 'neath the sky

Roams near the stream below,
And breathes forth many a gentle sigh,

Till I from hence can go.
And when she plucks a flow'ret blue,
And says "Forget-me-not!"--I, too,

Though far away, can feel it.

Ay, distance only swells love's might,

When fondly love a pair;
Though prison'd in the dungeon's night,

In life I linger there
And when my heart is breaking nigh,
"Forget-me-not!" is all I cry,

And straightway life returneth.

            1798.

SIR CURT'S WEDDING-JOURNEY.

WITH a bridegroom's joyous bearing,

Mounts Sir Curt his noble beast,
To his mistress' home repairing,

There to hold his wedding feast;

When a threatening foe advances

From a desert, rocky spot;
For the fray they couch their lances,

Not delaying, speaking not.

Long the doubtful fight continues,

Victory then for Curt declares;
Conqueror, though with wearied sinews,

Forward on his road he fares.
When he sees, though strange it may be,

Something 'midst the foliage move;
'Tis a mother, with her baby,

Stealing softly through the grove!

And upon the spot she beckons--

"Wherefore, love, this speed so wild?
Of the wealth thy storehouse reckons,

Hast thou nought to give thy child!"
Flames of rapture now dart through him,

And he longs for nothing more,
While the mother seemeth to him

Lovely as the maid of yore.

But he hears his servants blowing,

And bethinks him of his bride;
And ere long, while onward going,

Chances past a fair to ride;
In the booths he forthwith buys him

For his mistress many a pledge;
But, alas! some Jews surprise him,

And long-standing debts allege.

And the courts of justice duly

Send the knight to prison straight.
Oh accursed story, truly!

For a hero, what a fate!
Can my patience such things weather?

Great is my perplexity.
Women, debts, and foes together,--

Ah, no knight escapes scot free!

    1803.*

WEDDING SONG.

THE tale of the Count our glad song shall record

Who had in this castle his dwelling,
Where now ye are feasting the new-married lord,

His grandson of whom we are telling.
The Count as Crusader had blazon'd his fame,
Through many a triumph exalted his name,
And when on his steed to his dwelling he came,

His castle still rear'd its proud head,
But servants and wealth had all fled.

'Tis true that thou, Count, hast return'd to thy home,

But matters are faring there ill.
The winds through the chambers at liberty roam,

And blow through the windows at will
What's best to be done in a cold autumn night?
Full many I've pass'd in more piteous plight;
The morn ever settles the matter aright.

Then quick, while the moon shines so clear,

To bed on the straw, without fear,

And whilst in a soft pleasing slumber he lay,

A motion he feels 'neath his bed.
The rat, an he likes it, may rattle away!

Ay, had he but crumbs there outspread!
But lo! there appears a diminutive wight,
A dwarf 'tis, yet graceful, and bearing a light,
With orator-gestures that notice invite,

At the feet of the Count on the floor

Who sleeps not, though weary full sore.

"We've long been accustom'd to hold here our feast,

Since thou from thy castle first went;
And as we believed thou wert far in the East,

To revel e'en now we were bent.
And if thou'lt allow it, and seek not to chide,
We dwarfs will all banquet with pleasure and pride,
To honour the wealthy, the beautiful bride

Says the Count with a smile, half-asleep;--

"Ye're welcome your quarters to keep!"

Three knights then advance, riding all in a group,

Who under the bed were conceal'd;
And then is a singing and noise-making troop

Of strange little figures reveal'd;
And waggon on waggon with all kinds of things--
The clatter they cause through the ear loudly rings--
The like ne'er was seen save in castles of kings;

At length, in a chariot of gold,

The bride and the guests too, behold!

Then all at full gallop make haste to advance,

Each chooses his place in the hall;
With whirling and waltzing, and light joyous dance,

They begin with their sweethearts the ball.
The fife and the fiddle all merrily sound,
Thy twine, and they glide, and with nimbleness bound,
Thy whisper, and chatter, and, chatter around;

The Count on the scene casts his eye,

And seems in a fever to lie.

They hustle, and bustle, and rattle away

On table, on bench, and on stool;
Then all who had joined in the festival gay

With their partners attempt to grow cool.
The hams and the sausages nimbly they bear,
And meat, fish, and poultry in plenty are there,
Surrounded with wine of the vintage most rare:

And when they have revell'd full long,

They vanish at last with a song.

* * * * * *

And if we're to sing all that further occurr'd,

Pray cease ye to bluster and prate;
For what he so gladly in small saw and heard

He enjoy'd and he practis'd in great.
For trumpets, and singing, and shouts without end
On the bridal-train, chariots and horsemen attend,
They come and appear, and they bow and they bend,

In merry and countless array.

Thus was it, thus is it to-day.

1802.

THE TREASURE-DIGGER

ALL my weary days I pass'd

Sick at heart and poor in purse.

Poverty's the greatest curse,

  Riches are the highest good!
And to end my woes at last,

Treasure-seeking forth I sped.

"Thou shalt have my soul instead!"

  Thus I wrote, and with my blood.

Ring round ring I forthwith drew,

Wondrous flames collected there,

Herbs and bones in order fair,

  Till the charm had work'd aright.
Then, to learned precepts true,

Dug to find some treasure old,

In the place my art foretold

  Black and stormy was the night.

Coming o'er the distant plain,

With the glimmer of a star,

Soon I saw a light afar,

As the hour of midnight knell'd.
Preparation was in vain.

Sudden all was lighted up

With the lustre of a cup

That a beauteous boy upheld.

Sweetly seem'd his eyes to laugh

Neath his flow'ry chaplet's load;

With the drink that brightly glow'd,

He the circle enter'd in.
And he kindly bade me quaff:

Then methought "This child can ne'er,

With his gift so bright and fair,

To the arch-fiend be akin."

"Pure life's courage drink!" cried he:
"This advice to prize then learn,--

Never to this place return

Trusting in thy spells absurd;
Dig no longer fruitlessly.

Guests by night, and toil by day!

Weeks laborious, feast-days gay!

Be thy future magic-word!

    1797.

THE RAT-CATCHER.

I AM the bard known far and wide,
The travell'd rat-catcher beside;
A man most needful to this town,
So glorious through its old renown.
However many rats I see,
How many weasels there may be,
I cleanse the place from ev'ry one,
All needs must helter-skelter run.

Sometimes the bard so full of cheer
As a child-catcher will appear,
Who e'en the wildest captive brings,
Whene'er his golden tales he sings.
However proud each boy in heart,
However much the maidens start,
I bid the chords sweet music make,
And all must follow in my wake.

Sometimes the skilful bard ye view
In the form of maiden-catcher too;
For he no city enters e'er,
Without effecting wonders there.
However coy may be each maid,
However the women seem afraid,
Yet all will love-sick be ere long
To sound of magic lute and song.

   [Da Capo.]   1803.*

THE SPINNER.

As I calmly sat and span,

Toiling with all zeal,
Lo! a young and handsome man

Pass'd my spinning-wheel.

And he praised,--what harm was there?--

Sweet the things he said--
Praised my flax-resembling hair,

And the even thread.

He with this was not content,

But must needs do more;
And in twain the thread was rent,

Though 'twas safe before.

And the flax's stonelike weight

Needed to be told;
But no longer was its state

Valued as of old.

When I took it to the weaver,

Something felt I start,
And more quickly, as with fever,

Throbb'd my trembling heart.

Then I bear the thread at length

Through the heat, to bleach;
But, alas, I scarce have strength

To the pool to reach.

What I in my little room

Span so fine and slight,--
As was likely. I presume--

Came at last to light.

1800.*

BEFORE A COURT OF JUSTICE.

THE father's name ye ne'er shall be told

Of my darling unborn life;
"Shame, shame," ye cry, "on the strumpet bold!"

Yet I'm an honest wife.

To whom I'm wedded, ye ne'er shall be told,

Yet he's both loving and fair;
He wears on his neck a chain of gold,

And a hat of straw doth he wear.

If scorn 'tis vain to seek to repel,

On me let the scorn be thrown.
I know him well, and he knows me well,

And to God, too, all is known.

Sir Parson and Sir Bailiff, again,

I pray you, leave me in peace!
My child it is, my child 'twill remain,

So let your questionings cease!

1815.*

THE PAGE AND THE MILLER'S DAUGHTER.

PAGE.

WHERE goest thou? Where?

Miller's daughter so fair!

Thy name, pray?--

MILLER'S DAUGHTER.

  'Tis Lizzy.

PAGE.
Where goest thou? Where?
With the rake in thy hand?

MILLER'S DAUGHTER.
Father's meadows and land

To visit, I'm busy.

PAGE.
Dost go there alone?

MILLER'S DAUGHTER.
By this rake, sir, 'tis shown

That we're making the hay;
And the pears ripen fast
In the garden at last,

So I'll pick them to-day.

PAGE.
Is't a silent thicket I yonder view?

MILLER'S DAUGHTER.
Oh, yes! there are two;
There's one on each side.

PAGE.
I'll follow thee soon;
When the sun burns at noon
We'll go there, o'urselves from his rays to hide,
And then in some glade all-verdant and deep--

MILLER'S DAUGHTER.
Why, people would say--

PAGE.

Within mine arms thou gently wilt sleep.

MILLER'S DAUGHTER.

Your pardon, I pray!
Whoever is kiss'd by the miller-maid,
Upon the spot must needs be betray'd.

'Twould give me distress

To cover with white
Your pretty dark dress.
Equal with equal! then all is right!
That's the motto in which I delight.
I am in love with the miller-boy;
He wears nothing that I could destroy.

          1797.

THE YOUTH AND THE MILLSTREAM.

[This sweet Ballad, and the one entitled The Maid of the Mill's
Repentance, were written on the occasion of a visit paid by Goethe
to Switzerland. The Maid of the Mill's Treachery, to which the
latter forms the sequel, was not written till the following year.]

YOUTH.

SAY, sparkling streamlet, whither thou

    Art going!
With joyous mien thy waters now

    Are flowing.
Why seek the vale so hastily?
Attend for once, and answer me!

MILLSTREAM.

Oh youth, I was a brook indeed;

  But lately
My bed they've deepen'd, and my speed

  Swell'd greatly,
That I may haste to yonder mill.
And so I'm full and never still.

YOUTH.

The mill thou seekest in a mood

  Contented,
And know'st not how my youthful blood

  'S tormented.
But doth the miller's daughter fair
Gaze often on thee kindly there?

MILLSTREAM.

She opes the shutters soon as light

  Is gleaming;
And comes to bathe her features bright

  And beaming.
So full and snow-white is her breast,--
I feel as hot as steam suppress'd.

YOUTH.

If she in water can inflame

  Such ardour,
Surely, then, flesh and blood to tame

  Is harder.
When once is seen her beauteous face,
One ever longs her steps to trace.

MILLSTREAM.

Over the wheel I, roaring, bound,

      All-proudly,
And ev'ry spoke whirls swiftly round,

      And loudly.
Since I have seen the miller's daughter,
With greater vigour flows the water.

YOUTH.

Like others, then, can grief, poor brook,

      Oppress thee?
"Flow on!"--thus she'll, with smiling look,

      Address thee.
With her sweet loving glance, oh say,
Can she thy flowing current stay?

MILLSTREAM.

'Tis sad, 'tis sad to have to speed

      From yonder;
I wind, and slowly through the mead

      Would wander;
And if the choice remain'd with me,
Would hasten back there presently.

YOUTH.

Farewell, thou who with me dost prove

      Love's sadness!
Perchance some day thou'lt breathe of love

      And gladness.
Go, tell her straight, and often too,
The boy's mute hopes and wishes true.

              1797.

THE MAID OF THE MILL'S TREACHERY.

[This Ballad is introduced in the Wanderjahre, in a tale called
The Foolish Pilgrim.]

WHENCE comes our friend so hastily,

When scarce the Eastern sky is grey?
Hath he just ceased, though cold it be,

In yonder holy spot to pray?
The brook appears to hem his path,

Would he barefooted o'er it go?
Why curse his orisons in wrath,

Across those heights beclad with snow?

Alas! his warm bed he hath left,

Where he had look'd for bliss, I ween;
And if his cloak too, had been reft,

How fearful his disgrace had been!
By yonder villain sorely press'd,

His wallet from him has been torn;
Our hapless friend has been undress'd,

Left well nigh naked as when born.

The reason why he came this road,

Is that he sought a pair of eyes,
Which, at the mill, as brightly glow'd

As those that are in Paradise.
He will not soon again be there;

From out the house he quickly hied,
And when he gain'd the open air,

Thus bitterly and loudly cried

"Within her gaze, so dazzling bright,

No word of treachery I could read;
She seem'd to see me with delight,

Yet plann'd e'en then this cruel deed!
Could I, when basking in her smile,

Dream of the treason in her breast?
She bade kind Cupid stay awhile,

And he was there, to make us blest.

"To taste of love's sweet ecstasy

Throughout the night, that endless seem'd,
And for her mother's help to cry

Only when morning sunlight beam'd!
A dozen of her kith and kin,

A very human flood, in-press'd
Her cousins came, her aunts peer'd in,

And uncles, brothers, and the rest.

"Then what a tumult, fierce and loud!

Each seem'd a beast of prey to be;
The maiden's honour all the crowd,

With fearful shout, demand of me.
Why should they, madmen-like, begin

To fall upon a guiltless youth?
For he who such a prize would win,

Far nimbler needs must be, in truth.

"The way to follow up with skill

His freaks, by love betimes is known:

He ne'er will leave, within a mill,

Sweet flowers for sixteen years alone.--
They stole my clothes away,--yes, all!

And tried my cloak besides to steal.
How strange that any house so small

So many rascals could conceal!

"Then I sprang up, and raved, and swore,

To force a passage through them there.
I saw the treacherous maid once more,

And she was still, alas, so fair
They all gave way before my wrath,

Wild outcries flew about pell-mell;
At length I managed to rush forth,

With voice of thunder, from that hell.

"As maidens of the town we fly,

We'll shun you maidens of the village;
Leave it to those of quality

Their humble worshippers to pillage.
Yet if ye are of practised skill,

And of all tender ties afraid,
Exchange your lovers, if ye will,

But never let them be betray'd."

Thus sings he in the winter-night,

While not a blade of grass was green.
I laugh'd to see his piteous plight,

For it was well-deserved, I ween.
And may this be the fate of all,

Who treat by day their true loves ill,
And, with foolhardy daring, crawl

By night to Cupid's treacherous mill!

1798.

THE MAID OF THE MILL'S REPENTANCE.

YOUTH.

AWAY, thou swarthy witch! Go forth

 From out my house, I tell thee!
Or else I needs must, in my wrath,

 Expel thee!
What's this thou singest so falsely, forsooth,
Of love and a maiden's silent truth?

 Who'll trust to such a story!

GIPSY.

I sing of a maid's repentant fears,

 And long and bitter yearning;
Her levity's changed to truth and tears

 All-burning.
She dreads no more the threats of her mother,
She dreads far less the blows of her brother,

 Than the dearly loved-one's hatred.

YOUTH.

Of selfishness sing and treacherous lies,

 Of murder and thievish plunder!
Such actions false will cause no surprise,

Or wonder.
When they share their booty, both clothes and purse,--
As bad as you gipsies, and even worse,

Such tales find ready credence.

GIPSY.

"Alas, alas! oh what have I done?

 Can listening aught avail me?
I hear him toward my room hasten on,

 To hail me.
My heart beat high, to myself I said:
'O would that thou hadst never betray'd

 That night of love to thy mother!'"

YOUTH.

Alas! I foolishly ventured there,

 For the cheating silence misled me;
Ah, sweetest! let me to thee repair,--

 Nor dread me!
When suddenly rose a fearful din,
Her mad relations came pouring in.

 My blood still boils in my body!

GIPSY.

"Oh when will return an hour like this?

 I pine in silent sadness;
I've thrown away my only true bliss

 With madness.
Alas, poor maid! O pity my youth!
My brother was then full cruel in troth

 To treat the loved one so basely!"

THE POET.

The swarthy woman then went inside,

  To the spring in the courtyard yonder;
Her eyes from their stain she purified,

  And,--wonder!--
Her face and eyes were radiant and bright,
And the maid of the mill was disclosed to the sight

  Of the startled and angry stripling!

THE MAID OF THE MILL.

Thou sweetest, fairest, dearly-loved life!

  Before thine anger I cower;
But blows I dread not, nor sharp-edged knife,--

  This hour
Of sorrow and love to thee I'll sing,
And myself before thy feet I'll fling,

  And either live or die there!

YOUTH.

Affection, say, why buried so deep

  In my heart hast thou lain hidden?
By whom hast thou now to awake from thy sleep

  Been bidden?
Ah love, that thou art immortal I see!
Nor knavish cunning nor treachery

  Can destroy thy life so godlike.

THE MAID OF THE MILL.

If still with as fond and heartfelt love,

As thou once didst swear, I'm cherish'd,
Then nought of the rapture we used to prove

Is perish'd.
So take the woman so dear to thy breast!
In her young and innocent charms be blest,

For all are thine from henceforward!

BOTH.

Now, sun, sink to rest! Now, sun, arise!

Ye stars, be now shining, now darkling!
A star of love now gleams in the skies,

All-sparkling!
As long as the fountain may spring and run,
So long will we two be blended in one,

Upon each other's bosoms!

1797.

THE TRAVELLER AND THE FARM~MAIDEN.

HE.

CANST thou give, oh fair and matchless maiden,

'Neath the shadow of the lindens yonder,--

Where I'd fain one moment cease to wander,--
Food and drink to one so heavy laden?

SHE.

Wouldst thou find refreshment, traveller weary,

Bread, ripe fruit and cream to meet thy wishes,--

None but Nature's plain and homely dishes,--

Near the spring may soothe thy wanderings dreary.

HE.

Dreams of old acquaintance now pass through me,

Ne'er-forgotten queen of hours of blisses.

Likenesses I've often found, but this is
One that quite a marvel seemeth to me!

SHE.

Travellers often wonder beyond measure,

But their wonder soon see cause to smother;

Fair and dark are often like each other,
Both inspire the mind with equal pleasure.

HE.

Not now for the first time I surrender

To this form, in humble adoration;

It was brightest midst the constellation
In the hail adorn'd with festal splendour.

SHE.

Be thou joyful that 'tis in my power

To complete thy strange and merry story!

Silks behind her, full of purple glory,
Floated, when thou saw'st her in that hour.

HE.

No, in truth, thou hast not sung it rightly!

Spirits may have told thee all about it;

Pearls and gems they spoke of, do not doubt it,--
By her gaze eclipsed,--it gleam'd so brightly!

SHE.

This one thing I certainly collected:

That the fair one--(say nought, I entreat thee!)

Fondly hoping once again to meet thee,
Many a castle in the air erected.

HE.

By each wind I ceaselessly was driven,

Seeking gold and honour, too, to capture!

When my wand'rings end, then oh, what rapture,
If to find that form again 'tis given!

SHE.

'Tis the daughter of the race now banish'd

That thou seest, not her likeness only;

Helen and her brother, glad though lonely,
Till this farm of their estate now vanish'd.

HE.

But the owner surely is not wanting

Of these plains, with ev'ry beauty teeming?

Verdant fields, broad meads, and pastures gleaming,
Gushing springs, all heav'nly and enchanting.

SHE.

Thou must hunt the world through, wouldst thou find him!--

We have wealth enough in our possession,

And intend to purchase the succession,
When the good man leaves the world behind him.

HE.

I have learnt the owner's own condition,

And, fair maiden, thou indeed canst buy it;

But the cost is great, I won't deny it,--
Helen is the price,--with thy permission!

SHE.

Did then fate and rank keep us asunder,

And must Love take this road, and no other?

Yonder comes my dear and trusty brother;
What will he say to it all, I wonder?

    1803.*

EFFECTS AT A DISTANCE.

THE queen in the lofty hall takes her place,

The tapers around her are flaming;
She speaks to the page: "With a nimble pace

Go, fetch me my purse for gaming.

 'Tis lying, I'll pledge,

 On my table's edge."
Each nerve the nimble boy straineth,
And the end of the castle soon gaineth.

The fairest of maidens was sipping sherbet

Beside the queen that minute;
Near her mouth broke the cup,--and she got so wet!

The very devil seem'd in it

  What fearful distress

  'Tis spoilt, her gay dress.
She hastens, and ev'ry nerve straineth,
And the end of the castle soon gaineth.

The boy was returning, and quickly came,

And met the sorrowing maiden;
None knew of the fact,--and yet with Love's flame,

Those two had their hearts full laden.

  And, oh the bliss

  Of a moment like this!
Each falls on the breast of the other,
With kisses that well nigh might smother.

They tear themselves asunder at last,

To her chamber she hastens quickly,
To reach the queen the page hies him fast,

Midst the swords and the fans crowded thickly.

  The queen spied amain

  On his waistcoat a stain;
For nought was inscrutable to her,
Like Sheba's queen--Solomon's wooer.

To her chief attendant she forthwith cried

"We lately together contended,
And thou didst assert, with obstinate pride,

That the spirit through space never wended,--

  That traces alone

By the present were shown,--
That afar nought was fashion'd--not even
By the stars that illumine you heaven.

"Now see! while a goblet beside me they drain'd,

 They spilt all the drink in the chalice;
And straightway the boy had his waistcoat stain'd

 At the furthermost end of the palace.--

  Let them newly be clad!

   And since I am glad
That it served as a proof so decided,
The cost will by me be provided."

            1808.

THE WALKING BELL

A CHILD refused to go betimes

To church like other people;
He roam'd abroad, when rang the chimes

On Sundays from the steeple.

His mother said: "Loud rings the bell,

Its voice ne'er think of scorning;
Unless thou wilt behave thee well,

'Twill fetch thee without warning."

The child then thought: "High over head

The bell is safe suspended--"
So to the fields he straightway sped

As if 'twas school-time ended.

The bell now ceas'd as bell to ring,

Roused by the mother's twaddle;
But soon ensued a dreadful thing!--

The bell begins to waddle.

It waddles fast, though strange it seem;

The child, with trembling wonder,
Runs off, and flies, as in a dream;

The bell would draw him under.

He finds the proper time at last,

And straightway nimbly rushes
To church, to chapel, hastening fast

Through pastures, plains, and bushes.

Each Sunday and each feast as well,

His late disaster heeds he;
The moment that he bears the bell,

No other summons needs he.

   1813.

FAITHFUL ECKART,

"OH, would we were further! Oh, would we were home,
The phantoms of night tow'rd us hastily come,

The band of the Sorceress sisters.
They hitherward speed, and on finding us here,
They'll drink, though with toil we have fetch'd it, the beer,

And leave us the pitchers all empty."

Thus speaking, the children with fear take to flight,

When sudden an old man appears in their sight:

"Be quiet, child! children, be quiet!
From hunting they come, and their thirst they would still,
So leave them to swallow as much as they will,

And the Evil Ones then will be gracious."

As said, so 'twas done! and the phantoms draw near,
And shadowlike seem they, and grey they appear,

~Yet blithely they sip and they revel
The beer has all vanish'd, the pitchers are void;
With cries and with shouts the wild hunters, o'erjoy'd,

Speed onward o'er vale and o'er mountain.

The children in terror fly nimbly tow'rd home,
And with them the kind one is careful to come:

"My darlings, oh, be not so mournful!--
"They'll blame us and beat us, until we are dead."--
"No, no! ye will find that all goes well," he said;

"Be silent as mice, then, and listen!

"And he by whose counsels thus wisely ye're taught,
Is he who with children loves ever to sport.

The trusty and faithful old Eckart.
Ye have heard of the wonder for many a day,
But ne'er had a proof of the marvellous lay,--

Your hands hold a proof most convincing."

They arrive at their home, and their pitchers they place
By the side of their parents, with fear on their face,

Awaiting a beating and scolding.
But see what they're tasting: the choicest of beer!
Though three times and four times they quaff the good cheer

The pitchers remain still unemptied.

The marvel it lasts till the dawning of day;
All people who hear of it doubtless will say:

"What happen'd at length to the pitchers?"
In secret the children they smile, as they wait;
At last, though, they stammer, and stutter, and prate,

And straightway the pitchers were empty.

And if, children, with kindness address'd ye may be,
Whether father, or master, or alderman he,

Obey him, and follow his bidding!
And if 'tis unpleasant to bridle the tongue,
Yet talking is bad, silence good for the young--

And then will the beer fill your pitchers!

    1813.

THE DANCE OF DEATH.

THE warder looks down at the mid hour of night,

On the tombs that lie scatter'd below:
The moon fills the place with her silvery light,

And the churchyard like day seems to glow.
When see! first one grave, then another opes wide,
And women and men stepping forth are descried,

In cerements snow-white and trailing.

In haste for the sport soon their ankles they twitch,

And whirl round in dances so gay;
The young and the old, and the poor, and the rich,

But the cerements stand in their way;
And as modesty cannot avail them aught here,
They shake themselves all, and the shrouds soon appear

Scatter'd over the tombs in confusion.

Now waggles the leg, and now wriggles the thigh,

As the troop with strange gestures advance,
And a rattle and clatter anon rises high,

As of one beating time to the dance.
The sight to the warder seems wondrously queer,
When the villainous Tempter speaks thus in his ear:

"Seize one of the shrouds that lie yonder!"

Quick as thought it was done! and for safety he fled

Behind the church-door with all speed;
The moon still continues her clear light to shed

On the dance that they fearfully lead.
But the dancers at length disappear one by one,
And their shrouds, ere they vanish, they carefully don,

And under the turf all is quiet.

But one of them stumbles and shuffles there still,

And gropes at the graves in despair;
Yet 'tis by no comrade he's treated so ill

The shroud he soon scents in the air.
So he rattles the door--for the warder 'tis well
That 'tis bless'd, and so able the foe to repel,

All cover'd with crosses in metal.

The shroud he must have, and no rest will allow,

There remains for reflection no time;
On the ornaments Gothic the wight seizes now,

And from point on to point hastes to climb.
Alas for the warder! his doom is decreed!
Like a long-legged spider, with ne'er-changing speed,

Advances the dreaded pursuer.

The warder he quakes, and the warder turns pale,

The shroud to restore fain had sought;
When the end,--now can nothing to save him avail,--

In a tooth formed of iron is caught.
With vanishing lustre the moon's race is run,
When the bell thunders loudly a powerful One,

And the skeleton fails, crush'd to atoms.

        1813.

THE PUPIL IN MAGIC.

I AM now,--what joy to hear it!--

Of the old magician rid;
And henceforth shall ev'ry spirit

Do whate'er by me is bid;

  I have watch'd with rigour

    All he used to do,

  And will now with vigour

    Work my wonders too.

Wander, wander

  Onward lightly,

So that rightly

  Flow the torrent,

And with teeming waters yonder

In the bath discharge its current!

And now come, thou well-worn broom,

And thy wretched form bestir;
Thou hast ever served as groom,

So fulfil my pleasure, sir!

  On two legs now stand,

    With a head on top;

  Waterpail in hand,

    Haste, and do not stop!

Wander, wander

  Onward lightly,

So that rightly

  Flow the torrent,

And with teeming waters yonder

  In the bath discharge its current!

See! he's running to the shore,

And has now attain'd the pool,
And with lightning speed once more

Comes here, with his bucket full!

  Back he then repairs;

    See how swells the tide!

  How each pail he bears

Straightway is supplied!

Stop, for, lo!
　　All the measure
　　Of thy treasure
　　　Now is right!--
Ah, I see it! woe, oh woe!
　　I forget the word of might.

Ah, the word whose sound can straight
Make him what he was before!
Ah, he runs with nimble gait!
Would thou wert a broom once more!
　　Streams renew'd for ever
　　　Quickly bringeth he;
　　River after river
　　　Rusheth on poor me!

　Now no longer
　　Can I bear him;
　I will snare him,
　　Knavish sprite!
Ah, my terror waxes stronger!
　　What a look! what fearful sight
Oh, thou villain child of hell!

Shall the house through thee be drown'd
Floods I see that wildly swell,

O'er the threshold gaining ground.

  Wilt thou not obey,

    Oh, thou broom accurs'd?

  Be thou still I pray,

    As thou wert at first!

 Will enough

  Never please thee?

 I will seize thee,

  Hold thee fast,

And thy nimble wood so tough,

   With my sharp axe split at last.

See, once more he hastens back!

Now, oh Cobold, thou shalt catch it!
I will rush upon his track;

Crashing on him falls my hatchet.

  Bravely done, indeed!

   See, he's cleft in twain!

  Now from care I'm freed,

   And can breathe again.

 Woe, oh woe!

Both the parts,

Quick as darts,

Stand on end,

Servants of my dreaded foe!

Oh, ye gods protection send!

And they run! and wetter still

Grow the steps and grows the hail.
Lord and master hear me call!

Ever seems the flood to fill,

Ah, he's coming! see,

Great is my dismay!

Spirits raised by me

Vainly would I lay!

"To the side

Of the room

Hasten, broom,

As of old!

Spirits I have ne'er untied

Save to act as they are told."

1797.

THE BRIDE OF CORINTH.

[First published in Schiller's Horen, in connection with a friendly contest in the art of ballad-writing between the two great poets, to which many of their finest works are owing.]

ONCE a stranger youth to Corinth came,

  Who in Athens lived, but hoped that he
From a certain townsman there might claim,

  As his father's friend, kind courtesy.

    Son and daughter, they

    Had been wont to say

Should thereafter bride and bridegroom be.

But can he that boon so highly prized,

  Save tis dearly bought, now hope to get?
They are Christians and have been baptized,

  He and all of his are heathens yet.

    For a newborn creed,

    Like some loathsome weed,

  Love and truth to root out oft will threat.

Father, daughter, all had gone to rest,

  And the mother only watches late;
She receives with courtesy the guest,

  And conducts him to the room of state.

    Wine and food are brought,

    Ere by him besought;

Bidding him good night. she leaves him straight.

But he feels no relish now, in truth,

For the dainties so profusely spread;
Meat and drink forgets the wearied youth,

And, still dress'd, he lays him on the bed.

 Scarce are closed his eyes,

 When a form in-hies

Through the open door with silent tread.

By his glimmering lamp discerns he now

How, in veil and garment white array'd,
With a black and gold band round her brow,

Glides into the room a bashful maid.

 But she, at his sight,

 Lifts her hand so white,

And appears as though full sore afraid.

"Am I," cries she, "such a stranger here,

That the guest's approach they could not name?
Ah, they keep me in my cloister drear,

Well nigh feel I vanquish'd by my shame.

 On thy soft couch now

 Slumber calmly thou!

I'll return as swiftly as I came."

"Stay, thou fairest maiden!" cries the boy,

Starting from his couch with eager haste:
"Here are Ceres', Bacchus' gifts of joy;

Amor bringest thou, with beauty grac'd!

Thou art pale with fear!

Loved one let us here

Prove the raptures the Immortals taste."

"Draw not nigh, O Youth! afar remain!

Rapture now can never smile on me;
For the fatal step, alas! is ta'en,

Through my mother's sick-bed phantasy.

Cured, she made this oath:

'Youth and nature both

Shall henceforth to Heav'n devoted be.'

"From the house, so silent now, are driven

All the gods who reign'd supreme of yore;
One Invisible now rules in heaven,

On the cross a Saviour they adore.

Victims slay they here,

Neither lamb nor steer,

But the altars reek with human gore."

And he lists, and ev'ry word he weighs,

While his eager soul drinks in each sound:
"Can it be that now before my gaze

Stands my loved one on this silent ground?

Pledge to me thy troth!

Through our father's oath:

With Heav'ns blessing will our love be crown'd."

"Kindly youth, I never can be thine!

'Tis my sister they intend for thee.
When I in the silent cloister pine,

Ah, within her arms remember me!

Thee alone I love,

While love's pangs I prove;

Soon the earth will veil my misery."

"No! for by this glowing flame I swear,

Hymen hath himself propitious shown:
Let us to my fathers house repair,

And thoult find that joy is not yet flown,

Sweetest, here then stay,

And without delay

Hold we now our wedding feast alone!"

Then exchange they tokens of their truth;

She gives him a golden chain to wear,
And a silver chalice would the youth

Give her in return of beauty rare.

"That is not for me;

Yet I beg of thee,
One lock only give me of thy hair."

Now the ghostly hour of midnight knell'd,

And she seem'd right joyous at the sign;
To her pallid lips the cup she held,

But she drank of nought but blood-red wine.

For to taste the bread

There before them spread,

Nought he spoke could make the maid incline.

To the youth the goblet then she brought,--

He too quaff'd with eager joy the bowl.
Love to crown the silent feast he sought,

Ah! full love-sick was the stripling's soul.

From his prayer she shrinks,

Till at length he sinks

On the bed and weeps without control.

And she comes, and lays her near the boy:

"How I grieve to see thee sorrowing so!
If thou think'st to clasp my form with joy,

Thou must learn this secret sad to know;

Yes! the maid, whom thou

Call'st thy loved one now,

Is as cold as ice, though white as snow."

Then he clasps her madly in his arm,

While love's youthful might pervades his frame:
"Thou might'st hope, when with me, to grow warm,

E'en if from the grave thy spirit came!

   Breath for breath, and kiss!

   Overflow of bliss!

Dost not thou, like me, feel passion's flame?"

Love still closer rivets now their lips,

  Tears they mingle with their rapture blest,
From his mouth the flame she wildly sips,

  Each is with the other's thought possess'd.

   His hot ardour's flood

   Warms her chilly blood,

But no heart is beating in her breast.

In her care to see that nought went wrong,

  Now the mother happen'd to draw near;
At the door long hearkens she, full long,

  Wond'ring at the sounds that greet her ear.

   Tones of joy and sadness,

   And love's blissful madness,

As of bride and bridegroom they appear,

From the door she will not now remove

  'Till she gains full certainty of this;
And with anger hears she vows of love,

  Soft caressing words of mutual bliss.

   "Hush! the cock's loud strain!

   But thoult come again,

When the night returns!"--then kiss on kiss.

Then her wrath the mother cannot hold,

But unfastens straight the lock with ease
"In this house are girls become so bold,

As to seek e'en strangers' lusts to please?"

    By her lamp's clear glow

    Looks she in,--and oh!

Sight of horror!--'tis her child she sees.

Fain the youth would, in his first alarm,

With the veil that o'er her had been spread,
With the carpet, shield his love from harm;

But she casts them from her, void of dread,

    And with spirit's strength,

    In its spectre length,

Lifts her figure slowly from the bed.

"Mother! mother!"--Thus her wan lips say:

"May not I one night of rapture share?
From the warm couch am I chased away?

Do I waken only to despair?

    It contents not thee

    To have driven me

An untimely shroud of death to wear?

"But from out my coffin's prison-bounds

By a wond'rous fate I'm forced to rove,
While the blessings and the chaunting sounds

That your priests delight in, useless prove.

    Water, salt, are vain

    Fervent youth to chain,

Ah, e'en Earth can never cool down love!

"When that infant vow of love was spoken,

Venus' radiant temple smiled on both.
Mother! thou that promise since hast broken,

Fetter'd by a strange, deceitful oath.

    Gods, though, hearken ne'er,

    Should a mother swear

To deny her daughter's plighted troth.

From my grave to wander I am forc'd,

Still to seek The Good's long-sever'd link,
Still to love the bridegroom I have lost,

And the life-blood of his heart to drink;

    When his race is run,

    I must hasten on,

And the young must 'neath my vengeance sink,

"Beauteous youth! no longer mayst thou live;

Here must shrivel up thy form so fair;
Did not I to thee a token give,

Taking in return this lock of hair?

  View it to thy sorrow!

  Grey thoult be to-morrow,

Only to grow brown again when there.

"Mother, to this final prayer give ear!

Let a funeral pile be straightway dress'd;
Open then my cell so sad and drear,

That the flames may give the lovers rest!

   When ascends the fire

   From the glowing pyre,

To the gods of old we'll hasten, blest."

1797.

THE GOD AND THE BAYADERE.

AN INDIAN LEGEND.

[This very fine Ballad was also first given in the Horen.]
(MAHADEVA is one of the numerous names of Seeva, the destroyer,--
the great god of the Brahmins.)

MAHADEVA,* Lord of earth

  For the sixth time comes below,

As a man of mortal birth,--

  Like him, feeling joy and woe.

Hither loves he to repair,

  And his power behind to leave;

If to punish or to spare,

  Men as man he'd fain perceive.
And when he the town as a trav'ller hath seen,
Observing the mighty, regarding the mean,
He quits it, to go on his journey, at eve.

He was leaving now the place,

  When an outcast met his eyes,--

Fair in form, with painted face,--

  Where some straggling dwellings rise.

"Maiden, hail!"--"Thanks! welcome here!

  Stay!--I'll join thee in the road.'

"Who art thou?"--"A Bayadere,

  And this house is love's abode."
The cymbal she hastens to play for the dance,
Well skill'd in its mazes the sight to entrance,
Then by her with grace is the nosegay bestow'd.

Then she draws him, as in play,

  O'er the threshold eagerly:

"Beauteous stranger, light as day

  Thou shalt soon this cottage see.

I'll refresh thee, if thou'rt tired,

  And will bathe thy weary feet;

Take whate'er by thee's desired,

  Toying, rest, or rapture sweet."--

She busily seeks his feign'd suff'rings to ease;
Then smiles the Immortal; with pleasure he sees
That with kindness a heart so corrupted can beat.

And he makes her act the part

  Of a slave; he's straight obey'd.

What at first had been but art,

  Soon is nature in the maid.

By degrees the fruit we find,

  Where the buds at first obtain;

When obedience fills the mind,

  Love will never far remain.
But sharper and sharper the maiden to prove,
The Discerner of all things below and above,
Feigns pleasure, and horror, and maddening pain.

And her painted cheeks he kisses,

  And his vows her heart enthrall;

Feeling love's sharp pangs and blisses,

  Soon her tears begin to fall.

At his feet she now must sink,

  Not with thoughts of lust or gain,--

And her slender members shrink,

  And devoid of power remain.
And so the bright hours with gladness prepare
Their dark, pleasing veil of a texture so fair,
And over the couch softly, tranquilly reign.

Late she falls asleep, thus bless'd,--

  Early wakes, her slumbers fled,

And she finds the much-loved guest

  On her bosom lying dead.

Screaming falls she on him there,

  But, alas, too late to save!

And his rigid limbs they bear

  Straightway to their fiery grave.
Then hears she the priests and the funeral song,
Then madly she runs, and she severs the throng:
"Why press tow'rd the pile thus? Why scream thus, and rave?"

Then she sinks beside his bier,

  And her screams through air resound:

"I must seek my spouse so dear,

  E'en if in the grave he's bound.

Shall those limbs of grace divine

  Fall to ashes in my sight?

Mine he was! Yes, only mine!

  Ah, one single blissful night!"
The priests chaunt in chorus: "We bear out the old,
When long they've been weary, and late they've grown cold:
We bear out the young, too, so thoughtless and light.

"To thy priests' commands give ear!

  This one was thy husband ne'er;

Live still as a Bayadere,

  And no duty thou need'st share.

To deaths silent realms from life,

  None but shades attend man's frame,

With the husband, none but wife,--

  That is duty, that is fame.
Ye trumpets, your sacred lament haste to raise
Oh, welcome, ye gods, the bright lustre of days!
Oh, welcome to heaven the youth from the flame!"

Thus increased her torments are

  By the cruel, heartless quire;

And with arms outstretching far

  Leaps she on the glowing pyre.

But the youth divine outsprings

  From the flame with heav'nly grace,

And on high his flight he wings,

  While his arms his love embrace.
In the sinner repentant the Godhead feels joy;
Immortals delight thus their might to employ.
Lost children to raise to a heavenly place.

        1797.

THE PARIAH.

I. THE PARIAH S PRAYER.

DREADED Brama, lord of might!

All proceed from thee alone;
Thou art he who judgeth right!

Dost thou none but Brahmins own?
Do but Rajahs come from thee?

None but those of high estate?

Didst not thou the ape create,
Aye, and even such as we?

We are not of noble kind,

For with woe our lot is rife;
And what others deadly find

Is our only source of life.
Let this be enough for men,

Let them, if they will, despise us;

But thou, Brama, thou shouldst prize us,
All are equal in thy ken.

Now that, Lord, this prayer is said,

As thy child acknowledge me;
Or let one be born in-stead,

Who may link me on to thee!
Didst not thou a Bayadere

As a goddess heavenward raise?

And we too to swell thy praise,
Such a miracle would hear.

    1821.

II. LEGEND.

[The successful manner in which Goethe employs the simple rhymeless trochaic metre in this and in many other Poems will perhaps be remarked by the reader.]

WATER-FETCHING goes the noble
Brahmin's wife, so pure and lovely;
He is honour'd, void of blemish.
And of justice rigid, stern.
Daily from the sacred river
Brings she back refreshments precious;--
But where is the pail and pitcher?
She of neither stands in need.
For with pure heart, hands unsullied,
She the water lifts, and rolls it
To a wondrous ball of crystal
This she bears with gladsome bosom,
Modestly, with graceful motion,
To her husband in the house.

She to-day at dawn of morning
Praying comes to Ganges' waters,
Bends her o'er the glassy surface--
Sudden, in the waves reflected,
Flying swiftly far above her,
From the highest heavens descending,
She discerns the beauteous form
Of a youth divine, created
By the God's primeval wisdom
In his own eternal breast.

When she sees him, straightway feels she
Wondrous, new, confused sensations
In her inmost, deepest being;
Fain she'd linger o'er the vision,
Then repels it,--it returneth,--
And, perplex'd, she bends her flood-wards
With uncertain hands to draw it;
But, alas, she draws no more!
For the water's sacred billows
Seem to fly, to hasten from her;

She but sees the fearful chasm
Of a whirlpool black disclosed.

Arms drop down, and footsteps stumble,
Can this be the pathway homewards?
Shall she fly, or shall she tarry?
Can she think, when thought and counsel,
When assistance all are lost?
So before her spouse appears she--
On her looks he--look is judgment--
Proudly on the sword he seizes,
To the hill of death he drags her,
Where delinquents' blood pays forfeit.
What resistance could she offer?
What excuses could she proffer,
Guilty, knowing not her guilt?

And with bloody sword returns he,
Musing, to his silent dwelling,
When his son before him stands:
"Whose this blood? Oh, father! father!"
"The delinquent woman's!"--"Never!
For upon the sword it dries not,
Like the blood of the delinquent;
Fresh it flows, as from the wound.
Mother! mother! hither hasten!
Unjust never was my father,
Tell me what he now hath done."--
"Silence! silence! hers the blood is!"
"Whose, my father?"--"Silence! Silence!"
"What! oh what! my mother's blood!
What her crime? What did she? Answer!
Now, the sword! the sword now hold I;
Thou thy wife perchance might'st slaughter,
But my mother might'st not slay!
Through the flames the wife is able
Her beloved spouse to follow,
And his dear and only mother
Through the sword her faithful son."
"Stay! oh stay!" exclaim'd the father:
"Yet 'tis time, so hasten, hasten!
Join the head upon the body,
With the sword then touch the figure,
And, alive she'll follow thee."

Hastening, he, with breathless wonder,
Sees the bodies of two women
Lying crosswise, and their heads too;
Oh, what horror! which to choose!
Then his mother's head he seizes,--
Does not kiss it, deadly pale 'tis,--
On the nearest headless body
Puts it quickly, and then blesses
With the sword the pious work.
Then the giant form uprises,--
From the dear lips of his mother,
Lips all god-like--changeless--blissful,
Sound these words with horror fraught:
"Son, oh son! what overhast'ning!
Yonder is thy mother's body,
Near it lies the impious head
Of the woman who hath fallen
Victim to the judgment-sword!
To her body I am grafted
By thy hand for endless ages;
Wise in counsel, wild in action,
I shall be amongst the gods.
E'en the heav'nly boy's own image,
Though in eye and brow so lovely,
Sinking downwards to the bosom
Mad and raging lust will stir.

"'Twill return again for ever,
Ever rising, ever sinking,
Now obscured, and now transfigur'd,--
So great Brama hath ordain'd.
He 'twas sent the beauteous pinions,
Radiant face and slender members
Of the only God-begotten,
That I might be proved and tempted;
For from high descends temptation,
When the gods ordain it so.
And so I, the Brahmin woman,
With my head in Heaven reclining,
Must experience, as a Pariah,
The debasing power of earth.

Son, I send thee to thy father!

Comfort him! Let no sad penance,
Weak delay, or thought of merit,
Hold thee in the desert fast
Wander on through ev'ry nation,
Roam abroad throughout all ages,
And proclaim to e'en the meanest,
That great Brama hears his cry!

"None is in his eyes the meanest--
He whose limbs are lame and palsied,
He whose soul is wildly riven,
Worn with sorrow, hopeless, helpless,
Be he Brahmin, be he Pariah,
If tow'rd heaven he turns his gaze,
Will perceive, will learn to know it:
Thousand eyes are glowing yonder,
Thousand ears are calmly list'ning,
From which nought below is hid.

"If I to his throne soar upward,
If he sees my fearful figure
By his might transform'd to horror,
He for ever will lament it,--
May it to your good be found!
And I now will kindly warn him,
And I now will madly tell him
Whatsoe'er my mind conceiveth,
What within my bosom heaveth.
But my thoughts, my inmost feelings--
Those a secret shall remain."

           1821.

III. THE PARIAH'S THANKS.

MIGHTY Brama, now I'll bless thee!

'Tis from thee that worlds proceed!
As my ruler I confess thee,

For of all thou takest heed.

All thy thousand ears thou keepest

Open to each child of earth;
We, 'mongst mortals sunk the deepest,

Have from thee received new birth.

Bear in mind the woman's story,

Who, through grief, divine became;
Now I'll wait to view His glory,

Who omnipotence can claim.

    1821.

DEATH-LAMENT OF THE NOBLE WIFE OF ASAN AGA.

[From the Morlack.]

WHAT is yonder white thing in the forest?
Is it snow, or can it swans perchance be?
Were it snow, ere this it had been melted,
Were it swans, they all away had hastend.
Snow, in truth, it is not, swans it is not,
'Tis the shining tents of Asan Aga.
He within is lying, sorely wounded;
To him come his mother and his sister;
Bashfully his wife delays to come there.
When the torment of his wounds had lessen'd,
To his faithful wife he sent this message:
"At my court no longer dare to tarry,
At my court, or e'en amongst my people."

When the woman heard this cruel message,
Mute and full of sorrow stood that true one.
At the doors she hears the feet of horses,
And bethinks that Asan comes--her husband,
To the tower she springs, to leap thence headlong,
Her two darling daughters follow sadly,
And whilst weeping bitter tears, exclaim they:
These are not our father Asan's horses;

'Tis thy brother Pintorowich coming!"

So the wife of Asan turns to meet him,
Clasps her arms in anguish round her brother:
"See thy sister's sad disgrace, oh brother!
How I'm banish'd--mother of five children!"
Silently her brother from his wallet,
Wrapp'd in deep red-silk, and ready written,
Draweth forth the letter of divorcement,
To return home to her mother's dwelling,
Free to be another's wife thenceforward.

When the woman saw that mournful letter,
Fervently she kiss'd her two sons' foreheads,
And her two girls' cheeks with fervour kiss'd she,
But she from the suckling in the cradle
Could not tear herself, so deep her sorrow!
So she's torn thence by her fiery brother,
On his nimble steed he lifts her quickly,
And so hastens, with the heart-sad woman,
Straightway tow'rd his father's lofty dwelling.

Short the time was--seven days had pass'd not,--
Yet enough 'twas; many mighty princes
Sought the woman in her widow's-mourning.
Sought the woman,--as their wife they sought her.
And the mightiest was Imoski's Cadi,
And the woman weeping begg'd her brother:
By thy life, my brother, I entreat thee,
Let me not another's wife be ever,
Lest my heart be broken at the image
Of my poor, my dearly-cherish'd children!"

To her prayer her brother would not hearken,
Fix'd to wed her to Imoski's Cadi.
Yet the good one ceaselessly implored him:
"Send, at least a letter, oh, my brother,
With this message to Imoski's Cadi:
'The young widow sends thee friendly greeting;
Earnestly she prays thee, through this letter,
That, when thou com'st hither, with thy Suatians,
A long veil thou'lt bring me, 'neath whose shadow
I may hide, when near the house of Asan,
And not see my dearly cherish'd orphans.'"

Scarcely had the Cadi read this letter,
Than he gather'd all his Suatians round him,
And then tow'rd the bride his course directed,
And the veil she ask'd for, took he with him.

Happily they reach'd the princess' dwelling,
From the dwelling happily they led her.
But when they approach'd the house of Asan,
Lo! the children saw from high their mother,
And they shouted: "To thy halls return thou!
Eat thy supper with thy darling children!"
Mournfully the wife of Asan heard it,
Tow'rd the Suatian prince then turn'd she, saying:
"Let, I pray, the Suatians and the horses
At the loved ones' door a short time tarry,
That I may give presents to my children."

And before the loved ones' door they tarried,
And she presents gave to her poor children,
To the boys gave gold-embroider'd buskins,
To the girls gave long and costly dresses,
To the suckling, helpless in the cradle,
Gave a garment, to be worn hereafter.

This aside saw Father Asan Aga,--
Sadly cried he to his darling children:
"Hither come, ye dear unhappy infants,
For your mother's breast is turn'd to iron,
Lock'd for ever, closed to all compassion!"

When the wife of Asan heard him speak thus,
On the ground, all pale and trembling, fell she,
And her spirit fled her sorrowing bosom,
When she saw her children flying from her.

1775.

CANTATAS.

May the bard these numbers praise,
That are sung his fame to raise.

THE Poems composed by Goethe under this title are five in number, of which three are here given. The other two are entirely personal in their allusions, and not of general interest. One of them is a Requiem on the Prince de Ligne, who died in 1814, and whom Goethe calls "the happiest man of the century," and the other was composed in honour of the 70th birthday of his friend Zelter the composer, when Goethe was himself more than 79 (1828). The following sweet aria introduced in the latter is, however, worth giving:--

THE flowers so carefully rear'd,

In a garland for him I oft twin'd:
How sweet have they ever appear'd,

When wreath'd for a friend dear and kind.
Then incense sweet ascended,

Then new-horn blossoms rose,
With gentle zephyrs blended

In tones of soft repose.

IDYLL.

A village Chorus is supposed to be assembled, and about to commence its festive procession.

[Written for the birthday of the Duchess Louisa of Weimar.]

CHORUS.

THE festal day hail ye

With garlands of pleasure,

And dances' soft measure,
With rapture commingled
And sweet choral song.

DAMON.

Oh, how I yearn from out the crowd to flee!
What joy a secret glade would give to me!
Amid the throng, the turmoil here,
Confined the plain, the breezes e'en appear.

CHORUS.

Now order it truly,
That ev'ry one duly
May roam and may wander,
Now here, and now yonder,

The meadows along.

[The Chorus retreats gradually, and the song becomes fainter and fainter, till it dies away in the distance.]

DAMON.

In vain ye call, in vain would lure me on;
True my heart speaks,--but with itself alone.

And if I may view

  A blessing-fraught land,

The heaven's clear blue,

And the plain's verdant hue,

Alone I'll rejoice,

Undisturbed by man's voice.

And there I'll pay homage

To womanly merit,

  Observe it in spirit,

In spirit pay homage;

To echo alone

Shall my secret be known.

CHORUS.

[Faintly mingling with Damon's song in the distance.]

To echo--alone--

Shall my secret--be known.--

MENALCAS.

My friend, why meet I here with thee?

Thou hast'nest not to join the festal throng?
No longer stay, but come with me,

And mingle in the dance and song.

DAMON.

Thou'rt welcome, friend! but suffer me to roam

Where these old beeches hide me from man's view:
Love seeks in solitude a home,

And homage may retreat there too.

MENALCAS.

Thou seekest here a spurious fame,

And hast a mind to-day to grieve me.
Love as thy portion thou mayst claim

But homage thou must share with all, believe me!

When their voices thousands raise,
And the dawn of morning praise,

  Rapture bringing,

  Blithely singing

  On before us,
Heart and ear in pleasure vie;

  And when thousands join in chorus,

With the feelings brightly glowing,

And the wishes overflowing,
Forcibly they'll bear thee high.

[The Chorus gradually approaches, from the distance.]

DAMON.

Distant strains are hither wending,

And I'm gladden'd by the throng;
Yes, they're coming,--yes, descending

To the valley from the height,

MENALCAS.

Let us haste, our footsteps blending

With the rhythm of the song!
Yes, they come; their course they're bending

Tow'rd the wood's green sward so bright.

CHORUS.
[Gradually becoming louder.]

Yes, we hither come, attending

With the harmony of song,
As the hours their race are ending

On this day of blest delight.

ALL.

Let none reveal
The thoughts we feel,
The aims we own!
Let joy alone

Disclose the story!
She'll prove it right
And her delight

Includes the glory,
Includes the bliss
Of days like this!

    1813.

RINALDO.*

[This Cantata was written for Prince Frederick of Gotha, and set to music by Winter, the Prince singing the part of Rinaldo.--See the Annalen.]

(* See Tasso's Gerusalemme Liberata, Canto XVI.)

CHORUS.

To the strand! quick, mount the bark!

If no favouring zephyrs blow,

Ply the oar and nimbly row,
And with zeal your prowess mark!

O'er the sea we thus career.

RINALDO.

Oh, let me linger one short moment here!
'Tis heaven's decree, I may not hence away.
The rugged cliffs, the wood-encircled bay,
Hold me a prisoner, and my flight delay.

Ye were so fair, but now that dream is o'er;
The charms of earth, the charms of heaven are nought.
What keeps me in this spot so terror-fraught?

My only joy is fled for evermore.

Let me taste those days so sweet,

Heav'n-descended, once again!
Heart, dear heart! ay, warmly beat!

  Spirit true, recall those days

  Freeborn breath thy gentle lays

Mingled are with joy and pain.

Round the beds, so richly gleaming,

Rises up a palace fair;
All with rosy fragrance teeming,

As in dream thou saw'st it ne'er.

And this spacious garden round,

Far extend the galleries;
Roses blossom near the ground,

High in air, too, bloom the trees.

Wat'ry flakes and jets are falling.

Sweet and silv'ry strains arise;
While the turtle-dove is calling,

And the nightingale replies.

CHORUS.

Gently come! feel no alarm,

On a noble duty bent;
Vanish'd now is ev'ry charm

That by magic power was lent.
Friendly words and greetings calm
On his wounds will pour soft balm.

Fill his mind with sweet content.

RINALDO.

Hark! the turtle-dove is calling,

And the nightingale replies;
Wat'ry flakes and jets are falling,

Mingling with their melodies.

But all of them say:

Her only we mean;
But all fly away,

As soon as she's seen,--
The beauteous young maiden,

With graces so rife,

Then lily and rose

In wreaths are entwining;

In dancing combining,
Each zephyr that blows

Its brother is greeting,

All flying and meeting,

With balsam full laden,

When waken'd to life.

CHORUS.

No! no longer may we wait;
Rouse him from his vision straight!
Show the adamantine shield!

RINALDO.

Woe! what form is here reveal'd!

CHORUS.

'Twill disclose the cheat to thee.

RINALDO.

Am I doom'd myself to see
Thus degraded evermore?

CHORUS.

Courage take, and all is o'er.

RINALDO.

Be it so! I'll take fresh heart,
From the spot beloved depart,
Leave Armida once again,--
Come then! here no more remain.

CHORUS.

Yes, 'tis well! no more remain.

SEMI-CHORUS.

Away then! let's fly

O'er the zephyr-kiss'd ocean!
The soul-lighted eye

Sees armies in motion,
See proud banners wave

O'er the dust-sprinkled course.

CHORUS.

From his forefathers brave

Draws the hero new force.

RINALDO.

With sorrow laden,

Within this valley's

All-silent alleys
The fairest maiden

Again I see.

Twice can this be?
What! shall I hear it,
And not have spirit
To ease her pains?

CHORUS.

Unworthy chains?

RINALDO.

And now I've see her,

Alas! how changed!
With cold demeanour.

And looks estranged,
With ghostly tread,--
All hope is fled,
Yes, fled for ever.
The lightnings quiver,

Each palace falls;
The godlike halls,
Each joyous hour
Of spirit-power,
With love's sweet day
All fade away!

CHORUS.

Yes, fade away!

SEMI-CHORUS.

Already are heard

The prayers of the pious.

Why longer deny us?
The favouring zephyr

Forbids all delay.

CHORUS.

Away, then! away!

RINALDO.

With heart sadly stirr'd,

Your command I receive;

Ye force me to leave.
Unkind is the zephyr,--

Oh, wherefore not stay?

CHORUS.

Away, then! away!

1811.

THE FIRST WALPURGIS-NIGHT.

A DRUID.

SWEET smiles the May!

The forest gay

From frost and ice is freed;

No snow is found,

Glad songs resound

Across the verdant mead.

Upon the height

The snow lies light,

Yet thither now we go,
There to extol our Father's name,

Whom we for ages know.
Amid the smoke shall gleam the flame;

Thus pure the heart will grow.

THE DRUIDS.

Amid the smoke shall gleam the flame;
Extol we now our Father's name,

Whom we for ages know!

Up, up, then, let us go!

ONE OF THE PEOPLE.

Would ye, then, so rashly act?
Would ye instant death attract?

Know ye not the cruel threats

Of the victors we obey?
Round about are placed their nets

In the sinful heathen's way.
Ah! upon the lofty wall

Wife and children slaughter they;
And we all
Hasten to a certain fall.

CHORUS OF WOMEN.

Ay, upon the camp's high wall

All our children loved they slay.

Ah, what cruel victors they!
And we all
Hasten to a certain fall.

A DRUID.

 Who fears to-day

 His rites to pay,

Deserves his chains to wear.

 The forest's free!

 This wood take we,

And straight a pile prepare!

 Yet in the wood

 To stay 'tis good

By day, till all is still,
With watchers all around us plac'd

Protecting you from ill.
With courage fresh, then let us haste

Our duties to fulfil.

CHORUS OF WATCHERS.

Ye valiant watchers, now divide
Your numbers through the forest wide,

And see that all is still,

While they their rites fulfil.

A WATCHER.

Let us in a cunning wise,
Yon dull Christian priests surprise
With the devil of their talk

We'll those very priests confound.
Come with prong, and come with fork.

Raise a wild and rattling sound
Through the livelong night, and prowl

All the rocky passes round.
Screechowl, owl,
Join in chorus with our howl!

CHORUS OF WATCHERS.

Come with prong, and come with fork,
Like the devil of their talk,
And with wildly rattling sound,
Prowl the desert rocks around!
Screechowl, owl,
Join in chorus with our howl!

A DRUID.

  Thus far 'tis right.

That we by night

Our Father's praises sing;

  Yet when 'tis day,

  To Thee we may

A heart unsullied bring.

  'Tis true that now,

  And often, Thou

Fav'rest the foe in fight.
As from the smoke is freed the blaze,

So let our faith burn bright!
And if they crush our golden ways,

Who e'er can crush Thy light?

A CHRISTIAN WATCHER.

Comrades, quick! your aid afford!
All the brood of hell's abroad;
See how their enchanted forms

Through and through with flames are glowing!
Dragon-women, men-wolf swarms,

On in quick succession going!
Let us, let us haste to fly!

Wilder yet the sounds are growing,
And the archfiend roars on high;
From the ground
Hellish vapours rise around.

CHORUS OF CHRISTIAN WATCHERS.

Terrible enchanted forms,
Dragon-women, men-wolf swarms!
Wilder yet the sounds are growing!

See, the archfiend comes, all-glowing!
From the ground
Hellish vapours rise around!

CHORUS OF DRUIDS.

As from the smoke is freed the blaze,

So let our faith burn bright!
And if they crush our golden ways,

Who e'er can crush Thy light?

        1799.

ODES.

THESE are the most singular of all the Poems of Goethe, and to many will appear so wild and fantastic, as to leave anything but a pleasing impression. Those at the beginning, addressed to his friend Behrisch, were written at the age of eighteen, and most of the remainder were composed while he was still quite young. Despite, however, the extravagance of some of them, such as the Winter Journey over the Hartz Mountains, and the Wanderer's Storm-Song, nothing can be finer than the noble one entitled Mahomet's Song, and others, such as the Spirit Song' over the Waters, The God-like, and, above all, the magnificent sketch of Prometheus, which forms part of an unfinished piece bearing the same name, and called by Goethe a 'Dramatic Fragment.'

TO MY FRIEND.

[These three Odes are addressed to a certain Behrisch, who was tutor to Count Lindenau, and of whom Goethe gives an odd account at the end of the Seventh Book of his Autobiography.]

FIRST ODE.

TRANSPLANT the beauteous tree!

Gardener, it gives me pain;
A happier resting-place
Its trunk deserved.

Yet the strength of its nature
To Earth's exhausting avarice,
To Air's destructive inroads,
An antidote opposed.

See how it in springtime
Coins its pale green leaves!
Their orange-fragrance
Poisons each flyblow straight.

The caterpillar's tooth
Is blunted by them;
With silv'ry hues they gleam
In the bright sunshine,

Its twigs the maiden
Fain would twine in
Her bridal-garland;
Youths its fruit are seeking.

See, the autumn cometh!
The caterpillar
Sighs to the crafty spider,--
Sighs that the tree will not fade.

Hov'ring thither
From out her yew-tree dwelling,
The gaudy foe advances
Against the kindly tree,

And cannot hurt it,
But the more artful one
Defiles with nauseous venom
Its silver leaves;

And sees with triumph
How the maiden shudders,
The youth, how mourns he,
On passing by.

Transplant the beauteous tree!
Gardener, it gives me pain;
Tree, thank the gardener
Who moves thee hence!

   1767.

SECOND ODE.

THOU go'st! I murmur--
Go! let me murmur.
Oh, worthy man,
Fly from this land!

Deadly marshes,
Steaming mists of October
Here interweave their currents,
Blending for ever.

Noisome insects
Here are engender'd;
Fatal darkness
Veils their malice.

The fiery-tongued serpent,
Hard by the sedgy bank,
Stretches his pamper'd body,
Caress'd by the sun's bright beams.

Tempt no gentle night-rambles
Under the moon's cold twilight!
Loathsome toads hold their meetings
Yonder at every crossway.

Injuring not,
Fear will they cause thee.
Oh, worthy man,
Fly from this land!

   1767.

THIRD ODE.

BE void of feeling!
A heart that soon is stirr'd,
Is a possession sad
Upon this changing earth.

Behrisch, let spring's sweet smile
Never gladden thy brow!
Then winter's gloomy tempests
Never will shadow it o'er.

Lean thyself ne'er on a maiden's
Sorrow-engendering breast.
Ne'er on the arm,
Misery-fraught, of a friend.

Already envy
From out his rocky ambush
Upon thee turns
The force of his lynx-like eyes,

Stretches his talons,
On thee falls,
In thy shoulders
Cunningly plants them.

Strong are his skinny arms,
As panther-claws;
He shaketh thee,
And rends thy frame.

Death 'tis to part,
'Tis threefold death
To part, not hoping
Ever to meet again.

Thou wouldst rejoice to leave
This hated land behind,
Wert thou not chain'd to me
With friendships flowery chains.

Burst them! I'll not repine.
No noble friend
Would stay his fellow-captive,
If means of flight appear.

The remembrance
Of his dear friend's freedom
Gives him freedom
In his dungeon.

Thou go'st,--I'm left.
But e'en already
The last year's winged spokes
Whirl round the smoking axle.

I number the turns
Of the thundering wheel;
The last one I bless.--
Each bar then is broken, I'm free then as thou!

   1767.

MAHOMET'S SONG.

[This song was intended to be introduced in a dramatic poem entitled Mahomet, the plan of which was not carried out by Goethe. He mentions that it was to have been sung by Ali towards the end of the piece, in honor of his master, Mahomet, shortly before his death, and when at the height of his glory, of which it is typical.]

SEE the rock-born stream!
Like the gleam
Of a star so bright
Kindly spirits
High above the clouds
Nourished him while youthful
In the copse between the cliffs.

Young and fresh.
From the clouds he danceth
Down upon the marble rocks;

Then tow'rd heaven
Leaps exulting.

Through the mountain-passes
Chaseth he the colour'd pebbles,
And, advancing like a chief,
Tears his brother streamlets with him
In his course.

In the valley down below
'Neath his footsteps spring the flowers,
And the meadow
In his breath finds life.

Yet no shady vale can stay him,
Nor can flowers,
Round his knees all-softly twining
With their loving eyes detain him;
To the plain his course he taketh,
Serpent-winding,

Social streamlets
Join his waters. And now moves he
O'er the plain in silv'ry glory,
And the plain in him exults,
And the rivers from the plain,
And the streamlets from the mountain,
Shout with joy, exclaiming: "Brother,
Brother, take thy brethren with thee,
With thee to thine aged father,
To the everlasting ocean,
Who, with arms outstretching far,
Waiteth for us;
Ah, in vain those arms lie open
To embrace his yearning children;
For the thirsty sand consumes us
In the desert waste; the sunbeams
Drink our life-blood; hills around us
Into lakes would dam us! Brother,
Take thy brethren of the plain,
Take thy brethren of the mountain
With thee, to thy father's arms!

Let all come, then!--

And now swells he
Lordlier still; yea, e'en a people
Bears his regal flood on high!
And in triumph onward rolling,
Names to countries gives he,--cities
Spring to light beneath his foot.

Ever, ever, on he rushes,
Leaves the towers' flame-tipp'd summits,
Marble palaces, the offspring
Of his fullness, far behind.

Cedar-houses bears the Atlas
On his giant shoulders; flutt'ring
In the breeze far, far above him
Thousand flags are gaily floating,
Bearing witness to his might.

And so beareth he his brethren,
All his treasures, all his children,
Wildly shouting, to the bosom
Of his long-expectant sire.

1774.

SPIRIT SONG OVER THE WATERS.

THE soul of man
Resembleth water:
From heaven it cometh,
To heaven it soareth.
And then again
To earth descendeth,
Changing ever.

Down from the lofty
Rocky wall
Streams the bright flood,
Then spreadeth gently
In cloudy billows
O'er the smooth rock,
And welcomed kindly,

Veiling, on roams it,
Soft murmuring,
Tow'rd the abyss.

Cliffs projecting
Oppose its progress,--
Angrily foams it
Down to the bottom,
Step by step.

Now, in flat channel,
Through the meadowland steals it,
And in the polish'd lake
Each constellation
Joyously peepeth.

Wind is the loving
Wooer of waters;
Wind blends together
Billows all-foaming.

Spirit of man,
Thou art like unto water!
Fortune of man,
Thou art like unto wind!

   1789.*

MY GODDESS.

SAY, which Immortal
Merits the highest reward?
With none contend I,
But I will give it
To the aye-changing,
Ever-moving
Wondrous daughter of Jove.
His best-beloved offspring.
Sweet Phantasy.

For unto her
Hath he granted
All the fancies which erst
To none allow'd he

Saving himself;
Now he takes his pleasure
In the mad one.

She may, crowned with roses,
With staff twined round with lilies,
Roam thro' flow'ry valleys,
Rule the butterfly-people,
And soft-nourishing dew
With bee-like lips
Drink from the blossom:

Or else she may
With fluttering hair
And gloomy looks
Sigh in the wind
Round rocky cliffs,
And thousand-hued.
Like morn and even.
Ever changing,
Like moonbeam's light,
To mortals appear.

Let us all, then,
Adore the Father!
The old, the mighty,
Who such a beauteous
Ne'er-fading spouse
Deigns to accord
To perishing mortals!

To us alone
Doth he unite her,
With heavenly bonds,
While he commands her,
in joy and sorrow,
As a true spouse
Never to fly us.

All the remaining
Races so poor
Of life-teeming earth.
In children so rich.
Wander and feed

In vacant enjoyment,
And 'mid the dark sorrows
Of evanescent
Restricted life,--
Bow'd by the heavy
Yoke of Necessity.

But unto us he
Hath his most versatile,
Most cherished daughter
Granted,--what joy!

Lovingly greet her
As a beloved one!
Give her the woman's
Place in our home!

And oh, may the aged
Stepmother Wisdom
Her gentle spirit
Ne'er seek to harm!

Yet know I her sister,
The older, sedater,
Mine own silent friend;
Oh, may she never,
Till life's lamp is quench'd,
Turn away from me,--
That noble inciter,
Comforter,--Hope!

        1781.

WINTER JOURNEY OVER THE HARTZ MOUNTAINS.

[The following explanation is necessary, in order to make this
ode in any way intelligible. The Poet is supposed to leave his
companions, who are proceeding on a hunting expedition in winter,
in order himself to pay a visit to a hypochondriacal friend, and
also to see the mining in the Hartz mountains. The ode
alternately describes, in a very fragmentary and peculiar manner,
the naturally happy disposition of the Poet himself and the

unhappiness of his friend; it pictures the wildness of the road
and the dreariness of the prospect, which is relieved at one spot
by the distant sight of a town, a very vague allusion to which is
made in the third strophe; it recalls the hunting party on which
his companions have gone; and after an address to Love, concludes
by a contrast between the unexplored recesses of the highest peak
of the Hartz and the metalliferous veins of its smaller
brethren.]

LIKE the vulture
Who on heavy morning clouds
With gentle wing reposing
Looks for his prey,--
Hover, my song!

For a God hath
Unto each prescribed
His destined path,
Which the happy one
Runs o'er swiftly
To his glad goal:
He whose heart cruel
Fate hath contracted,
Struggles but vainly
Against all the barriers
The brazen thread raises,
But which the harsh shears
Must one day sever.

Through gloomy thickets
Presseth the wild deer on,
And with the sparrows
Long have the wealthy
Settled themselves in the marsh.

Easy 'tis following the chariot
That by Fortune is driven,
Like the baggage that moves
Over well-mended highways
After the train of a prince.

But who stands there apart?
In the thicket, lost is his path;
Behind him the bushes

Are closing together,
The grass springs up again,
The desert engulphs him.

Ah, who'll heal his afflictions,
To whom balsam was poison,
Who, from love's fullness,
Drank in misanthropy only?
First despised, and now a despiser,
He, in secret, wasteth
All that he is worth,
In a selfishness vain.
If there be, on thy psaltery,
Father of Love, but one tone
That to his ear may be pleasing,
Oh, then, quicken his heart!
Clear his cloud-enveloped eyes
Over the thousand fountains
Close by the thirsty one
In the desert.

Thou who createst much joy,
For each a measure o'erflowing,
Bless the sons of the chase
When on the track of the prey,
With a wild thirsting for blood,
Youthful and joyous
Avenging late the injustice
Which the peasant resisted
Vainly for years with his staff.

But the lonely one veil
Within thy gold clouds!
Surround with winter-green,
Until the roses bloom again,
The humid locks,
Oh Love, of thy minstrel!

With thy glimmering torch
Lightest thou him
Through the fords when 'tis night,
Over bottomless places
On desert-like plains;
With the thousand colours of morning

Gladd'nest his bosom;
With the fierce-biting storm
Bearest him proudly on high;
Winter torrents rush from the cliffs,--
Blend with his psalms;
An altar of grateful delight
He finds in the much-dreaded mountain's
Snow-begirded summit,
Which foreboding nations
Crown'd with spirit-dances.

Thou stand'st with breast inscrutable,
Mysteriously disclosed,
High o'er the wondering world,
And look'st from clouds
Upon its realms and its majesty,
Which thou from the veins of thy brethren
Near thee dost water.

1777.

TO FATHER* KRONOS.

[written in a post-chaise.]

(* In the original, Schwager, which has the twofold meaning of brother-in-law and postilion.)

HASTEN thee, Kronos!
On with clattering trot
Downhill goeth thy path;
Loathsome dizziness ever,
When thou delayest, assails me.
Quick, rattle along,
Over stock and stone let thy trot
Into life straightway lead

Now once more
Up the toilsome ascent
Hasten, panting for breath!
Up, then, nor idle be,--
Striving and hoping, up, up!

Wide, high, glorious the view
Gazing round upon life,
While from mount unto mount
Hovers the spirit eterne,
Life eternal foreboding.

Sideways a roof's pleasant shade
Attracts thee,
And a look that promises coolness
On the maidenly threshold.
There refresh thee! And, maiden,
Give me this foaming draught also,
Give me this health-laden look!

Down, now! quicker still, down!
See where the sun sets
Ere he sets, ere old age
Seizeth me in the morass,
Ere my toothless jaws mumble,
And my useless limbs totter;
While drunk with his farewell beam
Hurl me,--a fiery sea
Foaming still in mine eye,--
Hurl me, while dazzled and reeling,
Down to the gloomy portal of hell.

Blow, then, gossip, thy horn,
Speed on with echoing trot,
So that Orcus may know we are coming;
So that our host may with joy
Wait at the door to receive us.

1774.

THE WANDERER'S STORM-SONG.

[Goethe says of this ode, that it is the only one remaining out
of several strange hymns and dithyrambs composed by him at a
period of great unhappiness, when the love-affair between him and
Frederica had been broken off by him. He used to sing them while
wandering wildly about the country. This particular one was

caused by his being caught in a tremendous storm on one of these
occasions. He calls it a half-crazy piece (halkunsinn), and the
reader will probably agree with him.]

He whom thou ne'er leavest, Genius,
Feels no dread within his heart
At the tempest or the rain.
He whom thou ne'er leavest, Genius,
Will to the rain-clouds,
Will to the hailstorm,
Sing in reply
As the lark sings,
Oh thou on high!

Him whom thou ne'er leavest, Genius,
Thou wilt raise above the mud-track
With thy fiery pinions.
He will wander,
As, with flowery feet,
Over Deucalion's dark flood,
Python-slaying, light, glorious,
Pythius Apollo.

Him whom thou ne'er leavest, Genius,
Thou wilt place upon thy fleecy pinion
When he sleepeth on the rock,--
Thou wilt shelter with thy guardian wing
In the forest's midnight hour.

Him whom thou ne'er leavest, Genius,
Thou wilt wrap up warmly
In the snow-drift;
Tow'rd the warmth approach the Muses,
Tow'rd the warmth approach the Graces.

Ye Muses, hover round me!
Ye Graces also!
That is water, that is earth,
And the son of water and of earth
Over which I wander,
Like the gods.

Ye are pure, like the heart of the water,
Ye are pure like the marrow of earth,

Hov'ring round me, while I hover
Over water, o'er the earth
Like the gods.

Shall he, then, return,
The small, the dark, the fiery peasant?
Shall he, then, return, waiting
Only thy gifts, oh Father Bromius,
And brightly gleaming, warmth-spreading fire?
Return with joy?
And I, whom ye attended,
Ye Muses and ye Graces,
Whom all awaits that ye,
Ye Muses and ye Graces,
Of circling bliss in life
Have glorified--shall I
Return dejected?

Father Bromius!
Thourt the Genius,
Genius of ages,
Thou'rt what inward glow
To Pindar was,
What to the world
Phoebus Apollo.

Woe! Woe Inward warmth,
Spirit-warmth,
Central-point!
Glow, and vie with
Phoebus Apollo!
Coldly soon
His regal look
Over thee will swiftly glide,--

Envy-struck
Linger o'er the cedar's strength,
Which, to flourish,
Waits him not.

Why doth my lay name thee the last?
Thee, from whom it began,
Thee, in whom it endeth,
Thee, from whom it flows,

Jupiter Pluvius!
Tow'rd thee streams my song.
And a Castalian spring
Runs as a fellow-brook,
Runs to the idle ones,
Mortal, happy ones,
Apart from thee,
Who cov'rest me around,
Jupiter Pluvius!

Not by the elm-tree
Him didst thou visit,
With the pair of doves
Held in his gentle arm,--
With the beauteous garland of roses,--
Caressing him, so blest in his flowers,
Anacreon,
Storm-breathing godhead!
Not in the poplar grove,
Near the Sybaris' strand,
Not on the mountain's
Sun-illumined brow
Didst thou seize him,
The flower-singing,
Honey-breathing,
Sweetly nodding
Theocritus.

When the wheels were rattling,
Wheel on wheel tow'rd the goal,
High arose
The sound of the lash
Of youths with victory glowing,
In the dust rolling,
As from the mountain fall
Showers of stones in the vale--
Then thy soul was brightly glowing, Pindar--
Glowing? Poor heart!

There, on the hill,--
Heavenly might!
But enough glow
Thither to wend,
Where is my cot!

1771.

THE SEA-VOYAGE.

MANY a day and night my bark stood ready laden;
Waiting fav'ring winds, I sat with true friends round me,
Pledging me to patience and to courage,
In the haven.

And they spoke thus with impatience twofold:
"Gladly pray we for thy rapid passage,
Gladly for thy happy voyage; fortune
In the distant world is waiting for thee,
In our arms thoult find thy prize, and love too,
When returning."

And when morning came, arose an uproar,
And the sailors' joyous shouts awoke us;
All was stirring, all was living, moving,
Bent on sailing with the first kind zephyr.

And the sails soon in the breeze are swelling,
And the sun with fiery love invites us;
Fill'd the sails are, clouds on high are floating,
On the shore each friend exulting raises
Songs of hope, in giddy joy expecting
Joy the voyage through, as on the morn of sailing,
And the earliest starry nights so radiant.

But by God-sent changing winds ere long he's driven
Sideways from the course he had intended,
And he feigns as though he would surrender,
While he gently striveth to outwit them,

To his goal, e'en when thus press'd, still faithful.
But from out the damp grey distance rising,
Softly now the storm proclaims its advent,
Presseth down each bird upon the waters,
Presseth down the throbbing hearts of mortals.
And it cometh. At its stubborn fury,
Wisely ev'ry sail the seaman striketh;

With the anguish-laden ball are sporting
Wind and water.

And on yonder shore are gather'd standing,
Friends and lovers, trembling for the bold one:
"Why, alas, remain'd he here not with us!
Ah, the tempest! Cast away by fortune!
Must the good one perish in this fashion?
Might not he perchance.... Ye great immortals!"

Yet he, like a man, stands by his rudder;
With the bark are sporting wind and water,
Wind and water sport not with his bosom:
On the fierce deep looks he, as a master,--
In his gods, or shipwreck'd, or safe landed,
Trusting ever.

    1776.

THE EAGLE AND DOVE.

IN search of prey once raised his pinions
An eaglet;
A huntsman's arrow came, and reft
His right wing of all motive power.
Headlong he fell into a myrtle grove,
For three long days on anguish fed,
In torment writhed
Throughout three long, three weary nights;
And then was cured,
Thanks to all-healing Nature's
Soft, omnipresent balm.
He crept away from out the copse,
And stretch'd his wing--alas!
Lost is all power of flight--
He scarce can lift himself
From off the ground
To catch some mean, unworthy prey,
And rests, deep-sorrowing,
On the low rock beside the stream.
Up to the oak he looks,
Looks up to heaven,

While in his noble eye there gleams a tear.
Then, rustling through the myrtle boughs, behold,
There comes a wanton pair of doves,
Who settle down, and, nodding, strut
O'er the gold sands beside the stream,
And gradually approach;
Their red-tinged eyes, so full of love,
Soon see the inward-sorrowing one.
The male, inquisitively social, leaps
On the next bush, and looks
Upon him kindly and complacently.
"Thou sorrowest," murmurs he:
"Be of good cheer, my friend!
All that is needed for calm happiness
Hast thou not here?
Hast thou not pleasure in the golden bough
That shields thee from the day's fierce glow?
Canst thou not raise thy breast to catch,
On the soft moss beside the brook,
The sun's last rays at even?
Here thou mayst wander through the flowers' fresh dew,
Pluck from the overflow
The forest-trees provide,
Thy choicest food,--mayst quench
Thy light thirst at the silvery spring.
Oh friend, true happiness
Lies in contentedness,
And that contentedness
Finds everywhere enough."
"Oh, wise one!" said the eagle, while he sank
In deep and ever deep'ning thought--
"Oh Wisdom! like a dove thou speakest!"

1774.*

PROMETHEUS.

COVER thy spacious heavens, Zeus,
With clouds of mist,
And, like the boy who lops
The thistles' heads,
Disport with oaks and mountain-peaks,

Yet thou must leave
My earth still standing;
My cottage too, which was not raised by thee;
Leave me my hearth,
Whose kindly glow
By thee is envied.

I know nought poorer
Under the sun, than ye gods!
Ye nourish painfully,
With sacrifices
And votive prayers,
Your majesty:
Ye would e'en starve,
If children and beggars
Were not trusting fools.

While yet a child
And ignorant of life,
I turned my wandering gaze
Up tow'rd the sun, as if with him
There were an ear to hear my wailings,
A heart, like mine,
To feel compassion for distress.

Who help'd me
Against the Titans' insolence?
Who rescued me from certain death,
From slavery?
Didst thou not do all this thyself,
My sacred glowing heart?
And glowedst, young and good,
Deceived with grateful thanks
To yonder slumbering one?

I honour thee! and why?
Hast thou e'er lighten'd the sorrows
Of the heavy laden?
Hast thou e'er dried up the tears
Of the anguish-stricken?
Was I not fashion'd to be a man
By omnipotent Time,
And by eternal Fate,
Masters of me and thee?

Didst thou e'er fancy
That life I should learn to hate,
And fly to deserts,
Because not all
My blossoming dreams grew ripe?

Here sit I, forming mortals
After my image;
A race resembling me,
To suffer, to weep,
To enjoy, to be glad,
And thee to scorn,
As I!

    1773.

GANYMEDE.

How, in the light of morning,
Round me thou glowest,
Spring, thou beloved one!
With thousand-varying loving bliss
The sacred emotions
Born of thy warmth eternal
Press 'gainst my bosom,
Thou endlessly fair one!
Could I but hold thee clasp'd
Within mine arms!

Ah! upon thy bosom
Lay I, pining,
And then thy flowers, thy grass,
Were pressing against my heart.
Thou coolest the burning
Thirst of my bosom,
Beauteous morning breeze!
The nightingale then calls me
Sweetly from out of the misty vale.
I come, I come!
Whither? Ah, whither?

Up, up, lies my course.
While downward the clouds
Are hovering, the clouds
Are bending to meet yearning love.
For me,
Within thine arms
Upwards!
Embraced and embracing!
Upwards into thy bosom,
Oh Father all-loving!

   1789.*

THE BOUNDARIES OF HUMANITY.

WHEN the primeval
All-holy Father
Sows with a tranquil hand
From clouds, as they roll,
Bliss-spreading lightnings
Over the earth,
Then do I kiss the last
Hem of his garment,
While by a childlike awe
Fill'd is my breast.

For with immortals
Ne'er may a mortal
Measure himself.
If he soar upwards
And if he touch
With his forehead the stars,
Nowhere will rest then
His insecure feet,
And with him sport
Tempest and cloud.

Though with firm sinewy
Limbs he may stand
On the enduring
Well-grounded earth,
All he is ever

Able to do,
Is to resemble
The oak or the vine.

Wherein do gods
Differ from mortals?
In that the former
See endless billows
Heaving before them;
Us doth the billow
Lift up and swallow,
So that we perish.

Small is the ring
Enclosing our life,
And whole generations
Link themselves firmly
On to existence's
Chain never-ending.

   1789. *

THE GODLIKE.

NOBLE be man,
Helpful and good!
For that alone
Distinguisheth him
From all the beings
Unto us known.

Hail to the beings,
Unknown and glorious,
Whom we forebode!
From his example
Learn we to know them!

For unfeeling
Nature is ever:
On bad and on good
The sun alike shineth;
And on the wicked,

As on the best,
The moon and stars gleam.

Tempest and torrent,
Thunder and hail,
Roar on their path,
Seizing the while,
As they haste onward,
One after another.

Even so, fortune
Gropes 'mid the throng--
Innocent boyhood's
Curly head seizing,--
Seizing the hoary
Head of the sinner.

After laws mighty,
Brazen, eternal,
Must all we mortals
Finish the circuit
Of our existence.

Man, and man only
Can do the impossible;
He 'tis distinguisheth,
Chooseth and judgeth;
He to the moment
Endurance can lend.

He and he only
The good can reward,
The bad can he punish,
Can heal and can save;
All that wanders and strays
Can usefully blend.
And we pay homage
To the immortals
As though they were men,
And did in the great,
What the best, in the small,
Does or might do.

Be the man that is noble,

Both helpful and good.
Unweariedly forming
The right and the useful,
A type of those beings
Our mind hath foreshadow'd!

                    1782.

MISCELLANEOUS POEMS.

-----
in the wares before you spread,
Types of all things may be read.

THE GERMAN PARNASSUS.

'NEATH the shadow

Of these bushes,
On the meadow

Where the cooling water gushes.
Phoebus gave me, when a boy,
All life's fullness to enjoy.
So, in silence, as the God
Bade them with his sov'reign nod,
Sacred Muses train'd my days
To his praise.--
With the bright and silv'ry flood
Of Parnassus stirr'd my blood,
And the seal so pure and chaste
By them on my lips was placed.

With her modest pinions, see,
Philomel encircles me!
In these bushes, in yon grove,

Calls she to her sister-throng,

And their heavenly choral song
Teaches me to dream of love.

Fullness waxes in my breast
Of emotions social, blest;
Friendship's nurtured-love awakes,--
And the silence Phoebus breaks
Of his mountains, of his vales,
Sweetly blow the balmy gales;
All for whom he shows affection,
Who are worthy his protection,
Gladly follow his direction.

This one comes with joyous bearing

And with open, radiant gaze;
That a sterner look is wearing,
This one, scarcely cured, with daring

Wakes the strength of former days;
For the sweet, destructive flame
Pierced his marrow and his frame.
That which Amor stole before
Phoebus only can restore,
Peace, and joy, and harmony,
Aspirations pure and free.

Brethren, rise ye!
Numbers prize ye!
Deeds of worth resemble they.

Who can better than the bard
Guide a friend when gone astray?

If his duty he regard,
More he'll do, than others may.

Yes! afar I hear them sing!
Yes! I hear them touch the string,
And with mighty godlike stroke

Right and duty they inspire,
And evoke,

As they sing, and wake the lyre,
Tendencies of noblest worth,

To each type of strength give birth.

Phantasies of sweetest power
Flower
Round about on ev'ry bough,
Bending now
Like the magic wood of old,
'Neath the fruit that gleams like gold.

What we feel and what we view

In the land of highest bliss,--

This dear soil, a sun like this,--
Lures the best of women too.
And the Muses' breathings blest
Rouse the maiden's gentle breast,
Tune the throat to minstrelsy,
And with cheeks of beauteous dye,
Bid it sing a worthy song,
Sit the sister-band among;
And their strains grow softer still,
As they vie with earnest will.

One amongst the band betimes

Goes to wander
By the beeches, 'neath the limes,

Yonder seeking, finding yonder
That which in the morning-grove
She had lost through roguish Love,
All her breast's first aspirations,
And her heart's calm meditations,
To the shady wood so fair

Gently stealing,
Takes she that which man can ne'er

Duly merit,--each soft feeling,--
Disregards the noontide ray
And the dew at close of day,Ä

In the plain her path she loses.

Ne'er disturb her on her way!

Seek her silently, ye Muses

Shouts I hear, wherein the sound
Of the waterfall is drown'd.
From the grove loud clamours rise,
Strange the tumult, strange the cries.
See I rightly? Can it be?
To the very sanctuary,
Lo, an impious troop in-hies!

O'er the land
Streams the band;
Hot desire,
Drunken-fire
In their gaze
Wildly plays,--
Makes their hair
Bristle there.
And the troop,
With fell swoop,
Women, men,
Coming then,
Ply their blows
And expose,
Void of shame,
All the frame.
Iron shot,
Fierce and hot,
Strike with fear
On the ear;
All they slay
On their way.
O'er the land
Pours the band;
All take flight
At their sight.

Ah, o'er ev'ry plant they rush!
Ah, their cruel footsteps crush
All the flowers that fill their path!
Who will dare to stem their wrath?

Brethren, let us venture all!

Virtue in your pure cheek glows.
Phoebus will attend our call

When he sees our heavy woes;
And that we may have aright
Weapons suited to the fight,
He the mountain shaketh now--
From its brow
Rattling down
Stone on stone
Through the thicket spread appear.
Brethren, seize them! Wherefore fear?
Now the villain crew assail,
As though with a storm of hail,
And expel the strangers wild
From these regions soft and mild
Where the sun has ever smil'd!

What strange wonder do I see?
Can it be?
All my limbs of power are reft.
And all strength my hand has left.
Can it he?
None are strangers that I see!
And our brethren 'tis who go
On before, the way to show!
Oh, the reckless impious ones!
How they, with their jarring tones,
Beat the time, as on they hie!
Quick, my brethren!--let us fly!

To the rash ones, yet a word!
Ay, my voice shall now be heard,
As a peal of thunder, strong!

Words as poets' arms were made,--

When the god will he obey'd,
Follow fast his darts ere long.

Was it possible that ye
Thus your godlike dignity

Should forget? The Thyrsus rude

Must a heavy burden feel

To the hand but wont to steal
O'er the lyre in gentle mood.
From the sparkling waterfalls,
From the brook that purling calls,
Shall Silenus' loathsome beast
Be allow'd at will to feast?
Aganippe's * wave he sips
With profane and spreading lips,--
With ungainly feet stamps madly,
Till the waters flow on sadly.

Fain I'd think myself deluded

In the sadd'ning sounds I hear;
From the holy glades secluded

Hateful tones assail the ear.
Laughter wild (exchange how mournful!)

Takes the place of love's sweet dream;
Women-haters and the scornful

In exulting chorus scream.
Nightingale and turtle dove

Fly their nests so warm and chaste,
And, inflamed with sensual love,

Holds the Faun the Nymph embrac'd.
Here a garment's torn away,

Scoffs succeed their sated bliss,
While the god, with angry ray,

Looks upon each impious kiss.

Vapour, smoke, as from a fire,

And advancing clouds I view;
Chords not only grace the lyre,

For the bow its chords bath too.
Even the adorer's heart

Dreads the wild advancing hand,
For the flames that round them dart

 Show the fierce destroyer's hand.

Oh neglect not what I say,

For I speak it lovingly!
From our boundaries haste away,

From the god's dread anger fly!
Cleanse once more the holy place,

Turn the savage train aside!
Earth contains upon its face

Many a spot unsanctified;
Here we only prize the good.

Stars unsullied round us burn.

If ye, in repentant mood,

From your wanderings would return,--
If ye fail to find the bliss

That ye found with us of yore,--
Or when lawless mirth like this

Gives your hearts delight no more,--
Then return in pilgrim guise,

Gladly up the mountain go,
While your strains repentant rise,

And our brethren's advent show.

Let a new-born wreath entwine

Solemnly your temples round;

Rapture glows in hearts divine

When a long-lost sinner's found.
Swifter e'en than Lathe's flood

Round Death's silent house can play,
Ev'ry error of the good

Will love's chalice wash away.
All will haste your steps to meet,

As ye come in majesty,--
Men your blessing will entreat;--

Ours ye thus will doubly be!

           1798.
(* Aganippe--A spring in Boeotia, which arose out of Mount Helicon, and was sacred to Apollo and the Muses.)

LILY'S MENAGERIE.

[Goethe describes this much-admired Poem, which he wrote in honour of his love Lily, as being "designed to change his surrender of her into despair, by drolly-fretful images."]

THERE'S no menagerie, I vow,

Excels my Lily's at this minute;

She keeps the strangest creatures in it,
And catches them, she knows not how.

Oh, how they hop, and run, and rave,
And their clipp'd pinions wildly wave,--
Poor princes, who must all endure
The pangs of love that nought can cure.

What is the fairy's name?--Is't Lily?--Ask not me!
Give thanks to Heaven if she's unknown to thee.

Oh what a cackling, what a shrieking,

When near the door she takes her stand,

With her food-basket in her hand!
Oh what a croaking, what a squeaking!
Alive all the trees and the bushes appear,
While to her feet whole troops draw near;
The very fish within, the water clear
Splash with impatience and their heads protrude;
And then she throws around the food
With such a look!--the very gods delighting
(To say nought of beasts). There begins, then, a biting,
A picking, a pecking, a sipping,
And each o'er the legs of another is tripping,
And pushing, and pressing, and flapping,
And chasing, and fuming, and snapping,
And all for one small piece of bread,
To which, though dry, her fair hands give a taste,
As though it in ambrosia had been plac'd.

And then her look! the tone

With which she calls: Pipi! Pipi!
Would draw Jove's eagle from his throne;
Yes, Venus' turtle doves, I wean,
And the vain peacock e'en,
Would come, I swear,
Soon as that tone had reach'd them through the air.

E'en from a forest dark had she

Enticed a bear, unlick'd, ill-bred,

And, by her wiles alluring, led
To join the gentle company,
Until as tame as they was he:
(Up to a certain point, be't understood!)
How fair, and, ah, how good
She seem'd to be! I would have drain'd my blood
To water e'en her flow'rets sweet.

"Thou sayest: I! Who? How? And where?"--
Well, to be plain, good Sirs--I am the bear;

In a net-apron, caught, alas!

Chain'd by a silk-thread at her feet.

But how this wonder came to pass
I'll tell some day, if ye are curious;
Just now, my temper's much too furious.

Ah, when I'm in the corner plac'd,

And hear afar the creatures snapping,

And see the flipping and the flapping,

I turn around

With growling sound,

And backward run a step in haste,

And look around

With growling sound.

Then run again a step in haste,
And to my former post go round.

But suddenly my anger grows,
A mighty spirit fills my nose,
My inward feelings all revolt.
A creature such as thou! a dolt!
Pipi, a squirrel able nuts to crack!
I bristle up my shaggy back
Unused a slave to be.
I'm laughed at by each trim and upstart tree
To scorn. The bowling-green I fly,

With neatly-mown and well-kept grass:

The box makes faces as I pass,--
Into the darkest thicket hasten I,
Hoping to 'scape from the ring,
Over the palings to spring!
Vainly I leap and climb;

I feel a leaden spell.

That pinions me as well,
And when I'm fully wearied out in time,
I lay me down beside some mock-cascade,

And roll myself half dead, and foam, and cry,

And, ah! no Oreads hear my sigh,
Excepting those of china made!

But, ah, with sudden power

In all my members blissful feelings reign!
'Tis she who singeth yonder in her bower!

I hear that darling, darling voice again.
The air is warm, and teems with fragrance clear,
Sings she perchance for me alone to hear?

I haste, and trample down the shrubs amain;
The trees make way, the bushes all retreat,
And so--the beast is lying at her feet.

She looks at him: "The monster's droll enough!

He's, for a bear, too mild,

Yet, for a dog, too wild,
So shaggy, clumsy, rough!"
Upon his back she gently strokes her foot;

He thinks himself in Paradise.
What feelings through his seven senses shoot!

But she looks on with careless eyes.
I lick her soles, and kiss her shoes,

As gently as a bear well may;
Softly I rise, and with a clever ruse

Leap on her knee.--On a propitious day
She suffers it; my ears then tickles she,

And hits me a hard blow in wanton play;
I growl with new-born ecstasy;
Then speaks she in a sweet vain jest, I wot
"Allons lout doux! eh! la menotte!
Et faites serviteur
Comme un joli seigneur."
Thus she proceeds with sport and glee;

Hope fills the oft-deluded beast;
Yet if one moment he would lazy be,

Her fondness all at once hath ceas'd.

She doth a flask of balsam-fire possess,

Sweeter than honey bees can make,

One drop of which she'll on her finger take,
When soften'd by his love and faithfulness,

Wherewith her monster's raging thirst to slake;
Then leaves me to myself, and flies at last,
And I, unbound, yet prison'd fast
By magic, follow in her train,
Seek for her, tremble, fly again.
The hapless creature thus tormenteth she,

Regardless of his pleasure or his woe;
Ha! oft half-open'd does she leave the door for me,

And sideways looks to learn if I will fly or no.
And I--Oh gods! your hands alone
Can end the spell that's o'er me thrown;
Free me, and gratitude my heart will fill;

And yet from heaven ye send me down no aid--

Not quite in vain doth life my limbs pervade:
I feel it! Strength is left me still.

   1775.

TO CHARLOTTE.

'MIDST the noise of merriment and glee,

'Midst full many a sorrow, many a care,
Charlotte, I remember, we remember thee,

How, at evening's hour so fair,
Thou a kindly hand didst reach us,

When thou, in some happy place

Where more fair is Nature s face,

Many a lightly-hidden trace
Of a spirit loved didst teach us.

Well 'tis that thy worth I rightly knew,--

That I, in the hour when first we met,

While the first impression fill'd me yet,
Call'd thee then a girl both good and true.

Rear'd in silence, calmly, knowing nought,

On the world we suddenly are thrown;
Hundred thousand billows round us sport;

All things charm us--many please alone,
Many grieve us, and as hour on hour is stealing,

To and fro our restless natures sway;
First we feel, and then we find each feeling

By the changeful world-stream borne away.

Well I know, we oft within us find

Many a hope and many a smart.
Charlotte, who can know our mind?

Charlotte, who can know our heart?
Ah! 'twould fain be understood, 'twould fain o'erflow

In some creature's fellow-feelings blest,
And, with trust, in twofold measure know

All the grief and joy in Nature's breast.

Then thine eye is oft around thee cast,

But in vain, for all seems closed for ever.
Thus the fairest part of life is madly pass'd

Free from storm, but resting never:
To thy sorrow thou'rt to-day repell'd

By what yesterday obey'd thee.
Can that world by thee be worthy held

Which so oft betray'd thee?

Which, 'mid all thy pleasures and thy pains,

Lived in selfish, unconcern'd repose?
See, the soul its secret cells regains,

And the heart--makes haste to close.
Thus found I thee, and gladly went to meet thee;

"She's worthy of all love!" I cried,
And pray'd that Heaven with purest bliss might greet thee,

Which in thy friend it richly hath supplied.

1776.*

LOVE'S DISTRESSES.

WHO will hear me? Whom shall I lament to?
Who would pity me that heard my sorrows?
Ah, the lip that erst so many raptures
Used to taste, and used to give responsive,

Now is cloven, and it pains me sorely;
And it is not thus severely wounded
By my mistress having caught me fiercely,
And then gently bitten me, intending
To secure her friend more firmly to her:
No, my tender lip is crack'd thus, only
By the winds, o'er rime and frost proceeding,
Pointed, sharp, unloving, having met me.
Now the noble grape's bright juice commingled
With the bee's sweet juice, upon the fire
Of my hearth, shall ease me of my torment.
Ah, what use will all this be, if with it
Love adds not a drop of his own balsam?

    1789.*

THE MUSAGETES.

IN the deepest nights of Winter
To the Muses kind oft cried I:
"Not a ray of morn is gleaming,
Not a sign of daylight breaking;
Bring, then, at the fitting moment,
Bring the lamp's soft glimm'ring lustre,
'Stead of Phoebus and Aurora,
To enliven my still labours!"
Yet they left me in my slumbers,
Dull and unrefreshing, lying,
And to each late-waken'd morning
Follow'd days devoid of profit.

When at length return'd the spring-time,
To the nightingales thus spake I:
"Darling nightingales, oh, beat ye
Early, early at my window,--
Wake me from the heavy slumber
That chains down the youth so strongly!"
Yet the love-o'erflowing songsters
Their sweet melodies protracted
Through the night before my window,
Kept awake my loving spirit,
Rousing new and tender yearnings

In my newly-waken'd bosom.
And the night thus fleeted o'er me,
And Aurora found me sleeping,--
Ay, the sun could scarce arouse me.

Now at length is come the Summer,
And the early fly so busy
Draws me from my pleasing slumbers
At the first-born morning-glimmer.
Mercilessly then returns she,
Though the half-aroused one often
Scares her from him with impatience,
And she lures her shameless sisters,
So that from my weary eyelids
Kindly sleep ere long is driven.
From my couch then boldly spring I,
And I seek the darling Muses,
in the beechen-grove I find them,
Full of pieasure to receive me;
And to the tormenting insects
Owe I many a golden hour.
Thus be ye, unwelcome beings,
Highly valued by the poet,
As the flies my numbers tell of.

1798.

MORNING LAMENT.

OH thou cruel deadly-lovely maiden,
Tell me what great sin have I committed,
That thou keep'st me to the rack thus fasten'd,
That thou hast thy solemn promise broken?

'Twas but yestere'en that thou with fondness
Press'd my hand, and these sweet accents murmured:
"Yes, I'll come, I'll come when morn approacheth,
Come, my friend, full surely to thy chamber."

On the latch I left my doors, unfasten'd,
Having first with care tried all the hinges,
And rejoic'd right well to find they creak'd not.

What a night of expectation pass'd I!
For I watch'd, and ev'ry chime I number'd;
If perchance I slept a few short moments,
Still my heart remain'd awake forever,
And awoke me from my gentle slumbers.

Yes, then bless'd I night's o'erhanging darkness,
That so calmly cover'd all things round me;
I enjoy'd the universal silence,
While I listen'd ever in the silence,
If perchance the slightest sounds were stirring.

"Had she only thoughts, my thoughts resembling,
Had she only feelings, like my feelings,
She would not await the dawn of morning.
But, ere this, would surely have been with me."

Skipp'd a kitten on the floor above me,
Scratch'd a mouse a panel in the corner,
Was there in the house the slightest motion,
Ever hoped I that I heard thy footstep,
Ever thought I that I heard thee coming.
And so lay I long, and ever longer,
And already was the daylight dawning,
And both here and there were signs of movement.

"Is it yon door? Were it my door only!"
In my bed I lean'd upon my elbow,
Looking tow'rd the door, now half-apparent,
If perchance it might not be in motion.
Both the wings upon the latch continued,
On the quiet hinges calmly hanging.

And the day grew bright and brighter ever;
And I heard my neighbour's door unbolted,
As he went to earn his daily wages,
And ere long I heard the waggons rumbling,
And the city gates were also open'd,
While the market-place, in ev'ry corner,
Teem'd with life and bustle and confusion.

In the house was going now and coming
Up and down the stairs, and doors were creaking

Backwards now, now forwards,--footsteps clatter'd
Yet, as though it were a thing all-living,
From my cherish'd hope I could not tear me.

When at length the sun, in hated splendour.
Fell upon my walls, upon my windows,
Up I sprang, and hasten'd to the garden,
There to blend my breath, so hot and yearning,
With the cool refreshing morning breezes,
And, it might be, even there to meet thee:
But I cannot find thee in the arbour,
Or the avenue of lofty lindens.

    1789.*

THE VISIT.

FAIN had I to-day surprised my mistress,
But soon found I that her door was fasten'd.
Yet I had the key safe in my pocket,
And the darling door I open'd softly!
In the parlour found I not the maiden,
Found the maiden not within her closet,
Then her chamber-door I gently open'd,
When I found her wrapp'd in pleasing slumbers,
Fully dress'd, and lying on the sofa.

While at work had slumber stolen o'er her;
For her knitting and her needle found I
Resting in her folded hands so tender;
And I placed myself beside her softly,
And held counsel, whether I should wake her.

Then I looked upon the beauteous quiet
That on her sweet eyelids was reposing
On her lips was silent truth depicted,
On her cheeks had loveliness its dwelling,
And the pureness of a heart unsullied
In her bosom evermore was heaving.
All her limbs were gracefully reclining,
Set at rest by sweet and godlike balsam.
Gladly sat I, and the contemplation

Held the strong desire I felt to wake her
Firmer and firmer down, with mystic fetters.

"Oh, thou love," methought, "I see that slumber,
Slumber that betrayeth each false feature,
Cannot injure thee, can nought discover
That could serve to harm thy friend's soft feelings.

"Now thy beauteous eyes are firmly closed,
That, when open, form mine only rapture.
And thy sweet lips are devoid of motion,
Motionless for speaking or for kissing;
Loosen'd are the soft and magic fetters
Of thine arms, so wont to twine around me,
And the hand, the ravishing companion
Of thy sweet caresses, lies unmoving.
Were my thoughts of thee but based on error,
Were the love I bear thee self-deception,
I must now have found it out, since Amor
Is, without his bandage, placed beside me."

Long I sat thus, full of heartfelt pleasure
At my love, and at her matchless merit;
She had so delighted me while slumbering,
That I could not venture to awake her.

Then I on the little table near her
Softly placed two oranges, two roses;
Gently, gently stole I from her chamber.
When her eyes the darling one shall open,
She will straightway spy these colourd presents,
And the friendly gift will view with wonder,
For the door will still remain unopen'd.

If perchance I see to-night the angel,
How will she rejoice,--reward me doubly
For this sacrifice of fond affection!

      1765.

THE MAGIC NET.

Do I see a contest yonder?
See I miracles or pastimes?
Beauteous urchins, five in number,
'Gainst five sisters fair contending,--
Measured is the time they're beating--
At a bright enchantress' bidding.
Glitt'ring spears by some are wielded,
Threads are others nimbly twining,

So that in their snares, the weapons
One would think, must needs be captured,
Soon, in truth, the spears are prison'd;
Yet they, in the gentle war-dance,
One by one escape their fetters
In the row of loops so tender,
That make haste to seize a free one
Soon as they release a captive.

So with contests, strivings, triumphs,
Flying now, and now returning,
Is an artful net soon woven,
In its whiteness like the snow-flakes,
That, from light amid the darkness,
Draw their streaky lines so varied,
As e'en colours scarce can draw them.

Who shall now receive that garment
Far beyond all others wish'd-for?
Whom our much-loved mistress favour
As her own acknowledged servant?
I am blest by kindly Fortune's
Tokens true, in silence pray'd for!
And I feel myself held captive,
To her service now devoted.

Yet, e'en while I, thus enraptured,
Thus adorn'd, am proudly wand'ring,
See! yon wantons are entwining,
Void of strife, with secret ardour,
Other nets, each fine and finer,

Threads of twilight interweaving,
Moonbeams sweet, night-violets' balsam.

Ere the net is noticed by us,
Is a happier one imprison'd,
Whom we, one and all, together
Greet with envy and with blessings.

1803.

THE GOBLET.

ONCE I held a well-carved brimming goblet,--
In my two hands tightly clasp'd I held it,
Eagerly the sweet wine sipp'd I from it,
Seeking there to drown all care and sorrow.

Amor enter'd in, and found me sitting,
And he gently smiled in modest fashion,
Smiled as though the foolish one he pitied.

"Friend, I know a far more beauteous vessel,
One wherein to sink thy spirit wholly;
Say, what wilt thou give me, if I grant it,
And with other nectar fill it for thee?"

Oh, how kindly hath he kept his promise!
For to me, who long had yearn'd, he granted
Thee, my Lida, fill'd with soft affection.

When I clasp mine arms around thee fondly,
When I drink in love's long-hoarded balsam
From thy darling lips so true, so faithful,
Fill'd with bliss thus speak I to my spirit
"No! a vessel such as this, save Amor
Never god hath fashion'd or been lord of!
Such a form was ne'er produced by Vulcan
With his cunning, reason-gifted hammers!
On the leaf-crown'd mountains may Lyaeus
Bid his Fauns, the oldest and the wisest,
Pass the choicest clusters through the winepress,
And himself watch o'er the fermentation:

Such a draught no toil can e'er procure him!"

   1781.

TO THE GRASSHOPPER.

AFTER ANACREON.

[The strong resemblance of this fine poem to Cowley's Ode bearing the same name, and beginning "Happy insect! what can be," will be at once seen.]

HAPPY art thou, darling insect,
Who, upon the trees' tall branches,
By a modest draught inspired,
Singing, like a monarch livest!
Thou possessest as thy portion
All that on the plains thou seest,
All that by the hours is brought thee
'Mongst the husbandmen thou livest,
As a friend, uninjured by them,
Thou whom mortals love to honour,
Herald sweet of sweet Spring's advent!
Yes, thou'rt loved by all the Muses,

Phoebus' self, too, needs must love thee;
They their silver voices gave thee,
Age can never steal upon thee.
Wise and gentle friend of poets,
Born a creature fleshless, bloodless,
Though Earth's daughter, free from suff'ring,
To the gods e'en almost equal.

   1781.

FROM 'THE SORROWS OF YOUNG WERTHER.'

[Prefixed to the second edition.]

EV'RY youth for love's sweet portion sighs,

Ev'ry maiden sighs to win man's love;
Why, alas! should bitter pain arise

From the noblest passion that we prove?

Thou, kind soul, bewailest, lov'st him well,

From disgrace his memory's saved by thee;
Lo, his spirit signs from out its cell:

BE A MAN, NOR SEEK TO FOLLOW ME.

    1775.

TRILOGY OF PASSION.

I. TO WERTHER.

[This poem, written at the age of seventy-five, was appended to an edition of 'Werther,' published at that time.]

ONCE more, then, much-wept shadow, thou dost dare

 Boldly to face the day's clear light,
To meet me on fresh blooming meadows fair,

 And dost not tremble at my sight.
Those happy times appear return'd once more.

 When on one field we quaff'd refreshing dew,
And, when the day's unwelcome toils were o'er,

 The farewell sunbeams bless'd our ravish'd view;
Fate bade thee go,--to linger here was mine,--
Going the first, the smaller loss was thine.

The life of man appears a glorious fate:
The day how lovely, and the night how great!
And we 'mid Paradise-like raptures plac'd,
The sun's bright glory scarce have learn'd to taste.

When strange contending feelings dimly cover,
Now us, and now the forms that round us hover;
One's feelings by no other are supplied,
'Tis dark without, if all is bright inside;
An outward brightness veils my sadden'd mood,
When Fortune smiles,--how seldom understood!
Now think we that we know her, and with might
A woman's beauteous form instils delight;
The youth, as glad as in his infancy,
The spring-time treads, as though the spring were he
Ravish'd, amazed, he asks, how this is done?
He looks around, the world appears his own.
With careless speed he wanders on through space,
Nor walls, nor palaces can check his race;
As some gay flight of birds round tree-tops plays,
So 'tis with him who round his mistress strays;
He seeks from AEther, which he'd leave behind him,
The faithful look that fondly serves to bind him.

Yet first too early warn'd, and then too late,
He feels his flight restrain'd, is captur'd straight
To meet again is sweet, to part is sad,
Again to meet again is still more glad,
And years in one short moment are enshrin'd;
But, oh, the harsh farewell is hid behind!

Thou smilest, friend, with fitting thoughts inspired;
By a dread parting was thy fame acquired,
Thy mournful destiny we sorrow'd o'er,
For weal and woe thou left'st us evermore,
And then again the passions' wavering force
Drew us along in labyrinthine course;
And we, consumed by constant misery,
At length must part--and parting is to die!
How moving is it, when the minstrel sings,
To 'scape the death that separation brings!
Oh grant, some god, to one who suffers so,
To tell, half-guilty, his sad tale of woe

1824

II. ELEGY.

When man had ceased to utter his lament,

A god then let me tell my tale of sorrow.

WHAT hope of once more meeting is there now
In the still-closed blossoms of this day?
Both heaven and hell thrown open seest thou;
What wav'ring thoughts within the bosom play
No longer doubt! Descending from the sky,
She lifts thee in her arms to realms on high.

And thus thou into Paradise wert brought,

As worthy of a pure and endless life;
Nothing was left, no wish, no hope, no thought,

Here was the boundary of thine inmost strife:
And seeing one so fair, so glorified,
The fount of yearning tears was straightway dried.

No motion stirr'd the day's revolving wheel,

In their own front the minutes seem'd to go;
The evening kiss, a true and binding seal,

Ne'er changing till the morrow's sunlight glow.
The hours resembled sisters as they went.
Yet each one from another different.

The last hour's kiss, so sadly sweet, effac'd

A beauteous network of entwining love.
Now on the threshold pause the feet, now haste.

As though a flaming cherub bade them move;
The unwilling eye the dark road wanders o'er,
Backward it looks, but closed it sees the door.

And now within itself is closed this breast,

As though it ne'er were open, and as though,
Vying with ev'ry star, no moments blest

Had, in its presence, felt a kindling glow;
Sadness, reproach, repentance, weight of care,
Hang heavy on it in the sultry air.

Is not the world still left? The rocky steeps,

Are they with holy shades no longer crown'd?
Grows not the harvest ripe? No longer creeps

The espalier by the stream,--the copse around?
Doth not the wondrous arch of heaven still rise,
Now rich in shape, now shapeless to the eyes?

As, seraph-like, from out the dark clouds' chorus,

With softness woven, graceful, light, and fair,
Resembling Her, in the blue aether o'er us,

A slender figure hovers in the air,--
Thus didst thou see her joyously advance,
The fairest of the fairest in the dance.

Yet but a moment dost thou boldly dare

To clasp an airy form instead of hers;
Back to thine heart! thou'lt find it better there,

For there in changeful guise her image stirs
What erst was one, to many turneth fast,
In thousand forms, each dearer than the last.

As at the door, on meeting lingerd she,

And step by step my faithful ardour bless'd,
For the last kiss herself entreated me,

And on my lips the last last kiss impress'd,--
Thus clearly traced, the lov'd one's form we view,
With flames engraven on a heart so true,--

A heart that, firm as some embattled tower,

Itself for her, her in itself reveres,
For her rejoices in its lasting power,

Conscious alone, when she herself appears;
Feels itself freer in so sweet a thrall,
And only beats to give her thanks in all.

The power of loving, and all yearning sighs

For love responsive were effaced and drown'd;
While longing hope for joyous enterprise

Was form'd, and rapid action straightway found;
If love can e'er a loving one inspire,
Most lovingly it gave me now its fire;

And 'twas through her!--an inward sorrow lay

On soul and body, heavily oppress'd;
To mournful phantoms was my sight a prey,

In the drear void of a sad tortured breast;
Now on the well-known threshold Hope hath smil'd,
Herself appeareth in the sunlight mild.

Unto the peace of God, which, as we read,

Blesseth us more than reason e'er hath done,
Love's happy peace would I compare indeed,

When in the presence of the dearest one.
There rests the heart, and there that sweetest thought,
The thought of being hers, is check'd by nought.

In the pure bosom doth a yearning float,

Unto a holier, purer, unknown Being
Its grateful aspiration to devote,

The Ever-Nameless then unriddled seeing;
We call it: piety!--such blest delight
I feel a share in, when before her sight.

Before her sight, as 'neath the sun's hot ray,

Before her breath, as 'neath the spring's soft wind,

In its deep wintry cavern melts away

Self-love, so long in icy chains confin'd;
No selfishness and no self-will are nigh,
For at her advent they were forced to fly.

It seems as though she said: "As hours pass by

They spread before us life with kindly plan;
Small knowledge did the yesterday supply,

To know the morrow is conceal'd from man;
And if the thought of evening made me start,
The sun at setting gladden'd straight my heart.

"Act, then, as I, and look, with joyous mind,

The moment in the face; nor linger thou!
Meet it with speed, so fraught with life, so kind

In action, and in love so radiant now;
Let all things be where thou art, childlike ever,
Thus thoult be all, thus, thou'lt be vanquish'd never."

Thou speakest well, methought, for as thy guide

The moment's favour did a god assign,
And each one feels himself when by thy side,

Fate's fav'rite in a moment so divine;
I tremble at thy look that bids me go,
Why should I care such wisdom vast to know?

Now am I far! And what would best befit

The present minute? I could scarcely tell;
Full many a rich possession offers it,

These but offend, and I would fain repel.
Yearnings unquenchable still drive me on,
All counsel, save unbounded tears, is gone.

Flow on, flow on in never-ceasing course,

Yet may ye never quench my inward fire!
Within my bosom heaves a mighty force,

Where death and life contend in combat dire.
Medicines may serve the body's pangs to still;
Nought but the spirit fails in strength of will,--

Fails in conception; wherefore fails it so?

A thousand times her image it portrays;
Enchanting now, and now compell'd to go,

Now indistinct, now clothed in purest rays!
How could the smallest comfort here be flowing?
The ebb and flood, the coming and the going!

   * * * * * *

Leave me here now, my life's companions true!

Leave me alone on rock, in moor and heath;
But courage! open lies the world to you,

The glorious heavens above, the earth beneath;
Observe, investigate, with searching eyes,
And nature will disclose her mysteries.

To me is all, I to myself am lost,

Who the immortals' fav'rite erst was thought;
They, tempting, sent Pandoras to my cost,

So rich in wealth, with danger far more fraught;
They urged me to those lips, with rapture crown'd,
Deserted me, and hurl'd me to the ground.

    1823.

III. ATONEMENT.

[Composed, when 74 years old, for a Polish lady, who excelled in playing on the pianoforte.]

PASSION brings reason--who can pacify

An anguish'd heart whose loss hath been so great?
Where are the hours that fled so swiftly by?

In vain the fairest thou didst gain from fate;
Sad is the soul, confused the enterprise;

The glorious world, how on the sense it dies!

In million tones entwined for evermore,

Music with angel-pinions hovers there,
To pierce man's being to its inmost core,

Eternal beauty has its fruit to bear;
The eye grows moist, in yearnings blest reveres
The godlike worth of music as of tears.

And so the lighten'd heart soon learns to see

That it still lives, and beats, and ought to beat,
Off'ring itself with joy and willingly,

In grateful payment for a gift so sweet.
And then was felt,--oh may it constant prove!--
The twofold bliss of music and of love.

   1823.

THE remembrance of the Good
Keep us ever glad in mood.

The remembrance of the Fair
Makes a mortal rapture share.

The remembrance of one's Love
Blest Is, if it constant prove.

The remembrance of the One
Is the greatest joy that's known.

   1828.

[Written at the age of 77.]

WHEN I was still a youthful wight,

So full of enjoyment and merry,
The painters used to assert, in spite,

That my features were small--yes, very;
Yet then full many a beauteous child
With true affection upon me smil'd.

Now as a greybeard I sit here in state,

By street and by lane held in awe, sirs;
And may be seen, like old Frederick the Great,

On pipebowls, on cups, and on saucers.
Yet the beauteous maidens, they keep afar;
Oh vision of youth! Oh golden star!

1826.

FOR EVER.

THE happiness that man, whilst prison'd here,

Is wont with heavenly rapture to compare,--
The harmony of Truth, from wavering clear,--

Of Friendship that is free from doubting care,--
The light which in stray thoughts alone can cheer

The wise,--the bard alone in visions fair,--
In my best hours I found in her all this,
And made mine own, to mine exceeding bliss.

1820.*

FROM AN ALBUM OF 1604.

HOPE provides wings to thought, and love to hope.
Rise up to Cynthia, love, when night is clearest,
And say, that as on high her figure changeth,
So, upon earth, my joy decays and grows.
And whisper in her ear with modest softness,
How doubt oft hung its head, and truth oft wept.
And oh ye thoughts, distrustfully inclined,
If ye are therefore by the loved one chided,
Answer: 'tis true ye change, but alter not,
As she remains the same, yet changeth ever.
Doubt may invade the heart, but poisons not,
For love is sweeter, by suspicion flavour'd.
If it with anger overcasts the eye,
And heaven's bright purity perversely blackens,
Then zephyr-sighs straight scare the clouds away,
And, changed to tears, dissolve them into rain.
Thought, hope, and love remain there as before,
Till Cynthia gleams upon me as of old.

        1820.*

LINES ON SEEING SCHILLER'S SKULL.

[This curious imitation of the ternary metre of Dante was written at the age of 77.]

WITHIN a gloomy charnel-house one day

I view'd the countless skulls, so strangely mated,
And of old times I thought, that now were grey.

Close pack'd they stand, that once so fiercely hated,
And hardy bones, that to the death contended,

Are lying cross'd,--to lie for ever, fated.
What held those crooked shoulder-blades suspended?

No one now asks; and limbs with vigour fired,
The hand, the foot--their use in life is ended.

Vainly ye sought the tomb for rest when tired;
Peace in the grave may not be yours; ye're driven

Back into daylight by a force inspired;
But none can love the wither'd husk, though even

A glorious noble kernel it contained.
To me, an adept, was the writing given

Which not to all its holy sense explained,
When 'mid the crowd, their icy shadows flinging,

I saw a form, that glorious still remained.
And even there, where mould and damp were clinging,

Gave me a blest, a rapture-fraught emotion,
As though from death a living fount were springing.

What mystic joy I felt! What rapt devotion!
That form, how pregnant with a godlike trace!

A look, how did it whirl me tow'rd that ocean
Whose rolling billows mightier shapes embrace!

Mysterious vessel! Oracle how dear!
Even to grasp thee is my hand too base,

Except to steal thee from thy prison here
With pious purpose, and devoutly go

Back to the air, free thoughts, and sunlight clear.
What greater gain in life can man e'er know

Than when God-Nature will to him explain
How into Spirit steadfastness may flow,

How steadfast, too, the Spirit-Born remain.

    1826.

ROYAL PRAYER.

HA, I am the lord of earth! The noble,

Who're in my service, love me.
Ha, I am the lord of earth! The noble,

O'er whom my sway extendeth, love I.
Oh, grant me, God in Heaven, that I may ne'er

Dispense with loftiness and love!

        1815.*

HUMAN FEELINGS.

AH, ye gods! ye great immortals
In the spacious heavens above us!
Would ye on this earth but give us
Steadfast minds and dauntless courage
We, oh kindly ones, would leave you
All your spacious heavens above us!

        1815.*

ON THE DIVAN.

HE who knows himself and others

Here will also see,
That the East and West, like brothers,

Parted ne'er shall be.

Thoughtfully to float for ever

'Tween two worlds, be man's endeavour!
So between the East and West

To revolve, be my behest!

    1833.*

EXPLANATION OF AN ANCIENT WOODCUT, REPRESENTING HANS SACHS' POETICAL MISSION.

[I feel considerable hesitation in venturing to offer this
version of a poem which Carlyle describes to be 'a beautiful
piece (a very Hans Sacks beatified, both in character and style),
which we wish there was any possibility of translating.' The
reader will be aware that Hans Sachs was the celebrated Minstrel-
Cobbler of Nuremberg, who Wrote 208 plays, 1700 comic tales, and
between 4000 and 5000 lyric poems. He flourished throughout
almost the whole of the 16th century.]

EARLY within his workshop here,
On Sundays stands our master dear;
His dirty apron he puts away,
And wears a cleanly doublet to-day;
Lets wax'd thread, hammer, and pincers rest,
And lays his awl within his chest;
The seventh day he takes repose
From many pulls and many blows.

Soon as the spring-sun meets his view,
Repose begets him labour anew;
He feels that he holds within his brain
A little world, that broods there amain,
And that begins to act and to live,
Which he to others would gladly give.

He had a skilful eye and true,
And was full kind and loving too.
For contemplation, clear and pure,--
For making all his own again, sure;
He had a tongue that charm'd when 'twas heard,
And graceful and light flow'd ev'ry word;
Which made the Muses in him rejoice,
The Master-singer of their choice.

And now a maiden enter'd there,
With swelling breast, and body fair;
With footing firm she took her place,
And moved with stately, noble grace;
She did not walk in wanton mood,
Nor look around with glances lewd.

She held a measure in her hand,
Her girdle was a golden band,
A wreath of corn was on her head,
Her eye the day's bright lustre shed;
Her name is honest Industry,
Else, Justice, Magnanimity.

She enter'd with a kindly greeting;
He felt no wonder at the meeting,
For, kind and fair as she might be,
He long had known her, fancied he.

"I have selected thee," she said,
"From all who earth's wild mazes tread,
That thou shouldst have clear-sighted sense,
And nought that's wrong shouldst e'er commence.
When others run in strange confusion,
Thy gaze shall see through each illusion
When others dolefully complain,
Thy cause with jesting thou shalt gain,
Honour and right shalt value duly,
In everything act simply, truly,--
Virtue and godliness proclaim,
And call all evil by its name,
Nought soften down, attempt no quibble,
Nought polish up, nought vainly scribble.
The world shall stand before thee, then,
As seen by Albert Durer's ken,
In manliness and changeless life,
In inward strength, with firmness rife.
Fair Nature's Genius by the hand
Shall lead thee on through every land,
Teach thee each different life to scan,
Show thee the wondrous ways of man,
His shifts, confusions, thrustings, and drubbings,

Pushings, tearings, pressings, and rubbings;
The varying madness of the crew,
The anthill's ravings bring to view;
But thou shalt see all this express'd,
As though 'twere in a magic chest.
Write these things down for folks on earth,
In hopes they may to wit give birth."--
Then she a window open'd wide,
And show'd a motley crowd outside,
All kinds of beings 'neath the sky,
As in his writings one may spy.

Our master dear was, after this,
On Nature thinking, full of bliss,
When tow'rd him, from the other side
He saw an aged woman glide;
The name she bears, Historia,
Mythologia, Fabula;
With footstep tottering and unstable
She dragg'd a large and wooden carved-table,
Where, with wide sleeves and human mien,
The Lord was catechizing seen;
Adam, Eve, Eden, the Serpent's seduction,
Gomorrah and Sodom's awful destruction,
The twelve illustrious women, too,
That mirror of honour brought to view;
All kinds of bloodthirstiness, murder, and sin,
The twelve wicked tyrants also were in,
And all kinds of goodly doctrine and law;
Saint Peter with his scourge you saw,
With the world's ways dissatisfied,
And by our Lord with power supplied.
Her train and dress, behind and before,
And e'en the seams, were painted o'er
With tales of worldly virtue and crime.--
Our master view'd all this for a time;
The sight right gladly he survey'd,
So useful for him in his trade,
Whence he was able to procure
Example good and precept sure,
Recounting all with truthful care,
As though he had been present there.
His spirit seem'd from earth to fly,
He ne'er had turned away his eye,

Did he not just behind him hear
A rattle of bells approaching near.
And now a fool doth catch his eye,
With goat and ape's leap drawing nigh
A merry interlude preparing
With fooleries and jests unsparing.
Behind him, in a line drawn out,
He dragg'd all fools, the lean and stout,
The great and little, the empty and full,
All too witty, and all too dull,
A lash he flourish'd overhead,
As though a dance of apes he led,
Abusing them with bitterness,
As though his wrath would ne'er grow less.

While on this sight our master gazed,
His head was growing well-nigh crazed:
What words for all could he e'er find,
Could such a medley be combined?
Could he continue with delight
For evermore to sing and write?
When lo, from out a cloud's dark bed
In at the upper window sped
The Muse, in all her majesty,
As fair as our loved maids we see.
With clearness she around him threw
Her truth, that ever stronger grew.

"I, to ordain thee come," she spake:
"So prosper, and my blessing take!
The holy fire that slumb'ring lies
Within thee, in bright flames shall rise;
Yet that thine ever-restless life
May still with kindly strength be rife,
I, for thine inward spirit's calm.
Have granted nourishment and balm,
That rapture may thy soul imbue,
Like some fair blossom bathed in dew."--
Behind his house then secretly
Outside the doorway pointed she,
Where, in a shady garden-nook,
A beauteous maid with downcast look
Was sitting where a stream was flowing,
With elder bushes near it growing,

She sat beneath an apple tree,
And nought around her seem'd to see.
Her lap was full of roses fair,
Which in a wreath she twined with care.
And, with them, leaves and blossoms blended:
For whom was that sweet wreath intended?
Thus sat she, modest and retired,
Her bosom throbb'd, with hope inspired;
Such deep forebodings fill'd her mind,
No room for wishing could she find,
And with the thoughts that o'er it flew,
Perchance a sigh was mingled too.

"But why should sorrow cloud thy brow?
That, dearest love, which fills thee now
Is fraught with joy and ecstasy.
Prepared in one alone for thee,
That he within thine eye may find
Solace when fortune proves unkind,
And be newborn through many a kiss,
That he receives with inward bliss;
When'er he clasps thee to his breast.
May he from all his toils find rest
When he in thy dear arms shall sink,
May he new life and vigour drink:
Fresh joys of youth shalt thou obtain,
In merry jest rejoice again.
With raillery and roguish spite,
Thou now shalt tease him, now delight.
Thus Love will nevermore grow old,
Thus will the minstrel ne'er be cold!"

While he thus lives, in secret bless'd,
Above him in the clouds doth rest
An oak-wreath, verdant and sublime,
Placed on his brow in after-time;
While they are banish'd to the slough,
Who their great master disavow.

1776.

SONNETS.

Lovingly I'll sing of love;
Ever comes she from above.

THE FRIENDLY MEETING.

IN spreading mantle to my chin conceald,

I trod the rocky path, so steep and grey,

Then to the wintry plain I bent my way
Uneasily, to flight my bosom steel'd.

But sudden was the newborn day reveal'd:

A maiden came, in heavenly bright array,

Like the fair creatures of the poet's lay
In realms of song. My yearning heart was heal'd.

Yet turn'd I thence, till she had onward pass'd,

While closer still the folds to draw I tried,

  As though with heat self-kindled to grow warm;

But follow'd her. She stood. The die was cast!

No more within my mantle could I hide;

  I threw it off,--she lay within mine arm.

        1807-8.

IN A WORD.

THUS to be chain'd for ever, can I bear?

A very torment that, in truth, would be.

This very day my new resolve shall see.--
I'll not go near the lately-worshipp'd Fair.

Yet what excuse, my heart, can I prepare

In such a case, for not consulting thee?

But courage! while our sorrows utter we
In tones where love, grief, gladness have a share.

But see! the minstrel's bidding to obey,

Its melody pours forth the sounding lyre,

  Yearning a sacrifice of love to bring.

Scarce wouldst thou think it--ready is the lay;

Well, but what then? Methought in the first fire

  We to her presence flew, that lay to sing.

        1807Ä8.

THE MAIDEN SPEAKS.

How grave thou loookest, loved one! wherefore so?

Thy marble image seems a type of thee;

Like it, no sign of life thou giv'st to me;
Compared with thee, the stone appears to glow.

Behind his shield in ambush lurks the foe,

The friend's brow all-unruffled we should see.

I seek thee, but thou seek'st away to flee;
Fix'd as this sculptured figure, learn to grow!

Tell me, to which should I the preference pay?

Must I from both with coldness meet alone?

The one is lifeless, thou with life art blest.

In short, no longer to throw words away,

I'll fondy kiss and kiss and kiss this stone,

Till thou dost tear me hence with envious breast.

1807.

GROWTH.

O'ER field and plain, in childhood's artless days,

Thou sprang'st with me, on many a spring-morn fair.

"For such a daughter, with what pleasing care,
Would I, as father, happy dwellings raise!"

And when thou on the world didst cast thy gaze,

Thy joy was then in household toils to share.

"Why did I trust her, why she trust me e'er?
For such a sister, how I Heaven should praise!"

Nothing can now the beauteous growth retard;

Love's glowing flame within my breast is fann'd.

Shall I embrace her form, my grief to end?

Thee as a queen must I, alas, regard:

So high above me placed thou seem'st to stand;

Before a passing look I meekly bend.

1807-8.

FOOD IN TRAVEL.

IF to her eyes' bright lustre I were blind,

No longer would they serve my life to gild.

The will of destiny must be fulfilid,--
This knowing, I withdrew with sadden'd mind.

No further happiness I now could find:

The former longings of my heart were still'd;

I sought her looks alone, whereon to build
My joy in life,--all else was left behind.

Wine's genial glow, the festal banquet gay,

Ease, sleep, and friends, all wonted pleasures glad

 I spurn'd, till little there remain'd to prove.

Now calmly through the world I wend my way:

That which I crave may everywhere be had,

 With me I bring the one thing needful--love.

1807-8.

DEPARTURE.

WITH many a thousand kiss not yet content,

At length with One kiss I was forced to go;

After that bitter parting's depth of woe,
I deem'd the shore from which my steps I bent,

Its hills, streams, dwellings, mountains, as I went,

A pledge of joy, till daylight ceased to glow;

Then on my sight did blissful visions grow
In the dim-lighted, distant firmament,

And when at length the sea confined my gaze,

My ardent longing fill'd my heart once more;

  What I had lost, unwillingly I sought.

Then Heaven appear'd to shed its kindly rays:

Methought that all I had possess'd of yore

  Remain'd still mine--that I was reft of nought.

        1807Ä8.

THE LOVING ONE WRITES.

THE look that thy sweet eyes on mine impress

The pledge thy lips to mine convey,--the kiss,--

He who, like me, hath knowledge sure of this,
Can he in aught beside find happiness?

Removed from thee, friend-sever'd, in distress,

These thoughts I vainly struggle to dismiss:

They still return to that one hour of bliss,
The only one; then tears my grief confess.

But unawares the tear makes haste to dry:

He loves, methinks, e'en to these glades so still,--

  And shalt not thou to distant lands extend?

Receive the murmurs of his loving sigh;

My only joy on earth is in thy will,

  Thy kindly will tow'rd me; a token send!

        1807Ä8.

THE LOVING ONE ONCE MORE.

WHY do I o'er my paper once more bend?

Ask not too closely, dearest one, I pray

For, to speak truth, I've nothing now to say;
Yet to thy hands at length 'twill come, dear friend.

Since I can come not with it, what I send

My undivided heart shall now convey,

With all its joys, hopes, pleasures, pains, to-day:
All this hath no beginning, hath no end.

Henceforward I may ne'er to thee confide

How, far as thought, wish, fancy, will, can reach,

  My faithful heart with thine is surely blended.

Thus stood I once enraptured by thy side,

Gazed on thee, and said nought. What need of speech?

  My very being in itself was ended.

        1807Ä8.

SHE CANNOT END.

WHEN unto thee I sent the page all white,

Instead of first thereon inscribing aught,

The space thou doubtless filledst up in sport.
And sent it me, to make my joy grow bright.

As soon as the blue cover met my sight,

As well becomes a woman, quick as thought

I tore it open, leaving hidden nought,
And read the well-known words of pure delight:

MY ONLY BEING! DEAREST HEART! SWEET CHILD!

How kindly thou my yearning then didst still

  With gentle words, enthralling me to thee.

In truth methought I read thy whispers mild

Wherewith thou lovingly my soul didst fill,

  E'en to myself for aye ennobling me.

        1807Ä8.

NEMESIS.

WHEN through the nations stalks contagion wild,

We from them cautiously should steal away.

E'en I have oft with ling'ring and delay
Shunn'd many an influence, not to be defil'd.

And e'en though Amor oft my hours beguil'd,

At length with him preferr'd I not to play,

And so, too, with the wretched sons of clay,
When four and three-lined verses they compil'd.

But punishment pursues the scoffer straight,

As if by serpent-torch of furies led

  From bill to vale, from land to sea to fly.

I hear the genie's laughter at my fate;

Yet do I find all power of thinking fled

  In sonnet-rage and love's fierce ecstasy.

1807-8.

THE CHRISTMAS-BOX.

THIS box, mine own sweet darling, thou wilt find

With many a varied sweetmeat's form supplied;

The fruits are they of holy Christmas tide,
But baked indeed, for children's use design'd.

I'd fain, in speeches sweet with skill combin'd,

Poetic sweetmeats for the feast provide;

But why in such frivolities confide?
Perish the thought, with flattery to blind!

One sweet thing there is still, that from within,

Within us speaks,--that may be felt afar;

  This may be wafted o'er to thee alone.

If thou a recollection fond canst win,

As if with pleasure gleam'd each well-known star,

  The smallest gift thou never wilt disown.

        1807.

THE WARNING.

WHEN sounds the trumpet at the Judgment Day,

And when forever all things earthly die,

We must a full and true account supply
Of ev'ry useless word we dropp'd in play.

But what effect will all the words convey

Wherein with eager zeal and lovingly,

That I might win thy favour, labour'd I,
If on thine ear alone they die away?

Therefore, sweet love, thy conscience bear in mind,

Remember well how long thou hast delay'd,

  So that the world such sufferings may not know.

If I must reckon, and excuses find

For all things useless I to thee have said,

  To a full year the Judgment Day will grow

        1807Ä8.

THE EPOCHS.

ON Petrarch's heart, all other days before,

In flaming letters written, was impress d

GOOD FRIDAY. And on mine, be it confess'd,
Is this year's ADVENT, as it passeth o'er.

I do not now begin,--I still adore

Her whom I early cherish'd in my breast;,

Then once again with prudence dispossess'd,
And to whose heart I'm driven back once more.

The love of Petrarch, that all-glorious love,

Was unrequited, and, alas, full sad;

  One long Good Friday 'twas, one heartache drear

But may my mistress' Advent ever prove,

With its palm-jubilee, so sweet and glad,

  One endless Mayday, through the livelong year!

        1807.

THE DOUBTERS AND THE LOVERS.

THE DOUBTERS.

YE love, and sonnets write! Fate's strange behest!

The heart, its hidden meaning to declare,

Must seek for rhymes, uniting pair with pair:

Learn, children, that the will is weak, at best.

Scarcely with freedom the o'erflowing breast

As yet can speak, and well may it beware;

Tempestuous passions sweep each chord that's there,
Then once more sink to night and gentle rest.

Why vex yourselves and us, the heavy stone

Up the steep path but step by step to roll?

  It falls again, and ye ne'er cease to strive.

THE LOVERS.

But we are on the proper road alone!

If gladly is to thaw the frozen soul,

  The fire of love must aye be kept alive.

          1807Ä8.

CHARADE.

Two words there 'are, both short, of beauty rare,

Whose sounds our lips so often love to frame,

But which with clearness never can proclaim
The things whose own peculiar stamp they bear.

'Tis well in days of age and youth so fair,

One on the other boldly to inflame;

And if those words together link'd we name,
A blissful rapture we discover there.

But now to give them pleasure do I seek,

And in myself my happiness would find;

  I hope in silence, but I hope for this:

Gently, as loved one's names, those words to speak

To see them both within one image shrin'd,

  Both in one being to embrace with bliss.

        1807.

EPIGRAMS.

In these numbers be express'd
Meaning deep, 'neath merry jest.

TO ORIGINALS.

A FELLOW says: "I own no school or college;
No master lives whom I acknowledge;
And pray don't entertain the thought
That from the dead I e'er learnt aught."
This, if I rightly understand,
Means: "I'm a blockhead at first hand."

        1815.

THE SOLDIER'S CONSOLATION.

No! in truth there's here no lack:
White the bread, the maidens black!
To another town, next night:
Black the bread, the maidens white!

1815.*

GENIAL IMPULSE.

THUS roll I, never taking ease,
My tub, like Saint Diogenes,
Now serious am, now seek to please;
Now love and hate in turn one sees;
The motives now are those, now these;
Now nothings, now realities.
Thus roll I, never taking ease,
My tub, like Saint Diogenes.

1810.

NEITHER THIS NOR THAT.

IF thou to be a slave shouldst will,
Thou'lt get no pity, but fare ill;
And if a master thou wouldst be,
The world will view it angrily;
And if in statu quo thou stay,
That thou art but a fool, they'll say.

1815.*

THE WAY TO BEHAVE.

THOUGH tempers are bad and peevish folks swear,
Remember to ruffle thy brows, friend, ne'er;
And let not the fancies of women so fair
E'er serve thy pleasure in life to impair.

1815.*

THE BEST.

WHEN head and heart are busy, say,

What better can be found?
Who neither loves nor goes astray,

Were better under ground.

   1815.*

AS BROAD AS IT'S LONG.

MODEST men must needs endure,

And the bold must humbly bow;
Thus thy fate's the same, be sure,

Whether bold or modest thou.

   1815.*

THE RULE OF LIFE.

IF thou wouldst live unruffled by care,
Let not the past torment thee e'er;
As little as possible be thou annoy'd,
And let the present be ever enjoy'd;
Ne'er let thy breast with hate be supplied,
And to God the future confide.

   1815.*

THE SAME, EXPANDED.

IF thou wouldst live unruffled by care,
Let not the past torment thee e'er;
If any loss thou hast to rue,
Act as though thou wert born anew;
Inquire the meaning of each day,
What each day means itself will say;
In thine own actions take thy pleasure,
What others do, thou'lt duly treasure;
Ne'er let thy breast with hate be supplied,
And to God the future confide.

IF wealth is gone--then something is gone!

Quick, make up thy mind,

And fresh wealth find.
If honour is gone--then much is gone!

Seek glory to find,

And people then will alter their mind.
If courage is gone--then all is gone!
'Twere better that thou hadst never been born.

HE who with life makes sport,

Can prosper never;
Who rules himself in nought,

Is a slave ever.

MAY each honest effort be

Crown'd with lasting constancy.

EACH road to the proper end
Runs straight on, without a bend.

    1825.

CALM AT SEA.

SILENCE deep rules o'er the waters,

Calmly slumb'ring lies the main,
While the sailor views with trouble

Nought but one vast level plain.

Not a zephyr is in motion!

Silence fearful as the grave!
In the mighty waste of ocean

Sunk to rest is ev'ry wave.

    1795.

THE PROSPEROUS VOYAGE.

THE mist is fast clearing.
And radiant is heaven,
Whilst AEolus loosens
Our anguish-fraught bond.
The zephyrs are sighing,
Alert is the sailor.
Quick! nimbly be plying!
The billows are riven,
The distance approaches;
I see land beyond!

    1795.

COURAGE.

CARELESSLY over the plain away,
Where by the boldest man no path
Cut before thee thou canst discern,
Make for thyself a path!

Silence, loved one, my heart!
Cracking, let it not break!
Breaking, break not with thee!

        1776.*

MY ONLY PROPERTY.

I FEEL that I'm possess'd of nought,
Saving the free unfetterd thought

Which from my bosom seeks to flow,
And each propitious passing hour
That suffers me in all its power

A loving fate with truth to know.

        1814.

ADMONITION.

WHEREFORE ever ramble on?

For the Good is lying near,
Fortune learn to seize alone,

For that Fortune's ever here.

        1789.

OLD AGE.

OLD age is courteous--no one more:
For time after time he knocks at the door,
But nobody says, "Walk in, sir, pray!"
Yet turns he not from the door away,
But lifts the latch, and enters with speed.
And then they cry "A cool one, indeed!"

    1814.

EPITAPH.

As a boy, reserved and naughty;
As a youth, a coxcomb and haughty;
As a man, for action inclined;
As a greybeard, fickle in mind.--
Upon thy grave will people read:
This was a very man, indeed!

    1815.*

RULES FOR MONARCHS.

IF men are never their thoughts to employ,
Take care to provide them a life full of joy;
But if to some profit and use thou wouldst bend them,
Take care to shear them, and then defend them.

    1815.*

PAULO POST FUTURI.

WEEP ye not, ye children dear,

That as yet ye are unborn:
For each sorrow and each tear

Makes the father's heart to mourn.

Patient be a short time to it,

Unproduced, and known to none;
If your father cannot do it,

By your mother 'twill be done.

    1784.

THE FOOL'S EPILOGUE.

MANY good works I've done and ended,
Ye take the praise--I'm not offended;
For in the world, I've always thought
Each thing its true position hath sought.
When praised for foolish deeds am I,
I set off laughing heartily;
When blamed for doing something good,
I take it in an easy mood.
If some one stronger gives me hard blows,
That it's a jest, I feign to suppose:
But if 'tis one that's but my own like,
I know the way such folks to strike.
When Fortune smiles, I merry grow,
And sing in dulci jubilo;
When sinks her wheel, and tumbles me o'er,
I think 'tis sure to rise once more.

In the sunshine of summer I ne'er lament,
Because the winter it cannot prevent;
And when the white snow-flakes fall around,
I don my skates, and am off with a bound.
Though I dissemble as I will,
The sun for me will ne'er stand still;
The old and wonted course is run,
Until the whole of life is done;

Each day the servant like the lord,
In turns comes home, and goes abroad;
If proud or humble the line they take,
They all must eat, drink, sleep, and wake.
So nothing ever vexes me;
Act like the fool, and wise ye'll be!

   1804.

PARABLES.

Joy from that in type we borrow,
Which in life gives only sorrow.

JOY.

A DRAGON-FLY with beauteous wing
Is hov'ring o'er a silv'ry spring;
I watch its motions with delight,--
Now dark its colours seem, now bright;
Chameleon-like appear, now blue,
Now red, and now of greenish hue.
Would it would come still nearer me,
That I its tints might better see

It hovers, flutters, resting ne'er!

But hush! it settles on the mead.
I have it safe now, I declare!

 And when its form I closely view,

 'Tis of a sad and dingy blue--
Such, Joy-Dissector, is thy case indeed

   1767-9.

EXPLANATION OF AN ANTIQUE GEM,

A YOUNG fig-tree its form lifts high

Within a beauteous garden;
And see, a goat is sitting by.

As if he were its warden.

But oh, Quirites, how one errs!

The tree is guarded badly;
For round the other side there whirrs

And hums a beetle madly.

The hero with his well-mail'd coat

Nibbles the branches tall so;
A mighty longing feels the goat

Gently to climb up also.

And so, my friends, ere long ye see

The tree all leafless standing;
It looks a type of misery,

Help of the gods demanding.

Then listen, ye ingenuous youth,

Who hold wise saws respected:
From he-goat and from beetles-tooth

A tree should be protected!

1815.

CAT-PIE.

WHILE he is mark'd by vision clear

Who fathoms Nature's treasures,
The man may follow, void of fear,

Who her proportions measures.

Though for one mortal, it is true,

These trades may both be fitted,
Yet, that the things themselves are two

Must always be admitted.

Once on a time there lived a cook

Whose skill was past disputing,
Who in his head a fancy took

To try his luck at shooting.

So, gun in hand, he sought a spot

Where stores of game were breeding,
And there ere long a cat he shot

That on young birds was feeding.

This cat he fancied was a hare,

Forming a judgment hasty,
So served it up for people's fare,

Well-spiced and in a pasty.

Yet many a guest with wrath was fill'd

(All who had noses tender):
The cat that's by the sportsman kill'd

No cook a hare can render.

                1810.

LEGEND.

THERE lived in the desert a holy man

To whom a goat-footed Faun one day
Paid a visit, and thus began

To his surprise: "I entreat thee to pray
That grace to me and my friends may be given,
That we may be able to mount to Heaven,
For great is our thirst for heav'nly bliss."
The holy man made answer to this:
"Much danger is lurking in thy petition,
Nor will it be easy to gain admission;
Thou dost not come with an angel's salute;
For I see thou wearest a cloven foot."
The wild man paused, and then answer'd he:
"What doth my goat's foot matter to thee?
Full many I've known into heaven to pass
Straight and with ease, with the head of an ass!"

                1815.*

AUTHORS.

OVER the meadows, and down the stream,

And through the garden-walks straying,
He plucks the flowers that fairest seem;

His throbbing heart brooks no delaying.
His maiden then comes--oh, what ecstasy!
Thy flowers thou giv'st for one glance of her eye!

The gard'ner next door o'er the hedge sees the youth:

"I'm not such a fool as that, in good truth;
My pleasure is ever to cherish each flower,
And see that no birds my fruit e'er devour.
But when 'tis ripe, your money, good neighbour!
'Twas not for nothing I took all this labour!"
And such, methinks, are the author-tribe.

The one his pleasures around him strews,

That his friends, the public, may reap, if they choose;
The other would fain make them all subscribe,

    1776.*

THE CRITIC.

I HAD a fellow as my guest,
Not knowing he was such a pest,
And gave him just my usual fare;
He ate his fill of what was there,

And for desert my best things swallow'd,
Soon as his meal was o'er, what follow'd?
Led by the Deuce, to a neighbour he went,
And talk'd of my food to his heart's content:
"The soup might surely have had more spice,
The meat was ill-brown'd, and the wine wasn't nice."
A thousand curses alight on his head!
'Tis a critic, I vow! Let the dog be struck dead!

    1776.*

THE DILETTANTE AND THE CRITIC.

A BOY a pigeon once possess'd,
In gay and brilliant plumage dress'd;
He loved it well, and in boyish sport
Its food to take from his mouth he taught,
And in his pigeon he took such pride,

That his joy to others he needs must confide.

An aged fox near the place chanc'd to dwell,
Talkative, clever, and learned as well;
The boy his society used to prize,
Hearing with pleasure his wonders and lies.

"My friend the fox my pigeon must see
He ran, and stretch'd 'mongst the bushes lay he
"Look, fox, at my pigeon, my pigeon so fair!
His equal I'm sure thou hast look'd upon ne'er!"

"Let's see!"--The boy gave it.--"'Tis really not bad;
And yet, it is far from complete, I must add.
The feathers, for, instance, how short! 'Tis absurd!"
So he set to work straightway to pluck the poor bird.

The boy screamed.--"Thou must now stronger pinions supply,
Or else 'twill be ugly, unable to fly."--
Soon 'twas stripp'd--oh, the villain!--and torn all to pieces.
The boy was heart-broken,--and so my tale ceases.

* * * *

He who sees in the boy shadow'd forth his own case,
Should be on his guard 'gainst the fox's whole race.

1776.*

THE WRANGLER.

ONE day a shameless and impudent wight
Went into a shop full of steel wares bright,
Arranged with art upon ev'ry shelf.
He fancied they were all meant for himself;
And so, while the patient owner stood by,
The shining goods needs must handle and try,
And valued,--for how should a fool better know?--
The bad things high, and the good ones low,
And all with an easy self-satisfied face;
Then, having bought nothing, he left the place.

The tradesman now felt sorely vex'd,
So when the fellow went there next,
A lock of steel made quite red hot.
The other cried upon the spot:
"Such wares as these, who'd ever buy?
the steel is tarnish'd shamefully,"--
Then pull'd it, like a fool about,
But soon set up a piteous shout.
"Pray what's the matter?" the shopman spoke;
The other scream'd: "Faith, a very cool joke!"

   1815.*

THE YELPERS.

OUR rides in all directions bend,

For business or for pleasure,
Yet yelpings on our steps attend,

And barkings without measure.
The dog that in our stable dwells,

After our heels is striding,
And all the while his noisy yells

But show that we are riding.

   1815.*

THE STORK'S VOCATION.

THE stork who worms and frogs devours

That in our ponds reside,
Why should he dwell on high church-towers,

With which he's not allied?

Incessantly he chatters there,

And gives our ears no rest;
But neither old nor young can dare

To drive him from his nest.

I humbly ask it,--how can he

Give of his title proof,
Save by his happy tendency

To soil the church's roof?

CELEBRITY.

[A satire on his own Sorrows of Werther.]

ON bridges small and bridges great
Stands Nepomucks in ev'ry state,
Of bronze, wood, painted, or of stone,
Some small as dolls, some giants grown;
Each passer must worship before Nepomuck,
Who to die on a bridge chanced to have the ill luck,
When once a man with head and ears
A saint in people's eyes appears,
Or has been sentenced piteously
Beneath the hangman's hand to die,
He's as a noted person prized,
In portrait is immortalized.
Engravings, woodcuts, are supplied,
And through the world spread far and wide.
Upon them all is seen his name,
And ev'ry one admits his claim;
Even the image of the Lord
Is not with greater zeal ador'd.
Strange fancy of the human race!
Half sinner frail, half child of grace
We see HERR WERTHER of the story
In all the pomp of woodcut glory.
His worth is first made duly known,
By having his sad features shown

At ev'ry fair the country round;
In ev'ry alehouse too they're found.
His stick is pointed by each dunce
"The ball would reach his brain at once!"
And each says, o'er his beer and bread:
"Thank Heav'n that 'tis not we are dead!"

   1815.*

PLAYING AT PRIESTS.

WITHIN a town where parity
According to old form we see,--
That is to say, where Catholic
And Protestant no quarrels pick,
And where, as in his father's day,
Each worships God in his own way,
We Luth'ran children used to dwell,
By songs and sermons taught as well.
The Catholic clingclang in truth
Sounded more pleasing to our youth,
For all that we encounter'd there,
To us seem'd varied, joyous, fair.
As children, monkeys, and mankind
To ape each other are inclin'd,
We soon, the time to while away,
A game at priests resolved to play.
Their aprons all our sisters lent
For copes, which gave us great content;
And handkerchiefs, embroider'd o'er,
Instead of stoles we also wore;
Gold paper, whereon beasts were traced,
The bishop's brow as mitre graced.

Through house and garden thus in state
We strutted early, strutted late,
Repeating with all proper unction,
Incessantly each holy function.
The best was wanting to the game;

We knew that a sonorous ring

Was here a most important thing;
But Fortune to our rescue came,
For on the ground a halter lay;

We were delighted, and at once

Made it a bellrope for the nonce,
And kept it moving all the day;

In turns each sister and each brother

Acted as sexton to another;
All help'd to swell the joyous throng;

The whole proceeded swimmingly,

And since no actual bell had we,
We all in chorus sang, Ding dong!

* * * * *

Our guileless child's-sport long was hush'd

In memory's tomb, like some old lay;
And yet across my mind it rush'd

With pristine force the other day.
The New-Poetic Catholics
In ev'ry point its aptness fix!

    1815.*

SONGS.

SONGS are like painted window-panes!
In darkness wrapp'd the church remains,
If from the market-place we view it;
Thus sees the ignoramus through it.
No wonder that he deems it tame,--
And all his life 'twill be the same.

But let us now inside repair,
And greet the holy Chapel there!
At once the whole seems clear and bright,
Each ornament is bathed in light,
And fraught with meaning to the sight.
God's children! thus your fortune prize,
Be edified, and feast your eyes!

      1827.*

POETRY.

GOD to his untaught children sent

Law, order, knowledge, art, from high,
And ev'ry heav'nly favour lent,

The world's hard lot to qualify.
They knew not how they should behave,

For all from Heav'n stark-naked came;
But Poetry their garments gave,

And then not one had cause for shame.

      1816.

A PARABLE.

I PICKED a rustic nosegay lately,
And bore it homewards, musing greatly;
When, heated by my hand, I found
The heads all drooping tow'rd the ground.
I plac'd them in a well-cool'd glass,
And what a wonder came to pass
The heads soon raised themselves once more.
The stalks were blooming as before,
And all were in as good a case
As when they left their native place.

*   *   *   *

So felt I, when I wond'ring heard
My song to foreign tongues transferr'd.

        1828.

SHOULD E'ER THE LOVELESS DAY.

SHOULD e'er the loveless day remain
Obscured by storms of hail and rain,

Thy charms thou showest never;
I tap at window, tap at door:
Come, lov'd one, come! appear once more!

Thou art as fair as ever!

        1827.*

A PLAN THE MUSES ENTERTAINED.

A PLAN the Muses entertain'd

Methodically to impart

To Psyche the poetic art;
Prosaic-pure her soul remain'd.
No wondrous sounds escaped her lyre

E'en in the fairest Summer night;
But Amor came with glance of fire,--

The lesson soon was learn'd aright.

        1827.*

THE DEATH OF THE FLY.

WITH eagerness he drinks the treach'rous potion,

Nor stops to rest, by the first taste misled;
Sweet is the draught, but soon all power of motion

He finds has from his tender members fled;
No longer has he strength to plume his wing,
No longer strength to raise his head, poor thing!
E'en in enjoyment's hour his life he loses,
His little foot to bear his weight refuses;
So on he sips, and ere his draught is o'er,
Death veils his thousand eyes for evermore.

1810.

BY THE RIVER.

WHEN by the broad stream thou dost dwell,

Oft shallow is its sluggish flood;
Then, when thy fields thou tendest well,

It o'er them spreads its slime and mud.

The ships descend ere daylight wanes,

The prudent fisher upward goes;
Round reef and rock ice casts its chains,

And boys at will the pathway close.

To this attend, then, carefully,

And what thou wouldst, that execute!
Ne'er linger, ne'er o'erhasty be,

For time moves on with measured foot.

1821.*

THE FOX AND CRANE.

ONCE two persons uninvited

Came to join my dinner table;
For the nonce they lived united,

Fox and crane yclept in fable.

Civil greetings pass'd between us

Then I pluck'd some pigeons tender
For the fox of jackal-genius,

Adding grapes in full-grown splendour.

Long-neck'd flasks I put as dishes

For the crane, without delaying,
Fill'd with gold and silver fishes,

In the limpid water playing.

Had ye witness'd Reynard planted

At his flat plate, all demurely,
Ye with envy must have granted:

"Ne'er was such a gourmand, surely!"

While the bird with circumspection

On one foot, as usual, cradled,
From the flasks his fish-refection

With his bill and long neck ladled.

One the pigeons praised,--the other,

As they went, extoll'd the fishes,
Each one scoffing at his brother

For preferring vulgar dishes.

  * * *

If thou wouldst preserve thy credit,

When thou askest folks to guzzle
At thy hoard, take care to spread it

Suited both for bill and muzzle.

    1819.

THE FOX AND HUNTSMAN.

HARD 'tis on a fox's traces

To arrive, midst forest-glades;
Hopeless utterly the chase is,

If his flight the huntsman aids.

And so 'tis with many a wonder,

(Why A B make Ab in fact,)
Over which we gape and blunder,

And our head and brains distract.

    1821.*

THE FROGS.

A POOL was once congeal'd with frost;
The frogs, in its deep waters lost,

No longer dared to croak or spring;
But promised, being half asleep,
If suffer'd to the air to creep,

As very nightingales to sing.

A thaw dissolved the ice so strong,--
They proudly steer'd themselves along,
When landed, squatted on the shore,
And croak'd as loudly as before.

1821.*

THE WEDDING.

A FEAST was in a village spread,--
It was a wedding-day, they said.
The parlour of the inn I found,
And saw the couples whirling round,
Each lass attended by her lad,
And all seem'd loving, blithe, and glad;
But on my asking for the bride,
A fellow with a stare, replied:
"'Tis not the place that point to raise!

We're only dancing in her honour;
We now have danced three nights and days,

And not bestowed one thought upon her."

    *   *   *   *

Whoe'er in life employs his eyes
Such cases oft will recognise.

1821.*

BURIAL.

To the grave one day from a house they bore

A maiden;
To the window the citizens went to explore;
In splendour they lived, and with wealth as of yore

Their banquets were laden.
Then thought they: "The maid to the tomb is now borne;
We too from our dwellings ere long must be torn,
And he that is left our departure to mourn,

To our riches will be the successor,

For some one must be their possessor.

    1827.*

THREATENING SIGNS.

IF Venus in the evening sky
Is seen in radiant majesty,
If rod-like comets, red as blood,
Are 'mongst the constellations view'd,
Out springs the Ignoramus, yelling:
"The star's exactly o'er my dwelling!
What woeful prospect, ah, for me!
Then calls his neighbour mournfully:
"Behold that awful sign of evil,
Portending woe to me, poor devil!
My mother's asthma ne'er will leave her,
My child is sick with wind and fever;
I dread the illness of my wife,
A week has pass'd, devoid of strife,--
And other things have reach'd my ear;
The Judgment Day has come, I fear!"

His neighbour answered: "Friend, you're right!

Matters look very had to-night.
Let's go a street or two, though, hence,
And gaze upon the stars from thence."--
No change appears in either case.
Let each remain then in his place,
And wisely do the best he can,
Patient as any other man.

1821.*

THE BUYERS.

To an apple-woman's stall

Once some children nimbly ran;
Longing much to purchase all,
They with joyous haste began
Snatching up the piles there raised,
While with eager eyes they gazed
On the rosy fruit so nice;
But when they found out the price,
Down they threw the whole they'd got,
Just as if they were red hot.

*　*　*　*　*

The man who gratis will his goods supply
Will never find a lack of folks to buy!

1820.

THE MOUNTAIN VILLAGE.

"THE mountain village was destroy'd;
But see how soon is fill'd the void!
Shingles and boards, as by magic arise,
The babe in his cradle and swaddling-clothes lies;
How blest to trust to God's protection!"

Behold a wooden new erection,
So that, if sparks and wind but choose,
God's self at such a game must lose!

1827.*

<h1 style="text-align:center">SYMBOLS.</h1>

PALM Sunday at the Vatican

They celebrate with palms;
With reverence bows each holy man,

And chaunts the ancient psalms.
Those very psalms are also sung

With olive boughs in hand,
While holly, mountain wilds among,

In place of palms must stand:
In fine, one seeks some twig that's green,

And takes a willow rod,
So that the pious man may e'en

In small things praise his God.

And if ye have observed it well,

To gain what's fit ye're able,
If ye in faith can but excel;

Such are the myths of fable.

1827.*

THREE PALINODIAS.

I.

"Incense is but a tribute for the gods,--
To mortals 'tis but poison."

THE smoke that from thine altar blows,

Can it the gods offend?
For I observe thou hold'st thy nose--

Pray what does this portend?
Mankind deem incense to excel

Each other earthly thing,
So he that cannot bear its smell,

No incense e'er should bring.

With unmoved face by thee at least

To dolls is homage given;
If not obstructed by the priest,

The scent mounts up to heaven.

1827.*

II

CONFLICT OF WIT AND BEAUTY.

SIR Wit, who is so much esteem'd,

And who is worthy of all honour,
Saw Beauty his superior deem'd

By folks who loved to gaze upon her;
At this he was most sorely vex'd.

Then came Sir Breath (long known as fit

To represent the cause of wit),

Beginning, rudely, I admit,
To treat the lady with a text.
To this she hearken'd not at all,
But hasten'd to his principal:
"None are so wise, they say, as you,--
Is not the world enough for two?

If you are obstinate, good-bye!
If wise, to love me you will try,
For be assured the world can ne'er
Give birth to a more handsome pair."

   1827.*

=====

FAIR daughters were by Beauty rear'd,

Wit had but dull sons for his lot;
So for a season it appear'd

Beauty was constant, Wit was not.
But Wit's a native of the soil,

So he return'd, work'd, strove amain,
And found--sweet guerdon for his toil!--

Beauty to quicken him again.

   1827.*

III.

RAIN AND RAINBOW.

DURING a heavy storm it chanced
That from his room a cockney glanced

At the fierce tempest as it broke,
While to his neighbour thus he spoke:
"The thunder has our awe inspired,
Our barns by lightning have been fired,--
Our sins to punish, I suppose;
But in return, to soothe our woes,
See how the rain in torrents fell,
Making the harvest promise well!
But is't a rainbow that I spy
Extending o'er the dark-grey sky?
With it I'm sure we may dispense,
The colour'd cheat! The vain pretence!"
Dame Iris straightway thus replied:
"Dost dare my beauty to deride?
In realms of space God station'd me
A type of better worlds to be
To eyes that from life's sorrows rove
In cheerful hope to Heav'n above,
And, through the mists that hover here
God and his precepts blest revere.
Do thou, then, grovel like the swine,
And to the ground thy snout confine,
But suffer the enlighten'd eye
To feast upon my majesty."

1827.*

VALEDICTION.

I ONCE was fond of fools,

And bid them come each day;
Then each one brought his tools

The carpenter to play;
The roof to strip first choosing,

Another to supply,
The wood as trestles using,

To move it by-and-by,
While here and there they ran,

And knock'd against each other;
To fret I soon began,

My anger could not smother,
So cried, "Get out, ye fools!"

At this they were offended
Then each one took his tools,

And so our friendship ended.

Since that, I've wiser been,

And sit beside my door;
When one of them is seen,

I cry, "Appear no more!"
"Hence, stupid knave!" I bellow:

At this he's angry too:
"You impudent old fellow!

And pray, sir, who are you?
Along the streets we riot,

And revel at the fair;
But yet we're pretty quiet,

And folks revile us ne'er.
Don't call us names, then, please!"--
At length I meet with ease,

For now they leave my door--
'Tis better than before!

1827.*

THE COUNTRY SCHOOLMASTER.

I.

A MASTER of a country school
Jump'd up one day from off his stool,
Inspired with firm resolve to try
To gain the best society;
So to the nearest baths he walk'd,
And into the saloon he stalk'd.
He felt quite. startled at the door,
Ne'er having seen the like before.
To the first stranger made he now
A very low and graceful bow,
But quite forgot to bear in mind
That people also stood behind;
His left-hand neighbor's paunch he struck
A grievous blow, by great ill luck;
Pardon for this he first entreated,
And then in haste his bow repeated.
His right hand neighbor next he hit,
And begg'd him, too, to pardon it;
But on his granting his petition,
Another was in like condition;
These compliments he paid to all,
Behind, before, across the hall;
At length one who could stand no more,
Show'd him impatiently the door.

* * * *

May many, pond'ring on their crimes,
A moral draw from this betimes!

II.

As he proceeded on his way
He thought, "I was too weak to-day;
To bow I'll ne'er again be seen;
For goats will swallow what is green."
Across the fields he now must speed,
Not over stumps and stones, indeed,
But over meads and cornfields sweet,
Trampling down all with clumsy feet.
A farmer met him by-and-by,
And didn't ask him: how? or why?
But with his fist saluted him.

"I feel new life in every limb!"
Our traveller cried in ecstasy.
"Who art thou who thus gladden'st me?
May Heaven such blessings ever send!
Ne'er may I want a jovial friend!"

    1808.*

THE LEGEND OF THE HORSESHOE.

WHAT time our Lord still walk'd the earth,
Unknown, despised, of humble birth,
And on Him many a youth attended
(His words they seldom comprehended),
It ever seem'd to Him most meet
To hold His court in open street,
As under heaven's broad canopy
One speaks with greater liberty.
The teachings of His blessed word
From out His holy mouth were heard;
Each market to a fane turn'd He
With parable and simile.

One day, as tow'rd a town He roved,
In peace of mind with those He loved,
Upon the path a something gleam'd;
A broken horseshoe 'twas, it seem'd.
So to St. Peter thus He spake:
"That piece of iron prythee take!"
St. Peter's thoughts had gone astray,--
He had been musing on his way
Respecting the world's government,
A dream that always gives content,
For in the head 'tis check'd by nought;
This ever was his dearest thought,
For him this prize was far too mean
Had it a crown and sceptre been!
But, surely, 'twasn't worth the trouble
For half a horseshoe to bend double!
And so he turn'd away his head,
As if he heard not what was said,

The Lord, forbearing tow'rd all men,
Himself pick'd up the horseshoe then
(He ne'er again like this stoop'd down).
And when at length they reach'd the town,
Before a smithy He remain'd,
And there a penny for 't obtain'd.
As they the market-place went by,
Some beauteous cherries caught His eye:
Accordingly He bought as many
As could be purchased for a penny,
And then, as oft His wont had been,
Placed them within His sleeve unseen.

They went out by another gate,
O'er plains and fields proceeding straight,
No house or tree was near the spot,
The sun was bright, the day was hot;
In short, the weather being such,
A draught of water was worth much.
The Lord walk'd on before them all,
And let, unseen, a cherry fall.
St. Peter rush'd to seize it hold,
As though an apple 'twere of gold;
His palate much approv'd the berry;
The Lord ere long another cherry
Once more let fall upon the plain;
St. Peter forthwith stoop'd again.
The Lord kept making him thus bend
To pick up cherries without end.
For a long time the thing went on;
The Lord then said, in cheerful tone:
"Had'st thou but moved when thou wert bid,
Thou of this trouble had'st been rid;
The man who small things scorns, will next,
By things still smaller be perplex'd."

              1797.

A SYMBOL.

(This fine poem is given by Goethe amongst a small collection of (what he calls Loge (Lodge), meaning thereby Masonic pieces.)

THE mason's trade
Resembles life,
With all its strife,--
Is like the stir made
 By man on earth's face.
Though weal and woe
The future may hide,
Unterrified
We onward go
In ne'er changing race.
A veil of dread
Hangs heavier still.
Deep slumbers fill
The stars over-head,
And the foot-trodden grave.

Observe them well,
And watch them revealing
How solemn feeling
And wonderment swell
The hearts of the brave.
The voice of the blest,
And of spirits on high
Seems loudly to cry:
 "To do what is best,
Unceasing endeavour!
"In silence eterne
Here chaplets are twin'd,
That each noble mind
 Its guerdon may earn.--
Then hope ye for ever!"

1827.*

ART.

Artist, fashion! talk not long!
Be a breath thine only song!

THE DROPS OF NECTAR.

WHEN Minerva, to give pleasure
To Prometheus, her well-loved one,

Brought a brimming bowl of nectar
From the glorious realms of heaven
As a blessing for his creatures,
And to pour into their bosoms
Impulses for arts ennobling,
She with rapid footstep hasten'd,
Fearing Jupiter might see her,
And the golden goblet trembled,
And there fell a few drops from it
On the verdant plain beneath her.
Then the busy bees flew thither
Straightway, eagerly to drink them,
And the butterfly came quickly
That he, too, might find a drop there;
Even the misshapen spider
Thither crawl'd and suck'd with vigour.

To a happy end they tasted,
They, and other gentle insects!
For with mortals now divide they
ArtÄthat noblest gift of all.

1789.*

THE WANDERER.

[Published in the Gottingen Musen Almanach, having been written "to express his feelings and caprices" after his separation from Frederica.]

WANDERER.

YOUNG woman, may God bless thee,
Thee, and the sucking infant
Upon thy breast!
Let me, 'gainst this rocky wall,
Neath the elm-tree's shadow,
Lay aside my burden,
Near thee take my rest.

WOMAN.

What vocation leads thee,
While the day is burning,
Up this dusty path?
Bring'st thou goods from out the town
Round the country?
Smil'st thou, stranger,
At my question?

WANDERER.

From the town no goods I bring.
Cool is now the evening;
Show to me the fountain
'Whence thou drinkest,
Woman young and kind!

WOMAN.

Up the rocky pathway mount;
Go thou first! Across the thicket
Leads the pathway tow'rd the cottage
That I live in,
To the fountain
Whence I drink.

WANDERER.

Signs of man's arranging hand
See I 'mid the trees!
Not by thee these stones were join'd,
Nature, who so freely scatterest!

WOMAN.

Up, still up!

WANDERER.

Lo, a mossy architrave is here!
I discern thee, fashioning spirit!
On the stone thou hast impress'd thy seal.

WOMAN.

Onward, stranger!

WANDERER.

Over an inscription am I treading!
'Tis effaced!
Ye are seen no longer,
Words so deeply graven,
Who your master's true devotion
Should have shown to thousand grandsons!

WOMAN.

At these stones, why
Start'st thou, stranger?
Many stones are lying yonder
Round my cottage.

WANDERER.

Yonder?

WOMAN.

Through the thicket,
Turning to the left,
Here!

WANDERER.

Ye Muses and ye Graces!

WOMAN.

This, then, is my cottage.

WANDERER.

'Tis a ruin'd temple! *

WOMAN.

Just below it, see,
Springs the fountain

Whence I drink.

WANDERER.

Thou dost hover
O'er thy grave, all glowing,
Genius! while upon thee
Hath thy master-piece
Fallen crumbling,
Thou Immortal One!

WOMAN.

Stay, a cup I'll fetch thee
Whence to drink.

WANDERER.

Ivy circles thy slender
Form so graceful and godlike.
How ye rise on high
From the ruins,
Column-pair
And thou, their lonely sister yonder,--
How thou,
Dusky moss upon thy sacred head,--
Lookest down in mournful majesty
On thy brethren's figures
Lying scatter'd
At thy feet!
In the shadow of the bramble
Earth and rubbish veil them,
Lofty grass is waving o'er them
Is it thus thou, Nature, prizest
Thy great masterpiece's masterpiece?
Carelessly destroyest thou
Thine own sanctuary,
Sowing thistles there?

WOMAN.

How the infant sleeps!
Wilt thou rest thee in the cottage,
Stranger? Wouldst thou rather

In the open air still linger?
Now 'tis cool! take thou the child
While I go and draw some water.
Sleep on, darling! sleep!

WANDERER.

Sweet is thy repose!
How, with heaven-born health imbued,
Peacefully he slumbers!
Oh thou, born among the ruins
Spread by great antiquity,
On thee rest her spirit!
He whom it encircles
Will, in godlike consciousness,
Ev'ry day enjoy.
Full, of germ, unfold,
As the smiling springtime's
Fairest charm,
Outshining all thy fellows!
And when the blossom's husk is faded,
May the full fruit shoot forth
From out thy breast,
And ripen in the sunshine!

WOMAN.

God bless him!--Is he sleeping still?
To the fresh draught I nought can add,
Saving a crust of bread for thee to eat.

WANDERER.

I thank thee well.
How fair the verdure all around!
How green!

WOMAN.

My husband soon
Will home return
From labour. Tarry, tarry, man,
And with us eat our evening meal.

WANDERER.

Is't here ye dwell?

WOMAN.

Yonder, within those walls we live.
My father 'twas who built the cottage
Of tiles and stones from out the ruins.
'Tis here we dwell.
He gave me to a husbandman,
And in our arms expired.--
Hast thou been sleeping, dearest heart
How lively, and how full of play!
Sweet rogue!

WANDERER.

Nature, thou ever budding one,
Thou formest each for life's enjoyments,
And, like a mother, all thy children dear,
Blessest with that sweet heritage,--a home
The swallow builds the cornice round,
Unconscious of the beauties
She plasters up.
The caterpillar spins around the bough,
To make her brood a winter house;
And thou dost patch, between antiquity's
Most glorious relics,
For thy mean use,
Oh man, a humble cot,--
Enjoyest e'en mid tombs!--
Farewell, thou happy woman!

WOMAN.

Thou wilt not stay, then?

WANDERER.

May God preserve thee,
And bless thy boy!

WOMAN.

A happy journey!

WANDERER.

Whither conducts the path
Across yon hill?

WOMAN.

To Cuma.

WANDERER.

How far from hence?

WOMAN.

'Tis full three miles.

WANDERER.

Farewell!
Oh Nature, guide me on my way!
The wandering stranger guide,
Who o'er the tombs
Of holy bygone times
Is passing,
To a kind sheltering place,
From North winds safe,
And where a poplar grove
Shuts out the noontide ray!
And when I come
Home to my cot
At evening,
Illumined by the setting sun,
Let me embrace a wife like this,
Her infant in her arms!

    1772.

* Compare with the beautiful description contained in the subsequent lines, an account of a ruined temple of Ceres, given by Chamberlayne in his Pharonnida (published in 1659)

".... With mournful majesiy
A heap of solitary ruins lie,
Half sepulchred in dust, the bankrupt heir
To prodigal antiquity...."

LOVE AS A LANDSCAPE PAINTER.

ON a rocky peak once sat I early,
Gazing on the mist with eyes unmoving;
Stretch'd out like a pall of greyish texture,
All things round, and all above it cover'd.

Suddenly a boy appear'd beside me,
Saying "Friend, what meanest thou by gazing
On the vacant pall with such composure?
Hast thou lost for evermore all pleasure
Both in painting cunningly, and forming?"
On the child I gazed, and thought in secret:
"Would the boy pretend to be a master?"

"Wouldst thou be for ever dull and idle,"
Said the boy, "no wisdom thou'lt attain to;
See, I'll straightway paint for thee a figure,--
How to paint a beauteous figure, show thee."

And he then extended his fore-finger,--
(Ruddy was it as a youthful rosebud)
Tow'rd the broad and far outstretching carpet,
And began to draw there with his finger.

First on high a radiant sun he painted,
Which upon mine eyes with splendour glisten'd,
And he made the clouds with golden border,
Through the clouds he let the sunbeams enter;
Painted then the soft and feathery summits
Of the fresh and quicken'd trees, behind them
One by one with freedom drew the mountains;
Underneath he left no lack of water,
But the river painted so like Nature,
That it seem'd to glitter in the sunbeams,
That it seem'd against its banks to murmur.

Ah, there blossom'd flowers beside the river,
And bright colours gleam'd upon the meadow,
Gold, and green, and purple, and enamell'd,
All like carbuncles and emeralds seeming!

Bright and clear he added then the heavens,
And the blue-tinged mountains far and farther,
So that I, as though newborn, enraptured
Gazed on, now the painter, now the picture.

Then spake he: "Although I have convinced thee
That this art I understand full surely,
Yet the hardest still is left to show thee."

Thereupon he traced, with pointed finger,
And with anxious care, upon the forest,
At the utmost verge, where the strong sunbeams
From the shining ground appear'd reflected,

Traced the figure of a lovely maiden,
Fair in form, and clad in graceful fashion,
Fresh the cheeks beneath her brown locks' ambush,
And the cheeks possess'd the selfsame colour
As the finger that had served to paint them.

"Oh thou boy!" exclaim'd I then, "what master
In his school received thee as his pupil,
Teaching thee so truthfully and quickly
Wisely to begin, and well to finish?"

Whilst I still was speaking, lo, a zephyr
Softly rose, and set the tree-tops moving,
Curling all the wavelets on the river,
And the perfect maiden's veil, too, fill'd it,
And to make my wonderment still greater,
Soon the maiden set her foot in motion.
On she came, approaching tow'rd the station
Where still sat I with my arch instructor.

As now all, yes, all thus moved together,--
Flowers, river, trees, the veil,--all moving,--
And the gentle foot of that most fair one,
Can ye think that on my rock I linger'd,

Like a rock, as though fast-chain'd and silent?

1788.

GOD, SOUL, AND WORLD.

RHYMED DISTICHS.

[The Distichs, of which these are given as a specimen, are about forty in number.]

WHO trusts in God,
Fears not His rod.

THIS truth may be by all believed:
Whom God deceives, is well deceived.

HOW? when? and where?--No answer comes from high;
Thou wait'st for the Because, and yet thou ask'st not Why?

IF the whole is ever to gladden thee,
That whole in the smallest thing thou must see.

WATER its living strength first shows,
When obstacles its course oppose.

TRANSPARENT appears the radiant air,
Though steel and stone in its breast it may bear;
At length they'll meet with fiery power,
And metal and stones on the earth will shower.

WHATE'ER a living flame may surround,
No longer is shapeless, or earthly bound.
'Tis now invisible, flies from earth,
And hastens on high to the place of its birth.

1815.*

PROCEMION.

IN His blest name, who was His own creation,
Who from all time makes making his vocation;
The name of Him who makes our faith so bright,
Love, confidence, activity, and might;
In that One's name, who, named though oft He be,
Unknown is ever in Reality:
As far as ear can reach, or eyesight dim,
Thou findest but the known resembling Him;
How high so'er thy fiery spirit hovers,
Its simile and type it straight discovers
Onward thou'rt drawn, with feelings light and gay,
Where'er thou goest, smiling is the way;
No more thou numbrest, reckonest no time,
Each step is infinite, each step sublime.

1816.

WHAT God would outwardly alone control,
And on his finger whirl the mighty Whole?
He loves the inner world to move, to view
Nature in Him, Himself in Nature too,
So that what in Him works, and is, and lives,
The measure of His strength, His spirit gives.

1816.

WITHIN us all a universe doth dwell;
And hence each people's usage laudable,
That ev'ry one the Best that meets his eyes
As God, yea e'en his God, doth recognise;
To Him both earth and heaven surrenders he,
Fears Him, and loves Him too, if that may be.

1816.

THE METAMORPHOSIS OF PLANTS.

THOU art confused, my beloved, at, seeing the thousandfold union

Shown in this flowery troop, over the garden dispers'd;
any a name dost thou hear assign'd; one after another

Falls on thy list'ning ear, with a barbarian sound.
None resembleth another, yet all their forms have a likeness;

Therefore, a mystical law is by the chorus proclaim'd;
Yes, a sacred enigma! Oh, dearest friend, could I only

Happily teach thee the word, which may the mystery solve!
Closely observe how the plant, by little and little progressing,

Step by step guided on, changeth to blossom and fruit!
First from the seed it unravels itself, as soon as the silent

Fruit-bearing womb of the earth kindly allows Its escape,
And to the charms of the light, the holy, the ever-in-motion,

Trusteth the delicate leaves, feebly beginning to shoot.
Simply slumber'd the force in the seed; a germ of the future,

Peacefully lock'd in itself, 'neath the integument lay,
Leaf and root, and bud, still void of colour, and shapeless;

Thus doth the kernel, while dry, cover that motionless life.
Upward then strives it to swell, in gentle moisture confiding,

And, from the night where it dwelt, straightway ascendeth to light.
Yet still simple remaineth its figure, when first it appeareth;

And 'tis a token like this, points out the child 'mid the plants.
Soon a shoot, succeeding it, riseth on high, and reneweth,

Piling-up node upon node, ever the primitive form;
Yet not ever alike: for the following leaf, as thou seest,

Ever produceth itself, fashioned in manifold ways.
Longer, more indented, in points and in parts more divided,

Which. all-deform'd until now, slept in the organ below,
So at length it attaineth the noble and destined perfection,

Which, in full many a tribe, fills thee with wondering awe.
Many ribb'd and tooth'd, on a surface juicy and swelling,

Free and unending the shoot seemeth in fullness to be;
Yet here Nature restraineth, with powerful hands, the formation,

And to a perfecter end, guideth with softness its growth,
Less abundantly yielding the sap, contracting the vessels,

So that the figure ere long gentler effects doth disclose.
Soon and in silence is check'd the growth of the vigorous branches,

And the rib of the stalk fuller becometh in form.
Leafless, however, and quick the tenderer stem then up-springeth,

And a miraculous sight doth the observer enchant.
Ranged in a circle, in numbers that now are small, and now countless,

Gather the smaller-sized leaves, close by the side of their like.
Round the axis compress'd the sheltering calyx unfoldeth,

And, as the perfectest type, brilliant-hued coronals forms.
Thus doth Nature bloom, in glory still nobler and fuller,

Showing, in order arranged, member on member uprear'd.
Wonderment fresh dost thou feel, as soon as the stem rears the flower

Over the scaffolding frail of the alternating leaves.
But this glory is only the new creation's foreteller,

Yes, the leaf with its hues feeleth the hand all divine,
And on a sudden contracteth itself; the tenderest figures

Twofold as yet, hasten on, destined to blend into one.
Lovingly now the beauteous pairs are standing together,

Gather'd in countless array, there where the altar is raised.
Hymen hovereth o'er them, and scents delicious and mighty

Stream forth their fragrance so sweet, all things enliv'ning around.

Presently, parcell'd out, unnumber'd germs are seen swelling,

Sweetly conceald in the womb, where is made perfect the fruit.
Here doth Nature close the ring of her forces eternal;

Yet doth a new one, at once, cling to the one gone before,
So that the chain be prolonged for ever through all generations,

And that the whole may have life, e'en as enjoy'd by each part.
Now, my beloved one, turn thy gaze on the many-hued thousands

Which, confusing no more, gladden the mind as they wave.
Every plant unto thee proclaimeth the laws everlasting,

Every flowered speaks louder and louder to thee;
But if thou here canst decipher the mystic words of the goddess,

Everywhere will they be seen, e'en though the features are changed.
Creeping insects may linger, the eager butterfly hasten,--

Plastic and forming, may man change e'en the figure decreed!
Oh, then, bethink thee, as well, how out of the germ of acquaintance,

Kindly intercourse sprang, slowly unfolding its leaves;
Soon how friendship with might unveil'd itself in our bosoms,

And how Amor, at length, brought forth blossom and fruit
Think of the manifold ways wherein Nature hath lent to our feelings,

Silently giving them birth, either the first or the last!
Yes, and rejoice in the present day! For love that is holy

Seeketh the noblest of fruits,--that where the thoughts are the same,
Where the opinions agree,--that the pair may, in rapt contemplation,

Lovingly blend into one,--find the more excellent world.

    1797.

PROVERBS.

'TIS easier far a wreath to bind,
Than a good owner for't to find.

I KILL'D a thousand flies overnight,
Yet was waken'd by one, as soon as twas light.

To the mother I give;
For the daughter I live.

A BREACH is every day,

By many a mortal storm'd;
Let them fall in the gaps as they may,

Yet a heap of dead is ne'er form'd.

WHAT harm has thy poor mirror done, alas?
Look not so ugly, prythee, in the glass!

1815.*

TAME XENIA.

THE Epigrams bearing the title of XENIA were written by Goethe and Schiller together, having been first occasioned by some violent attacks made on them by some insignificant writers. They are extremely numerous, but scarcely any of them could be translated into English. Those here given are merely presented as a specimen.

GOD gave to mortals birth,

In his own image too;
Then came Himself to earth,

A mortal kind and true.

1821.*

BARBARIANS oft endeavour

Gods for themselves to make
But they're more hideous ever

Than dragon or than snake.

1821.*

WHAT shall I teach thee, the very first thing?--
Fain would I learn o'er my shadow to spring!

1827.*

"WHAT is science, rightly known?
'Tis the strength of life alone.
Life canst thou engender never,
Life must be life's parent ever.

1827.*

It matters not, I ween,

Where worms our friends consume,
Beneath the turf so green,

Or 'neath a marble tomb.
Remember, ye who live,

Though frowns the fleeting day,
That to your friends ye give

What never will decay.

1827.*

RELIGION AND CHURCH.

THOUGHTS ON JESUS CHRIST'S DESCENT INTO HELL.

[THE remarkable Poem of which this is a literal but faint representation, was written when Goethe was only sixteen years old. It derives additional interest from the fact of its being the very earliest piece of his that is preserved. The few other pieces included by Goethe under the title of Religion and Church are polemical, and devoid of interest to the English reader.]

WHAT wondrous noise is heard around!
Through heaven exulting voices sound,

A mighty army marches on
By thousand millions follow'd, lo,
To yon dark place makes haste to go

God's Son, descending from His throne!
He goes--the tempests round Him break,

As Judge and Hero cometh He;
He goes--the constellations quake,

The sun, the world quake fearfully.

I see Him in His victor-car,
On fiery axles borne afar,

Who on the cross for us expired.
The triumph to yon realms He shows,--
Remote from earth, where star ne'er glows,

The triumph He for us acquired.
He cometh, Hell to extirpate,

Whom He, by dying, wellnigh kill'd;
He shall pronounce her fearful fate

Hark! now the curse is straight fulfill'd.

Hell sees the victor come at last,
She feels that now her reign is past,

She quakes and fears to meet His sight;
She knows His thunders' terrors dread,
In vain she seeks to hide her head,

Attempts to fly, but vain is flight;
Vainly she hastes to 'scape pursuit

And to avoid her Judge's eye;
The Lord's fierce wrath restrains her foot

Like brazen chains,--she cannot fly.

Here lies the Dragon, trampled down,
He lies, and feels God's angry frown,

He feels, and grinneth hideously;
He feels Hell's speechless agonies,
A thousand times he howls and sighs:

"Oh, burning flames! quick, swallow me!"
There lies he in the fiery waves,

By torments rack'd and pangs infernal,
Instant annihilation craves,

And hears, those pangs will be eternal.

Those mighty squadrons, too, are here,
The partners of his cursed career,

Yet far less bad than he were they.
Here lies the countless throng combined,
In black and fearful crowds entwined,

While round him fiery tempests play;
He sees how they the Judge avoid,

He sees the storm upon them feed,
Yet is not at the sight o'erjoy'd,

Because his pangs e'en theirs exceed.

The Son of Man in triumph passes
Down to Hell's wild and black morasses,

And there unfolds His majesty.
Hell cannot bear the bright array,
For, since her first created day.

Darkness alone e'er govern'd she.
She lay remote from ev'ry light

With torments fill'd in Chaos here;
God turn'd for ever from her sight

His radiant features' glory clear.

Within the realms she calls her own,
She sees the splendour of the Son,

His dreaded glories shining forth;
She sees Him clad in rolling thunder,
She sees the rocks all quake with wonder,

When God before her stands in wrath.
She sees He comes her Judge to be,

She feels the awful pangs inside her,
Herself to slay endeavours she,

But e'en this comfort is denied her.

Now looks she back, with pains untold,
Upon those happy times of old,

When those glories gave her joy;
When yet her heart revered the truth,
When her glad soul, in endless youth

And rapture dwelt, without alloy.
She calls to mind with madden'd thought

How over man her wiles prevail'd;
To take revenge on God she sought,

And feels the vengeance it entail'd.

God was made man, and came to earth.
Then Satan cried with fearful mirth:

"E'en He my victim now shall be!"
He sought to slay the Lord Most High,
The world's Creator now must die;

But, Satan, endless woe to thee!
Thou thought'st to overcome Him then,

Rejoicing in His suffering;
But he in triumph comes again

To bind thee: Death! where is thy sting?

Speak, Hell! where is thy victory?
Thy power destroy'd and scatter'd see!

Know'st thou not now the Highest's might?
See, Satan, see thy rule o'erthrown!

By thousand-varying pangs weigh'd down,
Thou dwell'st in dark and endless night.

As though by lightning struck thou liest,
No gleam of rapture far or wide;

In vain! no hope thou there decriest,--
For me alone Messiah died!

A howling rises through the air,
A trembling fills each dark vault there,

When Christ to Hell is seen to come.
She snarls with rage, but needs must cower
Before our mighty hero's power;

He signs--and Hell is straightway dumb.
Before his voice the thunders break,

On high His victor-banner blows;
E'en angels at His fury quake,

When Christ to the dread judgment goes.

Now speaks He, and His voice is thunder,
He speaks, the rocks are rent in sunder,

His breath is like devouring flames.
Thus speaks He: "Tremble, ye accurs'd!
He who from Eden hurl'd you erst,

Your kingdom's overthrow proclaims.
Look up! My children once were ye,

Your arms against Me then ye turn'd,
Ye fell, that ye might sinners be,

Ye've now the wages that ye earn'd.

"My greatest foeman from that day,
Ye led my dearest friends astray,--

As ye had fallen, man must fall.
To kill him evermore ye sought,
'They all shall die the death,' ye thought;

But howl! for Me I won them all.
For them alone did I descend,

For them pray'd, suffer'd, perish'd I.
Ye ne'er shall gain your wicked end;

Who trusts in Me shall never die.

"In endless chains here lie ye now,
Nothing can save you from the slough.

Not boldness, not regret for crime.
Lie, then, and writhe in brimstone fire!
'Twas ye yourselves drew down Mine ire,

Lie and lament throughout all time!
And also ye, whom I selected,

E'en ye forever I disown,

For ye My saving grace rejected

Ye murmur? blame yourselves alone!

"Ye might have lived with Me in bliss,
For I of yore had promis'd this;

Ye sinn'd, and all My precepts slighted
Wrapp'd in the sleep of sin ye dwelt,
Now is My fearful judgment felt,

By a just doom your guilt requited."--
Thus spake He, and a fearful storm

From Him proceeds, the lightnings glow,
The thunders seize each wicked form,

And hurl them in the gulf below.

The God-man closeth Hell's sad doors,
In all His majesty He soars

From those dark regions back to light.
He sitteth at the Father's side;
Oh, friends, what joy doth this betide!

For us, for us He still will fight!
The angels sacred quire around

Rejoice before the mighty Lord,
So that all creatures hear the sound:

"Zebaoth's God be aye ador'd!"

    1765.

ANTIQUES.

LEOPOLD, DUKE OF BRUNSWICK.

[Written on the occasion of the death, by drowning, of the Prince.]

THOU wert forcibly seized by the hoary lord of the river,--

Holding thee, ever he shares with thee his streaming domain,
Calmly sleepest thou near his urn as it silently trickles,

Till thou to action art roused, waked by the swift-rolling flood.
Kindly be to the people, as when thou still wert a mortal,

Perfecting that as a god, which thou didst fail in, as man.

    1785.

TO THE HUSBANDMAN.

SMOOTHLY and lightly the golden seed by the furrow is cover'd;

Yet will a deeper one, friend, cover thy bones at the last.
Joyously plough'd and sow'd! Here food all living is budding,

E'en from the side of the tomb Hope will not vanish away.

    1789.*

ANACREON'S GRAVE.

HERE where the roses blossom, where vines round the laurels are twining,

Where the turtle-dove calls, where the blithe cricket is heard,
Say, whose grave can this be, with life by all the Immortals

Beauteously planted and deck'd?--Here doth Anacreon sleep
Spring and summer and autumn rejoiced the thrice-happy minstrel,

And from the winter this mound kindly hath screen'd him at last.

1789.*

THE BRETHREN.

SLUMBER and Sleep, two brethren ordain'd by the gods to their service,

Were by Prometheus implored, comfort to give to his race;
But though so light to the gods, too heavy for man was their burden,

We in their slumber find sleep, we in their sleep meet with death.

1789.*

MEASURE OF TIME.

EROS, what mean'st thou by this? In each of thine hands is an hourglass!

What, oh thou frivolous god! twofold thy measure of time?
"Slowly run from the one, the hours of lovers when parted;

While through the other they rush swiftly, as soon as they meet."

1789.*

WARNING.

WAKEN not Amor from sleep! The beauteous urchin still slumbers;

Go, and complete thou the task, that to the day is assign'd!
Thus doth the prudent mother with care turn time to her profit,

While her babe is asleep, for 'twill awake but too soon.

1785.*

SOLITUDE.

OH ye kindly nymphs, who dwell 'mongst the rocks and the thickets,

Grant unto each whatsoe'er he may in silence desire!
Comfort impart to the mourner, and give to the doubter instruction,

And let the lover rejoice, finding the bliss that he craves.

For from the gods ye received what they ever denied unto mortals,

Power to comfort and aid all who in you may confide.

    1782.

THE CHOSEN CLIFF.

HERE in silence the lover fondly mused on his loved one;

Gladly he spake to me thus: "Be thou my witness, thou stone!
Yet thou must not be vainglorious, thou hast many companions;

Unto each rock on the plain, where I, the happy one, dwell,
Unto each tree of the wood that I cling to, as onward I ramble,

'Be thou a sign of my bliss!' shout I, and then 'tis ordain'd.
Yet to thee only I lend a voice, as a Muse from the people

Chooseth one for herself, kissing his lips as a friend."

    1782.

THE CONSECRATED SPOT.

WHEN in the dance of the Nymphs, in the moonlight so holy assembled,

Mingle the Graces, down from Olympus in secret descending,
Here doth the minstrel hide, and list to their numbers enthralling,

Here doth he watch their silent dances' mysterious measure.
All that is glorious in Heaven, and all that the earth in her beauty

Ever hath brought into life, the dreamer awake sees before him;
All he repeats to the Muses, and lest the gods should be anger'd,

How to tell of secrets discreetly, the Muses instruct him.

    1789.*

THE INSTRUCTORS.

WHEN Diogenes quietly sunn'd himself in his barrel,

When Calanus with joy leapt in the flame-breathing grave,
Oh, what noble lessons were those for the rash son of Philip,

Were not the lord of the world e'en for instruction too great!

    1789.*

THE UNEQUAL MARRIAGE,

EVEN this heavenly pair were unequally match'd when united:

Psyche grew older and wise, Amor remain'd still a child,

    1789.*

EXCUSE.

THOU dost complain of woman for changing from one to another?

Censure her not: for she seeks one who will constant remain.

    1789.*

SAKONTALA.

WOULDST thou the blossoms of spring, as well as the fruits of the autumn,

Wouldst thou what charms and delights, wouldst thou what

plenteously, feeds,
Would thou include both Heaven and earth in one designation,

All that is needed is done, when I Sakontala name.

    1792.

THE MUSE'S MIRROR.

EARLY one day, the Muse, when eagerly bent on adornment,
Follow'd a swift-running streamlet, the quietest nook by it seeking.
Quickly and noisily flowing, the changeful surface distorted
Ever her moving form; the goddess departed in anger.
Yet the stream call'd mockingly after her, saying: "What, truly!
Wilt thou not view, then, the truth, in my mirror so clearly depicted?"

But she already was far away, on the brink of the ocean,
In her figure rejoicing, and duly arranging her garland.

   1799.*

PHOEBUS AND HERMES.

DELOS' stately ruler, and Maia's son, the adroit one,

Warmly were striving, for both sought the great prize to obtain.
Hermes the lyre demanded, the lyre was claim'd by Apollo,

Yet were the hearts of the foes fruitlessly nourish'd by hope.
For on a sudden Ares burst in, with fury decisive,

Dashing in twain the gold toy, brandishing wildly his sword.
Hermes, malicious one, laughed beyond measure; yet deep-seated sorrow

Seized upon Phoebus's heart, seized on the heart of each Muse.

   1799.*

THE NEW AMOR.

AMOR, not the child, the youthful lover of Psyche,
Look'd round Olympus one day, boldly, to triumph inured;
There he espied a goddess, the fairest amongst the immortals,--
Venus Urania she,--straight was his passion inflamed.
Even the holy one powerless proved, alas! 'gainst his wooing,--
Tightly embraced in his arm, held her the daring one fast.
Then from their union arose a new, a more beauteous Amor,
Who from his father his wit, grace from his mother derives.
Ever thou'lt find him join'd in the kindly Muses' communion,
And his charm-laden bolt foundeth the love of the arts.

   1792.

THE GARLANDS.

KLOPSTOCK would lead us away from Pindus; no longer for laurel
May we be eager--the homely acorn alone must content us;
Yet he himself his more-than-epic crusade is conducting
High on Golgotha's summit, that foreign gods he may honour!
Yet, on what hill he prefers, let him gather the angels together,

Suffer deserted disciples to weep o'er the grave of the just one:
There where a hero and saint hath died, where a bard breath'd his numbers,
Both for our life and our death an ensample of courage resplendent
And of the loftiest human worth to bequeath,--ev'ry nation
There will joyously kneel in devotion ecstatic, revering
Thorn and laurel garland, and all its charms and its tortures.

       1815.*

THE SWISS ALPS.

YESTERDAY brown was still thy head, as the locks of my loved one,

Whose sweet image so dear silently beckons afar.
Silver-grey is the early snow to-day on thy summit,

Through the tempestuous night streaming fast over thy brow.
Youth, alas, throughout life as closely to age is united

As, in some changeable dream, yesterday blends with to-day.

    Uri, October 7th, 1797.

DISTICHS.

CHORDS are touch'd by Apollo,--the death-laden bow, too, he bendeth;

While he the shepherdess charms, Python he lays in the dust.

WHAT is merciful censure? To make thy faults appear smaller?

May be to veil them? No, no! O'er them to raise thee on high!

DEMOCRATIC food soon cloys on the multitude's stomach;
But I'll wager, ere long, other thou'lt give them instead.

WHAT in France has pass'd by, the Germans continue to practise,

For the proudest of men flatters the people and fawns.

WHO is the happiest of men? He who values the merits of others,
 And in their pleasure takes joy, even as though 'twere his own.

NOT in the morning alone, not only at mid-day he charmeth;

Even at setting, the sun is still the same glorious planet.

VENETIAN EPIGRAMS.
(Written in 1790.)

URN and sarcophagus erst were with life adorn'd by the heathen

Fauns are dancing around, while with the Bacchanal troop
Chequerd circles they trace; and the goat-footed, puffy-cheekd player

Wildly produceth hoarse tones out of the clamorous horn.
Cymbals and drums resound; we see and we hear, too, the marble.

Fluttering bird! oh how sweet tastes the ripe fruit to thy bill!
Noise there is none to disturb thee, still less to scare away Amor,

Who, in the midst of the throng, learns to delight in his torch.
Thus doth fullness overcome death; and the ashes there cover'd

Seem, in that silent domain, still to be gladdend with life.
Thus may the minstrel's sarcophagus be hereafter surrounded

With such a scroll, which himself richly with life has adorn'd.

CLASP'D in my arms for ever eagerly hold I my mistress,

Ever my panting heart throbs wildly against her dear breast,
And on her knees forever is leaning my head, while I'm gazing

Now on her sweet-smiling mouth, now on her bright sparkling eyes.
"Oh thou effeminate!" spake one, "and thus, then, thy days thou

art spending?"

Ah, they in sorrow are spent. List while I tell thee my tale:
Yes! I have left my only joy in life far behind me,

Twenty long days hath my car borne me away from her sight.
Vettrini defy me, while crafty chamberlains flatter,

And the sly Valet de place thinks but of lies and deceit.
If I attempt to escape, the Postmaster fastens upon me,

Postboys the upper hand get, custom-house duties enrage.
"Truly, I can't understand thee! thou talkest enigmas! thou seemest

Wrapp'd in a blissful repose, glad as Rinaldo of yore:
Ah, I myself understand full well; 'tis my body that travels,

And 'tis my spirit that rests still in my mistress's arms.

I WOULD liken this gondola unto the soft-rocking cradle,

And the chest on its deck seems a vast coffin to be.
Yes! 'tween the cradle and coffin, we totter and waver for ever

On the mighty canal, careless our lifetime is spent.

WHY are the people thus busily moving? For food they are seeking,

Children they fain would beget, feeding them well as they can.
Traveller, mark this well, and when thou art home, do thou likewise!

More can no mortal effect, work with what ardour he will.

I WOULD compare to the land this anvil, its lord to the hammer,

And to the people the plate, which in the middle is bent.
Sad is the poor tin-plate's lot, when the blows are but given at random:

Ne'er will the kettle be made, while they uncertainly fall.

WHAT is the life of a man? Yet thousands are ever accustom'd
Freely to talk about man,--what he has done, too, and how.
Even less is a poem; yet thousands read and enjoy it,
Thousands abuse it.--My friend, live and continue to rhyme!

MERRY'S the trade of a poet; but somewhat a dear one, I fear me

For, as my book grows apace, all of my sequins I lose.

Is' thou'rt in earnest, no longer delay, but render me happy;
Art thou in jest? Ah, sweet love! time for all jesting is past.

ART thou, then, vex'd at my silence? What shall I speak of? Thou markest

Neither my sorrowful sigh, nor my soft eloquent look.
Only one goddess is able the seal of my lips to unloosen,--

When by Aurora I'm found, slumbering calm on thy breast.
Ah, then my hymn in the ears of the earliest gods shall be chaunted,

As the Memnonian form breath'd forth sweet secrets in song.

IN the twilight of morning to climb to the top of the mountain,--

Thee to salute, kindly star, earliest herald of day,--
And to await, with impatience, the gaze of the ruler of heaven,--

Youthful delight, oh oft lur'st thou me out in the night!
Oh ye heralds of day, ye heavenly eyes of my mistress,

Now ye appear, and the sun evermore riseth too soon.

THOU art amazed, and dost point to the ocean. It seems to be burning,
Flame-crested billows in play dart round our night-moving bark.
Me it astonisheth not,--of the ocean was born Aphrodite,--
Did not a flame, too, proceed from her for us, in her son?

GLEAMING the ocean appear'd, the beauteous billows were smiling,

While a fresh, favouring wind, filling the sails, drove us on.
Free was my bosom from yearning; yet soon my languishing glances

Turn'd themselves backward in haste, seeking the snow-cover'd hills.
Treasures unnumber'd are southwards lying. Yet one to the northwards

Draws me resistlessly back, like the strong magnet in force.

SPACIOUS and fair is the world; yet oh! how I thank the kind heavens

That I a garden possess, small though it be, yet mine own.
One which enticeth me homewards; why should a gardener wander?

Honour and pleasure he finds, when to his garden he looks.

AH, my maiden is going! she mounts the vessel! My monarch,

AEolus! potentate dread! keep ev'ry storm far away!
"Oh, thou fool!" cried the god:"ne'er fear the blustering tempest;

When Love flutters his wings, then mayst thou dread the soft breeze."

ELEGIES.

PART I.

ROMAN ELEGIES.

[The Roman Elegies were written in the same year as the Venetian Epigrams--viz. 1790.]

SPEAK, ye stones, I entreat! Oh speak, ye palaces lofty!

Utter a word, oh ye streets! Wilt thou not, Genius, awake?
All that thy sacred walls, eternal Rome, hold within them

Teemeth with life; but to me, all is still silent and dead.
Oh, who will whisper unto me,--when shall I see at the casement

That one beauteous form, which, while it scorcheth, revives?
Can I as yet not discern the road, on which I for ever

To her and from her shall go, heeding not time as it flies?
Still do I mark the churches, palaces, ruins, and columns,

As a wise traveller should, would he his journey improve.
Soon all this will be past; and then will there be but one temple,

Amor's temple alone, where the Initiate may go.
Thou art indeed a world, oh Rome; and yet, were Love absent,

Then would the world be no world, then would e'en Rome be no Rome.

Do not repent, mine own love, that thou so soon didst surrender

Trust me, I deem thee not bold! reverence only I feel.
Manifold workings the darts of Amor possess; some but scratching,

Yet with insidious effect, poison the bosom for years.
Others mightily feather'd, with fresh and newly-born sharpness

Pierce to the innermost bone, kindle the blood into flame.
In the heroical times, when loved each god and each goddess,

Longing attended on sight; then with fruition was bless'd.
Think'st thou the goddess had long been thinking of love and its pleasures

When she, in Ida's retreats, own'd to Anchises her flame?
Had but Luna delayd to kiss the beautiful sleeper,

Oh, by Aurora, ere long, he had in envy been rous'd!
Hero Leander espied at the noisy feast, and the lover

Hotly and nimbly, ere long, plunged in the night-cover'd flood.
Rhea Silvia, virgin princess, roam'd near the Tiber,

Seeking there water to draw, when by the god she was seiz'd.
Thus were the sons of Mars begotten! The twins did a she-wolf

Suckle and nurture,--and Rome call'd herself queen of the world,

-----

ALEXANDER, and Caesar, and Henry, and Fred'rick, the mighty,

On me would gladly bestow half of the glory they earn'd,
Could I but grant unto each one night on the couch where I'm lying;

But they, by Orcus's night, sternly, alas! are held down.
Therefore rejoice, oh thou living one, blest in thy love-lighted homestead,

Ere the dark Lethe's sad wave wetteth thy fugitive foot.

THESE few leaves, oh ye Graces, a bard presents, in your honour,

On your altar so pure, adding sweet rosebuds as well,
And he does it with hope. The artist is glad in his workshop,

When a Pantheon it seems round him for ever to bring.
Jupiter knits his godlike brow,--her's, Juno up-lifteth;

Phoebus strides on before, shaking his curly-lock'd head
Calmly and drily Minerva looks down, and Hermes the light one,

Turneth his glances aside, roguish and tender at once.
But tow'rds Bacchus, the yielding, the dreaming, raiseth Cythere

Looks both longing and sweet, e'en in the marble yet moist.
Of his embraces she thinks with delight, and seems to be asking

"Should not our glorious son take up his place by our side?"

AMOR is ever a rogue, and all who believe him are cheated!

To me the hypocrite came: "Trust me, I pray thee, this once.
Honest is now my intent,--with grateful thanks I acknowledge

That thou thy life and thy works hast to my worship ordain'd.
See, I have follow'd thee thither, to Rome, with kindly intention,

Hoping to give thee mine aid, e'en in the foreigner's land.
Every trav'ller complains that the quarters he meets with are wretched

Happily lodged, though, is he, who is by Amor receiv'd.
Thou dost observe the ruins of ancient buildings with wonder,

Thoughtfully wandering on, over each time-hallow'd spot.
Thou dost honour still more the worthy relics created

By the few artists--whom I loved in their studios to seek.
I 'twas fashion'd those forms! thy pardon,--I boast not at present;

Presently thou shalt confess, that what I tell thee is true.
Now that thou serv'st me more idly, where are the beauteous figures,

Where are the colours, the light, which thy creations once fill'd?
Hast thou a mind again to form? The school of the Grecians

Still remains open, my friend; years have not barr'd up its doors.
I, the teacher, am ever young, and love all the youthful,

Love not the subtle and old; Mother, observe what I say!
Still was new the Antique, when yonder blest ones were living;

Happily live,--and, in thee, ages long vanish'd will live!
Food for song, where hop'st thou to find it? I only can give it,

And a more excellent style, love, and love only can teach."
Thus did the Sophist discourse. What mortal, alas! could resist him?

And when a master commands, I have been train'd to obey.
Now he deceitfully keeps his word, gives food for my numbers,

But, while he does so, alas! robs me of time, strength, and mind.
Looks, and pressure of hands, and words of kindness, and kisses,

Syllables teeming with thought, by a fond pair are exchang'd.
Then becomes whispering, talk,--and stamm'ring, a language enchanting;

Free from all prosody's rules, dies such a hymn on the ear.
Thee, Aurora, I used to own as the friend of the Muses;

Hath, then, Amor the rogue cheated, Aurora, e'en thee?
Thou dost appear to me now as his friend, and again dost awake me

Unto a day of delight, while at his altar I kneel.
All her locks I find on my bosom, her head is reposing,

Pressing with softness the arm, which round her neck is entwin'd;
Oh! what a joyous awak'ning, ye hours so peaceful, succeeded,

Monument sweet of the bliss which had first rock'd us to sleep
In her slumber she moves, and sinks, while her face is averted,

Far on the breadth of the couch, leaving her hand still in mine
Heartfelt love unites us for ever, and yearnings unsullied,

And our cravings alone claim for themselves the exchange.
One faint touch of the hand, and her eyes so heavenly see I

Once more open. Ah, no! let me still look on that form!
Closed still remain! Ye make me confused and drunken, ye rob me

Far too soon of the bliss pure contemplation affords.
Mighty, indeed, are these figures! these limbs, how gracefully rounded!

Theseus, could'st thou e'er fly, whilst Ariadne thus slept?
Only one single kiss on these lips! Oh, Theseus, now leave us!

Gaze on her eyes! she awakes--Firmly she holds thee embrac'd

PART II.

ALEXIS AND DORA.

[This beautiful poem was first published in Schiller's Horen.]

FARTHER and farther away, alas! at each moment the vessel

Hastens, as onward it glides, cleaving the foam-cover'd flood!
Long is the track plough'd up by the keel where dolphins are sporting,

Following fast in its rear, while it seems flying pursuit.
All forebodes a prosperous voyage; the sailor with calmness

Leans 'gainst the sail, which alone all that is needed performs.
Forward presses the heart of each seamen, like colours and streamers;

Backward one only is seen, mournfully fix'd near the mast,
While on the blue tinged mountains, which fast are receding, he gazeth,

And as they sink in the sea, joy from his bosom departs.
Vanish'd from thee, too, oh Dora, is now the vessel that robs thee

Of thine Alexis, thy friend,--ah, thy betrothed as well!
Thou, too, art after me gazing in vain. Our hearts are still throbbing,

Though, for each other, yet ah! 'gainst one another no more.
Oh, thou single moment, wherein I found life! thou outweighest

Every day which had else coldly from memory fled.
'Twas in that moment alone, the last, that upon me descended

Life, such as deities grant, though thou perceived'st it not.
Phoebus, in vain with thy rays dost thou clothe the ether in glory:

Thine all-brightening day hateful alone is to me.
Into myself I retreat for shelter, and there, in the silence,

Strive to recover the time when she appear'd with each day.
Was it possible beauty like this to see, and not feel it?

Work'd not those heavenly charms e'en on a mind dull as thine?
Blame not thyself, unhappy one! Oft doth the bard an enigma

Thus propose to the throng, skillfully hidden in words.
Each one enjoys the strange commingling of images graceful,

Yet still is wanting the word which will discover the sense.
When at length it is found, the heart of each hearer is gladden'd,

And in the poem he sees meaning of twofold delight.
Wherefore so late didst thou remove the bandage, oh Amor,

Which thou hadst placed o'er mine eyes,--wherefore remove it so late?
Long did the vessel, when laden, lie waiting for favouring breezes,

'Till in kindness the wind blew from the land o'er the sea.
Vacant times of youth! and vacant dreams of the future!

Ye all vanish, and nought, saving the moment, remains.
Yes! it remains,--my joy still remains! I hold thee; my Dora,

And thine image alone, Dora, by hope is disclos'd.
Oft have I seen thee go, with modesty clad, to the temple,

While thy mother so dear solemnly went by thy side.
Eager and nimble thou wert, in bearing thy fruit to the market,

Boldly the pail from the well didst thou sustain on thy head.
Then was reveal'd thy neck, then seen thy shoulders so beauteous,

Then, before all things, the grace filling thy motions was seen.
Oft have I fear'd that the pitcher perchance was in danger of falling,

Yet it ever remain'd firm on the circular cloth.
Thus, fair neighbour, yes, thus I oft was wont to observe thee,

As on the stars I might gaze, as I might gaze on the moon,
Glad indeed at the sight, yet feeling within my calm bosom

Not the remotest desire ever to call them mine own.
Years thus fleeted away! Although our houses were only

Twenty paces apart, yet I thy threshold ne'er cross'd.
Now by the fearful flood are we parted! Thou liest to Heaven,

Billow! thy beautiful blue seems to me dark as the night.
All were now in movement; a boy to the house of my father

Ran at full speed and exclaim'd: "Hasten thee quick to the strand
Hoisted the sail is already, e'en now in the wind it is flutt'ring,

While the anchor they weigh, heaving it up from the sand;
Come, Alexis, oh come!"--My worthy stout-hearted father

Press'd, with a blessing, his hand down on my curly-lock'd head,
While my mother carefully reach'd me a newly-made bundle,

"Happy mayst thou return!" cried they--" both happy and rich!"
Then I sprang away, and under my arm held the bundle,

Running along by the wall. Standing I found thee hard by,
At the door of thy garden. Thou smilingly saidst then "Alexis!

Say, are yon boisterous crew going thy comrades to be?
Foreign coasts will thou visit, and precious merchandise purchase,

Ornaments meet for the rich matrons who dwell in the town.
Bring me, also, I praythee, a light chain; gladly I'll pay thee,

Oft have I wish'd to possess some stich a trinket as that."
There I remain'd, and ask'd, as merchants are wont, with precision

After the form and the weight which thy commission should have.
Modest, indeed, was the price thou didst name! I meanwhile was gazing

On thy neck which deserv'd ornaments worn but by queens.
Loudly now rose the cry from the ship; then kindly thou spakest

"Take, I entreat thee, some fruit out of the garden, my friend
Take the ripest oranges, figs of the whitest; the ocean

Beareth no fruit, and, in truth, 'tis not produced by each land."
So I entered in. Thou pluckedst the fruit from the branches,

And the burden of gold was in thine apron upheld.
Oft did I cry, Enough! But fairer fruits were still falling

Into the hand as I spake, ever obeying thy touch.

Presently didst thou reached the arbour; there lay there a basket,

Sweet blooming myrtle trees wav'd, as we drew nigh, o'er our heads.
Then thou began'st to arrange the fruit with skill and in silence:

First the orange, which lay heavy as though 'twere of gold,
Then the yielding fig, by the slightest pressure disfigur'd,

And with myrtle the gift soon was both cover'd and grac'd.
But I raised it not up. I stood. Our eyes met together,

And my eyesight grew dim, seeming obscured by a film,
Soon I felt thy bosom on mine! Mine arm was soon twining

Round thy beautiful form; thousand times kiss'd I thy neck.
On my shoulder sank thy head; thy fair arms, encircling,

Soon rendered perfect the ring knitting the rapturous pair.
Amor's hands I felt: he press'd us together with ardour,

And, from the firmament clear, thrice did it thunder; then tears
Stream'd from mine eyes in torrents, thou weptest, I wept, both were weeping,

And, 'mid our sorrow and bliss, even the world seem'd to die.
Louder and louder they call'd from the strand; my feet would no longer

Bear my weight, and I cried:--"Dora! and art thou not mine?"
"Thine forever!" thou gently didst say. Then the tears we were shedding

Seem'd to be wiped from our eyes, as by the breath of a god.
Nearer was heard the cry "Alexis!" The stripling who sought me

Suddenly peep'd through the door. How he the basket snatch'd up!
How he urged me away! how press'd I thy hand! Wouldst thou ask me

How the vessel I reach'd? Drunken I seem'd, well I know.
Drunken my shipmates believed me, and so had pity upon me;

And as the breeze drove us on, distance the town soon obscur'd.
"Thine for ever!" thou, Dora, didst murmur; it fell on my senses

With the thunder of Zeus! while by the thunderer's throne
Stood his daughter, the Goddess of Love; the Graces were standing

Close by her side! so the bond beareth an impress divine!
Oh then hasten, thou ship, with every favouring zephyr!

Onward, thou powerful keel, cleaving the waves as they foam!
Bring me unto the foreign harbour, so that the goldsmith

May in his workshop prepare straightway the heavenly pledge!
Ay, of a truth, the chain shall indeed be a chain, oh my Dora!

Nine times encircling thy neck, loosely around it entwin'd
Other and manifold trinkets I'll buy thee; gold-mounted bracelets,

Richly and skillfully wrought, also shall grace thy fair hand.
There shall the ruby and emerald vie, the sapphire so lovely

Be to the jacinth oppos'd, seeming its foil; while the gold
Holds all the jewels together, in beauteous union commingled.

Oh, how the bridegroom exults, when he adorns his betroth'd!
Pearls if I see, of thee they remind me; each ring that is shown me

Brings to my mind thy fair hand's graceful and tapering form.
I will barter and buy; the fairest of all shalt thou choose thee,

Joyously would I devote all of the cargo to thee.
Yet not trinkets and jewels alone is thy loved one procuring;

With them he brings thee whate'er gives to a housewife delight.
Fine and woollen coverlets, wrought with an edging of purple,

Fit for a couch where we both, lovingly, gently may rest;
Costly pieces of linen. Thou sittest and sewest, and clothest

Me, and thyself, and, perchance, even a third with it too.
Visions of hope, deceive ye my heart! Ye kindly Immortals,

Soften this fierce-raging flame, wildly pervading my breast!
Yet how I long to feel them again, those rapturous torments.

When, in their stead, care draws nigh, coldly and fearfully calm.
Neither the Furies' torch, nor the hounds of hell with their harking

Awe the delinquent so much, down in the plains of despair,
As by the motionless spectre I'm awed, that shows me the fair one

Far away: of a truth, open the garden-door stands!
And another one cometh! For him the fruit, too, is falling,

And for him, also, the fig strengthening honey doth yield!
Doth she entice him as well to the arbour? He follows? Oh, make me

Blind, ye Immortals! efface visions like this from my mind!
Yes, she is but a maiden! And she who to one doth so quickly

Yield, to another ere long, doubtless, Will turn herself round.
Smile not, Zeus, for this once, at an oath so cruelly broken!

Thunder more fearfully! Strike!--Stay--thy fierce lightnings withhold!
Hurl at me thy quivering bolt! In the darkness of midnight

Strike with thy lightning this mast, make it a pitiful wreck!
Scatter the planks all around, and give to the boisterous billows

All these wares, and let me be to the dolphins a prey
Now, ye Muses, enough! In vain would ye strive to depicture

How, in a love-laden breast, anguish alternates with bliss.
Ye cannot heal the wounds, it is true, that love hath inflicted;

Yet from you only proceeds, kindly ones, comfort and balm.

       1796.

HERMANN AND DOROTHEA.

IN NINE CANTOS.

I. KALLIOPE.

FATE AND SYMPATHY.

"NE'ER have I seen the market and streets so thoroughly empty!
Still as the grave is the town, clear'd out! I verily fancy
Fifty at most of all our inhabitants still may be found there.
People are so inquisitive! All are running and racing
Merely to see the sad train of poor fellows driven to exile.

Down to the causeway now building, the distance nearly a league is,
And they thitherward rush, in the heat and the dust of the noonday.
As for me, I had rather not stir from my place just to stare at
Worthy and sorrowful fugitives, who, with what goods they can carry,
Leaving their own fair land on the further side of the Rhine-stream,
Over to us are crossing, and wander through the delightful
Nooks of this fruitful vale, with all its twistings and windings.
Wife, you did right well to bid our son go and meet them,
Taking with him old linen, and something to eat and to drink too,
Just to give to the poor; the rich are bound to befriend them.
How he is driving along! How well he holds in the horses!
Then the new little carriage looks very handsome; inside it
Four can easily sit, besides the one on the coachbox.
This time he is alone; how easily-turns it the corner!"
Thus to his wife the host of the Golden Lion discoursed,
Sitting at ease in the porch of his house adjoining the market.
Then replied as follows the shrewd and sensible hostess
"Father, I don't like giving old linen away, for I find it
Useful in so many ways, 'tis not to he purchased for money
Just when it's wanted. And yet to-day I gladly have given
Many excellent articles, shirts and covers and suchlike;
For I have heard of old people and children walking half-naked.
Will you forgive me, too, for having ransacked your presses?
That grand dressing-gown, cover'd with Indian flowers all over,
Made of the finest calico, lined with excellent flannel,
I have despatch'd with the rest; 'tis thin, old, quite out of fashion."

But the worthy landlord only smiled, and then answer'd
I shall dreadfully miss that ancient calico garment,
Genuine Indian stuff! They're not to be had any longer.
Well! I shall wear it no more. And your poor husband henceforward
Always must wear a surtout, I suppose, or commonplace jacket,
Always must put on his boots; good bye to cap and to slippers!"

"See," continued his wife, "a few are already returning
Who have seen the procession, which long ago must have pass'd by.
See how dusty their shoes are, and how their faces are glowing
Each one carries a handkerchief, wiping the sweat from his forehead.
I, for one, wouldn't hurry and worry myself in such weather
Merely to see such a sight! I'm certain to hear all about it."

And the worthy father, speaking with emphasis, added
"Such fine weather seldom lasts through the whole of the harvest
And we're bringing the fruit home, just as the hay we brought lately,

Perfectly dry; the sky is clear, no cloud's in the heavens,
And the whole day long delicious breezes are blowing.
Splendid weather I call it! The corn already too ripe is,
And to-morrow begin we to gather the plentiful harvest."

Whilst he was thus discoursing, the number of men and of women
Crossing the market and going towards home kept ever increasing;
And there return'd amongst others, bringing with him his daughters,
On the other side of the market, their prosperous neighbour,
Going full speed to his newbuilt house, the principal merchant,
Riding inside an open carriage (in Landau constructed).
All the streets were alive; for the town, though small, was well peopled,
Many a factory throve there, and many a business also.

Long sat the excellent couple under the doorway, exchanging
Many a passing remark on the people who happen'd to pass them.
Presently thus to her husband exclaim'd the good-natured hostess
"See! Yon comes the minister; with him is walking the druggist:
They'll be able to give an account of all that has happen'd,
What they witness'd, and many a sight I fear which was painful."

Both of them came in a friendly manner, and greeted the couple,
Taking their seats on the wooden benches under the doorway,
Shaking the dust from their feet, their handkerchiefs using to fan them.
Presently, after exchanging reciprocal greetings, the druggist
Open'd his mouth, and almost peevishly vented his feelings
"What strange creatures men are! They all resemble each other,
All take pleasure in staring, when troubles fall on their neighbours.
Ev'ry one runs to see the flames destroying a dwelling,
Or a poor criminal led in terror and shame to the scaffold.
All the town has been out to gaze at the sorrowing exiles,
None of them bearing in mind that a like misfortune hereafter,
Possibly almost directly, may happen to be their own portion.
I can't pardon such levity; yet 'tis the nature of all men."
Thereupon rejoin'd the noble and excellent pastor,
He, the charm of the town, in age scarce more than a stripling:--
(He was acquainted with life, and knew the wants of his hearers,
Fully convinced of the worth of the Holy Scriptures, whose mission
Is to reveal man's fate, his inclinations to fathom;
He was also well read in the best of secular writings.)
"I don't like to find fault with any innocent impulse
Which in the mind of man Dame Nature has ever implanted;
For what reason and intellect ne'er could accomplish, is often
Done by some fortunate, quite irresistible instinct within him.

If mankind were never by curiosity driven,
Say, could they e'er have found out for themselves the wonderful manner
Things in the world range in order? For first they Novelty look for,
Then with untiring industry seek to discover the Useful,
Lastly they yearn for the Good, which makes them noble and worthy.
All through their youth frivolity serves as their joyous companion,
Hiding the presence of danger, and. swiftly effacing the traces
Caused by misfortune and grief, as soon as their onslaught is over.
Truly the man's to be praised who, as years roll onward, develops
Out of such glad disposition an intellect settled and steady,--
Who, in good fortune as well as misfortune, strives zealously, nobly;
For what is Good he brings forth, replacing whatever is injured."
Then in a friendly voice impatiently spoke thus the hostess:--
"Tell us what have you seen; I am eagerly longing to hear it."

Then with emphasis answer'd the druggist:--" The terrible stories
Told me to-day will serve for a long time to make me unhappy.
Words would fail to describe the manifold pictures of mis'ry.
Far in the distance saw we the dust, before we descended
Down to the meadows; the rising hillocks hid the procession
Long from our eyes, and little could we distinguish about it.
When, however, we reach'd the road that winds thro' the valley,
Great was the crowd and the noise of the emigrants mix'd with the waggons.
We unhappily saw poor fellows passing in numbers,
Some of them showing how bitter the sense of their sorrowful flight was,
Some with a feeling of joy at saving their lives in a hurry.
Sad was the sight of the manifold goods and chattels pertaining
Unto a well-managed house, which the careful owner's accustom'd
Each in its proper position to place, and in regular order,
Always ready for use, for all are wanted and useful.--
Sad was the sight of them now, on many a waggon and barrow
Heap'd in thorough confusion, and hurriedly huddled together.
Over a cupboard was placed a sieve and a coverlet woollen;
Beds in the kneeding troughs lay, and linen over the glasses.
Ah! and the danger appear'd to rob the men of their senses,
Just as in our great fire of twenty years ago happen'd,
When what was worthless they saved, and left all the best things behind them.
So on the present occasion with heedless caution they carried
Many valueless chattels, o'erlading the cattle and horses,--
Common old boards and barrels, a birdcage next to a goosepen.
Women and children were gasping beneath the weight of their bundles,
Baskets and tubs full of utterly useless articles, bearing.
(Man is always unwilling the least of his goods to abandon.)
Thus on its dusty way advanced the crowded procession,

All in hopeless confusion. First one, whose cattle were weaker,
Fain would slowly advance, while others would eagerly hasten.
Then there arose a scream of half-crush'd women and children,
And a lowing of cattle, with yelping of dogs intermingled,
And a wailing of aged and sick, all sitting and shaking,
Ranged in their beds on the top of the waggon too-heavily laden.
Next some lumbering wheel, push'd out of the track by the pressure,
Went to the edge of the roadway; the vehicle fell in the ditch then,
Rolling right over, and throwing, in falling, the men who were in it
Far in the field, screaming loudly, their persons however uninjured.
Then the boxes roll'd off and tumbled close to the waggon.
Those who saw them failing full surely expected to see them
Smash'd to pieces beneath the weight of the chests and the presses.
So the waggon lay broken, and those that it carried were helpless,
For the rest of the train went on, and hurriedly pass'd them,
Thinking only of self, and carried away by the current.
So we sped to the spot, and found the sick and the aged
Who, when at home and in bed, could scarcely endure their sad ailments,
Lying there on the ground, all sighing and groaning in anguish,
Stifled by clouds of dust, and scorch'd by the fierce sun of summer.

Then replied in tones of compassion the sensitive landlord
Hermann I trust will find them and give them refreshment and clothing.
I should unwillingly see them: I grieve at the eight of such sorrow.
Touch'd by the earliest news of the sad extent of the suffering,
Hastily sent we a trifle from out of our superabundance,
Just to comfort a few, and then our minds were more easy.
Now let us cease to discourse on such a sorrowful subject,
For men's hearts are easily overshadow'd by terror,
And by care, more odious far to me than misfortune.
Now let us go to a cooler place, the little back-parlour;
There the sun never shines, and the walls are so thick that the hot air
Never can enter; and mother shall forthwith bring us a glass each
Full of fine Eighty-three, well fitted to drive away trouble.
This is a bad place for drinking; the flies will hum round the glasses."
So they all went inside, enjoying themselves in the coolness.
Then in a well-cut flask the mother carefully brought them
Some of that clear good wine, upon a bright metal waiter
With those greenish rummers, the fittingest goblets for Rhine wine.
So the three sat together, around the glistening polish'd
Circular large brown table-Äon massive feet it was planted.
Merrily clink'd together the glasses of host and of pastor,
But the other one thoughtfully held his glass without moving,
And in friendly fashion the host thus ask'd him to join them:--

"Drink, good neighbour, I pray! A merciful God has protected
Us in the past from misfortune, and will protect us in future.
All must confess that since He thought fit to severely chastise us,
When that terrible fire occurr'd, He has constantly bless'd us.
And watch'd over us constantly, just as man is accustom'd
His eye's precious apple to guard, that dearest of members.
Shall He not for the future preserve us, and be our Protector?
For 'tis in danger we learn to appreciate duly His Goodness.
This so flourishing town, which He built again from its ashes
By the industrious hands of its burghers, and bless'd it so richly,
Will He again destroy it, and render their toil unavailing?"

Cheerfully answer'd the excellent pastor, in accents of mildness
"Steadfastly cling to this faith, and cherish such worthy opinions;
In good fortune they'll make you prudent, and then in misfortune
Well-grounded hopes they'll supply, and furnish you true consolation."

Then continued the host, with thoughts full of manhood and wisdom
"Oft have I greeted with wonder the rolling flood of the Rhine stream,
When, on my business trav'lling, I've once more come to its borders.
Grand has it ever appear'd, exalting my feelings and senses;
But I could never imagine that soon its beautiful margin
Into a wall would be turn'd, to keep the French from our country,
And its wide-spreading bed a ditch to hinder and check them.
So by Nature we're guarded, we're guarded by valorous Germans,
And by the Lord we're guarded; who then would foolishly tremble?
Weary the combatants are, and all things indicate peace soon;
And when at length the long-expected festival's holden
Here in our church, and the bells chime in with the organ in chorus,
And the trumpets are blowing, the noble Te Deum upraising,
Then on that selfsame day I fain would see, my good pastor,
Our dear Hermann kneel with his bride at the altar before you,
And the glad festival held through the length and breadth of the country
Will henceforward to me be a glad anniversary also!
But I am grieved to observe that the youth, who is always so active
When he is here at home, abroad is so slow and so timid.
Little at any time cares he to mix with the rest of the people;
Yes, he even avoids young maidens' society ever,
And the frolicsome dance, that great delight of young people."

Thus he spake, and then listen'd. The sound of the stamping of horses
Drawing nearer was heard; and then the roll of the carriage,
Which, with impetuous speed, now thunder'd under the gateway.

II. TERPSICHORE.

HERMANN.

THEN when into the room the well-built son made his entry,
Straightway with piercing glances the minister eyed him intently,
And with carefulness watch'd his looks and the whole of his bearing,
With an inquiring eye which easily faces decyphers;
Then he smiled, and with cordial words address'd him as follows
"How you are changed in appearance, my friend! I never have seen you
Half so lively before; your looks are thoroughly cheerful.
You have return'd quite joyous and merry. You've doubtless divided
All of the presents amongst the poor, their blessings receiving."

Then in calm accents replied the son, with gravity speaking
"Whether I've laudably acted, I know not; I follow'd the impulse
Of my own heart, as now I'll proceed to describe with exactness.
Mother, you rummaged so long, in looking over old pieces,
And in making your choice, that 'twas late when the bundle was ready,
And the wine and the beer were slowly and carefully pack'd up.
When I at length emerged at the gate, and came on the highway,
Streams of citizens met I returning, with women and children,
For the train of the exiles had long disappear'd in the distance.
So I quicken'd my pace, and hastily drove to the village
Where I had heard that to-night to rest and to sleep they intended.
Well, as I went on my way, the newly-made causeway ascending,
Suddenly saw I a waggon, of excellent timber constructed,
Drawn by a couple of oxen, the best and the strongest of foreign.
Close beside it there walk'd, with sturdy footsteps, a maiden,
Guiding the two strong beasts with a long kind of staff, which with skill she
Knew how to use, now driving, and now restraining their progress.
When the maiden observed me, she quietly came near the horses,
And address'd me as follows:--'Our usual condition, believe me,
Is not so sad as perchance you might judge from our present appearance.
I am not yet accustom'd to ask for alms from a stranger,
Who so often but gives, to rid himself of a beggar.
But I'm compell'd to speak by necessity. Here on the straw now
Lies the lately-confined poor wife of a wealthy landowner,
Whom with much trouble I managed to save with oxen and waggon.
We were late in arriving, and scarcely with life she escaped.
Now the newly-born child in her arms is lying, all naked,
And our friends will be able to give them but little assistance,
E'en if in the next village, to which to-night we are going,

We should still find them, although I fear they have left it already.
If you belong to the neighbourhood, any available linen
These poor people will deem a most acceptable present.

"Thus she spake, and wearily raised herself the pale patient
Up from the straw and gazed upon me, while thus I made answer
'Oft doth a heavenly spirit whisper to kind-hearted people,
So that they feel the distress o'er their poorer brethren impending;
For my mother, your troubles foreboding, gave me a bundle
Ready prepared for relieving the wants of those who were naked.'
Then I loosen'd the knots of the cord, and the dressing-gown gave her
Which belong'd to my father, and gave her some shirts and some linen,
And she thank'd me with joy and said:--'The fortunate know not
How 'tis that miracles happen; we only discover in sorrow
God's protecting finger and hand, extended to beckon
Good men to good. May your kindness to us by Him be requited.'
And I saw the poor patient joyfully handling the linen,
Valuing most of all the soft flannel, the dressing-gown lining.
Then the maid thus address'd her:--'Now let us haste to the village
Where our friends are resting, to-night intending to sleep there
There I will straightway attend to what e'er for the infant is needed.'
Then she saluted me too, her thanks most heartily giving,
Drove the oxen, the waggon went on. I lingerd behind them,
Holding my horses rein'd back, divided between two opinions,
Whether to hasten ahead, reach the village, the viands distribute
'Mongst the rest of the people, or give them forthwith to the maiden,
So that she might herself divide them amongst them with prudence
Soon I made up my mind, and follow'd after her softly,
Overtook her without delay, and said to her quickly
'Maiden, it was not linen alone that my mother provided
And in the carriage placed, as clothing to give to the naked,
But she added meat, and many an excellent drink too;
And I have got quite a stock stow'd away in the boot of the carriage.
Well, I have taken a fancy the rest of the gifts to deposit
In your hands, and thus fulfil to the best my commission;
You will divide them with prudence, whilst I my fate am obeying.'
Then the maiden replied:--'With faithfulness I will distribute
All your gifts, and the needy shall surely rejoice at your bounty.'
Thus she spake, and I hastily open'd the boot of the carriage,
Took out the hams (full heavy they were) and took out the bread-stuffs,
Flasks of wine and beer, and handed the whole of them over.
Gladly would I have given her more, but empty the boot was.
Straightway she pack'd them away at the feet of the patient, and forthwith
Started again, whilst I hasten'd back to the town with my horses."

Then when Hermann had ended his story, the garrulous neighbour
Open'd his mouth and exclaim'd:--"I only deem the man happy
Who lives alone in his house in these days of flight and confusion,
Who has neither wife nor children cringing beside him
I feel happy at present; I hate the title of father;
Care of children and wife in these days would be a sad drawback.
Often have I bethought me of flight, and have gather'd together
All that I deem most precious, the antique gold and the jewels
Worn by my late dear mother, not one of which has been sold yet.
Much indeed is left out, that is not so easily carried.
Even the herbs and the roots, collected with plenty of trouble,
I should he sorry to lose, though little in value they may be.
If the dispenser remains, I shall leave my house in good spirits
If my ready money is saved, and my body, why truly
All is saved, for a bachelor easily flies when 'tis needed."

"Neighbour," rejoin'd forthwith young Hermann, with emphasis speaking
"Altogether I differ, and greatly blame your opinions.
Can that man be deem'd worthy, who both in good and ill fortune
Thinks alone of himself, and knows not the secret of sharing
Sorrows and joys with others, and feels no longing to do so?
I could more easily now than before determine to marry
Many an excellent maiden needs a husband's protection,
Many a man a cheerful wife, when sorrow's before him."
Smilingly said then the father:--"I'm pleas'd to hear what you're saying,
Words of such wisdom have seldom been utter'd by you in my presence.

Then his good mother broke in, in her turn, with vivacity speaking
"Son, you are certainly right. We parents set the example.
'Twas not in time of pleasure that we made choice of each other,
And 'twas the saddest of hours, that knitted us closely together.
Monday morning,--how well I remember! the very day after
That most terrible fire occurr'd which burnt down the borough,
Twenty years ago now; the day, like to-day, was a Sunday,
Hot and dry was the weather, and little available water.
All the inhabitants, clothed in their festival garments, were walking,
Scatter'd about in the inns and the mills of the neighbouring hamlets.
At one end of the town the fire broke out, and the flames ran
Hastily all through the streets, impell'd by the draught they created.
And the barns were consumed, where all the rich harvest was gather'd
And all the streets as far as the market; the dwelling house also
Of my father hard by was destroy'd, as likewise was this one.
Little indeed could we save; I sat the sorrowful night through

On the green of the town, protecting the beds and the boxes.
Finally sleep overtook me, and when by the cool breeze of morning
Which dies away when the sun arises I was awaken'd,
Saw I the smoke and the glow, and the half-consumed walls and the chimneys.
Then my heart was sorely afflicted; but soon in his glory
Rose the sun more brilliant than ever, my spirits reviving.
Then in haste I arose, impell'd the site to revisit
Where our dwelling had stood, to see if the chickens were living
Which I especially loved; for childlike I still was by nature.
But when over the ruins of courtyard and house I was climbing,
Which still smoked, and saw my dwelling destroy'd and deserted,
You came up on the other side, the ruins exploring.
You had a horse shut up in his stall; the still-glowing rafters
Over it lay, and rubbish, and nought could be seen of the creature.
Over against each other we stood, in doubt and in sorrow,
For the wall had fallen which used to sever our courtyards;
And you grasp'd my hand, addressing me softly as follows
'Lizzy, what here are you doing? Away! Your soles you are burning,
For the rubbish is hot, and is scorching my boots which are thicker.'
Then you lifted me up, and carried me off through your courtyard.
There still stood the gateway before the house, with its arch'd roof,
Just as it now is standing, the only thing left remaining.
And you sat me down and kiss'd me, and I tried to stop you,
But you presently said, with kindly words full of meaning
'See, my house is destroy'd! Stop here and help me to build it,
I in return will help to rebuild the house of your father.'
I understood you not, till you sent to my father your mother,
And ere long our marriage fulfilid the troth we soon plighted.
Still to this day I remember with pleasure the half-consumed rafters,
Still do I see the sun in all his majesty rising,
For on that day I gain'd my husband; the son of my youth too
Gained I during that earliest time of the wild desolation.
Therefore commend I you, Hermann, for having with confidence guileless
Turn'd towards marriage your thoughts in such a period of mourning,
And for daring to woo in war and over the ruins.--"

Then the father straightway replied, with eagerness speaking:--
"Sensible is your opinion, and true is also the story
Which you have told us, good mother, for so did ev'rything happen.
But what is better is better. 'Tis not the fortune of all men
All their life and existence to find decided beforehand;
All are not doom'd to such troubles as we and others have suffer'd.
O, how happy is he whose careful father and mother
Have a house ready to give him, which he can successfully manage!

All beginnings are hard, and most so the landlords profession.
Numberless things a man must have, and ev'rything daily
Dearer becomes, so he needs to scrape together more money.
So I am hoping that you, dear Hermann, will shortly be bringing
Home to us a bride possessing an excellent dowry,
For a worthy husband deserves a girl who is wealthy,
And 'tis a capital thing for the wish'd-for wife to bring with her
Plenty of suitable articles stow'd in her baskets and boxes.
Not in vain for years does the mother prepare for her daughter
Stocks of all kinds of linen, both finest and strongest in texture;
Not in vain do god-parents give them presents of silver,
Or the father lay by in his desk a few pieces of money.
For she hereafter will gladden, with all her goods and possessions,
That happy youth who is destined from out of all others to choose her.
Yes! I know how pleasant it makes a house for a young wife,
When she finds her own property placed in the rooms and the kitchen,
And when she herself has cover'd the bed and the table.
Only well-to-do brides should be seen in a house, I consider,
For a poor one is sure at last to be scorn'd by her husband,
And he'll deem her a jade who as jade first appear'd with her bundle.
Men are always unjust, but moments of love are but transient.
Yes, my Hermann, you greatly would cheer the old age of your father
If you soon would bring home a daughter-in-law to console me,
Out of the neighbourhood too,--yes, out of yon dwelling, the green one!
Rich is the man, in truth his trade and his manufactures
Make him daily richer, for when does a merchant not prosper?
He has only three daughters; the whole of his wealth they'll inherit.
True the eldest's already engaged; but then there's the second,
And the third, who still (not for long) may be had for the asking.
Had I been in your place, I should not till this time have waited;
Bring home one of the girls, as I brought your mother before you.

Then, with modesty, answer'd the son his impetuous father
"Truly my wish was, like yours, to marry one of the daughters
Of our neighbour. We all, in fact, were brought up together,
Sported in youthful days near the fountain adjoining the market,
And from the rudeness of boys I often managed to save them.
But those days have long pass'd the maidens grew up, and with reason
Stop now at home and avoid the rougher pastimes of childhood.
Well brought up with a vengeance they are! To please you, I sometimes
Went to visit them, just for the sake of olden acquaintance
But I was never much pleased at holding intercourse with them,
For they were always finding fault, and I had to bear it
First my coat was too long, the cloth too coarse, and the colour

Far too common, my hair was cut and curl'd very badly.
I at last was thinking of dressing myself like the shop-boys,
Who are accustom'd on Sundays to show off their persons up yonder,
And round whose coats in summer half-silken tatters are hanging.
But ere long I discover'd they only intended to fool me
This was very annoying, my pride was offended, but more still
Felt I deeply wounded that they so mistook the good feelings
Which I cherish'd towards them, especially Minnie, the youngest.
Well, I went last Easter, politely to pay them a visit,
And I wore the new coat now hanging up in the closet,
And was frizzled and curld, like all the rest of the youngsters.
When I enter'd, they titter'd; but that didn't very much matter.
Minnie sat at the piano, the father was present amongst them,
Pleased with his daughter's singing, and quite in a jocular humour.
Little could I understand of the words in the song she was singing,
But I constantly heard of Pamina, and then of Tamino,*

(* Characters In Mozart's Zauberflote.)
And I fain would express my opinion; so when she had ended,
I ask'd questions respecting the text, and who were the persons.
All were silent and smiled; but presently answer'd the father
'Did you e'er happen, my friend, to hear of Eve or of Adam?'
Then no longer restrain'd they themselves, the girls burst out laughing,
All the boys laugh'd loudly, the old man's sides appear'd splitting.
In my confusion I let my hat fall down, and the titt'ring
Lasted all the time the singing and playing continued.
Then I hasten'd home, ashamed and full of vexation,
Hung up my coat in the closet, and put my hair in disorder
With my fingers, and swore ne'er again to cross o'er their threshold.
And I'm sure I was right; for they are all vain and unloving.
And I hear they're so rude as to give me the nickname Tamino."
Then the mother rejoin'd:--"You're wrong, dear Hermann, to harbour
Angry feelings against the children, for they are but children.
Minnie's an excellent girl, and has a tenderness for you;
Lately she ask'd how you were. Indeed, I wish you would choose her!"

Then the son thoughtfully answer'd:--"I know not why, but the fact is
My annoyance has graven itself in my mind, and hereafter
I could not bear at the piano to see her, or list to her singing."

But the father sprang up, and said, in words full of anger
"Little comfort you give me, in truth! I always have said it,
When you took pleasure in horses, and cared for nothing but fieldwork;
That which the servants of prosperous people perform as their duty,

You yourself do; meanwhile the father his son must dispense with,
Who in his honour was wont to court the rest of the townsfolk.
Thus with empty hopes your mother early deceived me,
When your reading, and writing, and learning at school ne'er succeeded
Like the rest of the boys, and so you were always the lowest.
This all comes from a youth not possessing a due sense of honour,
And not having the spirit to try and raise his position.
Had my father but cared for me, as I have for you, sir,
Sent me to school betimes, and given me proper instructors,
I should not merely have been the host of the famed Golden Lion."

But the son arose, and approach'd the doorway in silence,
Slowly, and making no noise: but then the father in dudgeon
After him shouted:--"Be off! I know you're an obstinate fellow!
Go and look after the business; else I shall scold you severely;
But don't fancy I'll ever allow you to bring home in triumph
As my daughter-in-law any boorish impudent hussy.
Long have I lived in the world, and know how to manage most people,
Know how to entertain ladies and gentlemen, so that they leave me
In good humour, and know how to flatter a stranger discreetly.
But my daughter-in-law must have useful qualities also,
And be able to soften my manifold cares and vexations.
She must also play on the piano, that all the best people
Here in the town may take pleasure in often coming to see us,
As in the house of our neighbour the merchant happens each Sunday."
Softly the son at these words raised the latch, and left the apartment.

III. THALIA.

THE BURGHERS.

THUS did the prudent son escape from the hot conversation,
But the father continued precisely as he had begun it
What is not in a man can never come out of him, surely!
Never, I fear, shall I see fulfill'd my dearest of wishes,
That my son should be unlike his father, but better.
What would be the fate of a house or a town, if its inmates
Did not all take pride in preserving, renewing, improving,
As we are taught by the age, and by the wisdom of strangers?
Man is not born to spring out of the ground, just like a mere mushroom,
And to rot away soon in the very place that produced him!
Leaving behind him no trace of what he has done in his lifetime.
One can judge by the look of a house of the taste of its master,
As on ent'ring a town, one can judge the authorities' fitness.

For where the towers and walls are falling, where in the ditches
Dirt is collected, and dirt in every street is seen lying,
Where the stones come out of their groove, and are not replaced there,
Where the beams are rotting, and vainly the houses are waiting
New supports; that town is sure to be wretchedly managed.
For where order and cleanliness reign not supreme in high places,
Then to dirt and delay the citizens soon get accustom'd,
Just as the beggar's accustom'd to wear his cloths full of tatters.
Therefore I often have wish'd that Hermann would start on his travels
Ere he's much older, and visit at any rate Strasburg and Frankfort,
And that pleasant town, Mannheim, so evenly built and so cheerful.
He who has seen such large and cleanly cities rests never
Till his own native town, however small, he sees better'd.
Do not all strangers who visit us praise our well-mended gateways,
And the well-whited tower, the church so neatly repair'd too?
Do not all praise our pavements? Our well-arranged cover'd-in conduits,
Always well furnish'd with water, utility blending with safety,
So that a fire, whenever it happens, is straightway extinguish'd,--
Is not this the result of that conflagration so dreadful?
Six times in Council I superintended the town's works, receiving
Hearty thanks and assistance from every well-disposed burgher.
How I design'd, follow'd up, and ensured the completion of measures
Worthy men had projected, and afterwards left all unfinish'd!
Finally, every man in the Council took pleasure in working.
All put forth their exertions, and now they have finally settled
That new highway to make, which will join our town with the main road.
But I am greatly afraid that the young generation won't act thus;
Some on the one hand think only of pleasure and trumpery dresses,
Others wont stir out of doors, and pass all their time by the fireside,
And our Hermann, I fear, will always be one of this last sort."

Forthwith to him replied the excellent sensible mother
"Father, you're always unjust whenever you speak of your son, and
That is the least likely way to obtain your wishes' fulfillment,
For we cannot fashion our children after our fancy.
We must have them and love them, as God has given them to us,
Bring them up for the best, and let each do as he listeth.
One has one kind of gift, another possesses another,
Each one employs them, and each in turn in his separate fashion
Good and happy becomes. My Hermann shall not be upbraided,
For I know that he well deserves the wealth he'll inherit;
He'll be an excellent landlord, a pattern to burghers and peasants,
And, as I clearly foresee, by no means the last in the Council.
But with your blame and reproaches, you daily dishearten him sadly,

As you have done just now, and make the poor fellow unhappy."

Then she left the apartment, and after her son hasten'd quickly,
Hoping somewhere to find him, and with her words of affection
Gladden his heart, for he, the excellent son, well deserved it.
Smilingly, when she had closed the door, continued the father
"What a wonderful race of people are women and children.
All of them fain would do whatever pleases their fancy,
And we're only alow'd to praise them and flatter them freely.
Once for all there's truth in the ancient proverb which tells us:
He who moves not forward, goes backward! a capital saying!"

Speaking with much circumspection, the druggist made answer as follows
"What you say, good neighbour, is certainly true, and my plan is
Always to think of improvement, provided tho' new, 'tis not costly.
But what avails it in truth, unless one has plenty of money,
Active and fussy to he, improving both inside and outside?
Sadly confined are the means of a burgher; e'en when he knows it,
Little that's good he is able to do, his purse is too narrow,
And the sum wanted too great; and so he is always prevented.
I have had plenty of schemes! but then I was terribly frighten'd
At the expense, especially during a time of such danger.
Long had my house smiled upon me, deck'd out in modish exterior,
Long had my windows with large panes of glass resplendently glitterd.
Who can compete with a merchant, however, who, rolling in riches,
Also knows the manner in which what is best can be purchased?
Only look at the house up yonder, the new one: how handsome
Looks the stucco of those white scrolls on the green-colour'd panels!
Large are the plates of the windows--how shining and brilliant the panes are,
Quite eclipsing the rest of the houses that stand in the market!
Yet at the time of the fire, our two were by far the most handsome,
Mine at the sign of the Angel, and yours at the old Golden Lion.
Then my garden was famous throughout the whole country, and strangers
Used to stop as they pass'd and peep through my red-colour'd palings
At my beggars of stone, and at my dwarfs, which were painted,
He to whom I gave coffee inside my beautiful grotto,
Which, alas! is now cover'd with dust and tumbling to pieces,
Used to rejoice in the colour'd glimmering light of the mussels,
Ranged in natural order around it, and connoisseurs even
Used with dazzled eyes to gaze at the spars and the coral.
Then, in the drawing-room, people look'd with delight on the painting,
Where the prim ladies and gentlemen walked in the garden demurely,
And with pointed fingers presented the flowers, and held them.
Ah, if only such things were now to be seen! Little care I

Now to go out; for everything needs to be alter'd and tasteful,
As it is call'd; and white are the benches of wood and the palings;
All things are simple and plain; and neither carving not gilding
Now are employ'd, and foreign timber is now all the fashion.
I should be only too pleased to possess some novelty also,
So as to march with the times, and my household furniture alter.
But we all are afraid to make the least alteration,
For who is able to pay the present charges of workmen?
Lately a fancy possess'd me, the angel Michael, whose figure
Hangs up over my shop, to treat to a new coat of gilding,
And the terrible Dragon, who round his feet is entwining;
But I have left him all brown; as he is; for the cost quite alarm'd me."

IV. EUTERPE.

MOTHER AND SON.

THUS the men discourse together; and meanwhile the mother
Went in search of her son,--at first in front of the dwelling
On the bench of stone, for he was accustom'd to sit there.
When she found him not there, she went to look in the stable,
Thinking perchance he was feeding his splendid horses, the stallions
Which he had bought when foals, and which he entrusted to no one.
But the servant inform'd her that he had gone to the garden.
Then she nimbly strode across the long double courtyard,
Left the stables behind, and the barns all made of good timber,
Enter'd the garden which stretch'd far away to the walls of the borough,
Walk'd across it, rejoicing to see how all things were growing,
Carefully straighten'd the props, on which the apple-tree's branches,
Heavily loaded, reposed, and the weighty boughs of the pear-tree,
Took a few caterpillars from off the strong-sprouting cabbage;
For a bustling woman is never idle one moment.
In this manner she came to the end of the long-reaching garden,
Where was the arbour all cover'd with woodbine: she found not her son there,
Nor was he to be seen in any part of the garden.
But she found on the latch the door which out of the arbour
Through the wall of the town had been made by special permission
During their ancestor's time, the worthy old burgomaster.
So she easily stepp'd across the dry ditch at the spot where
On the highway abutted their well-inclosed excellent vineyard.
Rising steeply upwards, its face tow'rd the sun turn'd directly.
Up the hill she proceeded, rejoicing, as farther she mounted,
At the size of the grapes, which scarcely were hid by the foliage.
Shady and well-cover'd in, the middle walk at the top was,

Which was ascended by steps of rough flat pieces constructed.
And within it were hanging fine chasselas and muscatels also,
And a reddish-blue grape, of quite an exceptional bigness,
All with carefulness planted, to give to their guests after dinner.
But with separate stems the rest of the vineyard was planted,
Smaller grapes producing, from which the finest wine made is.
So she constantly mounted, enjoying in prospect the autumn.
And the festal day, when the neighbourhood met with rejoicing,
Picking and treading the grapes, and putting the must in the wine-vats,
Every corner and nook resounding at night with the fireworks,
Blazing and cracking away, due honour to pay to the harvest.
But she uneasy became, when she in vain had been calling
Twice and three times her son, and when the sole answer that reach'd her
Came from the garrulous echo which out of the town towers issued.
Strange it appear'd to have to seek him; he never went far off,
(As he before had told her) in order to ward off all sorrow
From his dear mother, and her forebodings of coming disaster.
But she still was expecting upon the highway to find him,
For the doors at the bottom, like those at the top, of the vineyard
Stood wide open; and so at length she enter'd the broad field
Which, with its spreading expanse, o'er the whole of the hill's back extended.
On their own property still she proceeded, greatly rejoicing
At their own crops, and at the corn which nodded so bravely,
Over the whole field in golden majesty waving.
Then on the border between the fields she follow'd the footpath,
Keeping her eye on the pear-tree fix'd, the big one, which standing
Perch'd by itself on the top of the hill, their property bounded.
Who had planted it, no one knew; throughout the whole country
Far and wide was it visible; noted also its fruit was.
Under its shadow the reaper ate his dinner at noonday,
And the herdsman was wont to lie, when tending his cattle.
Benches made of rough stones and of turf were placed all about it.
And she was not mistaken; there sat her Hermann and rested
On his arm he was leaning, and seem'd to be looking cross country
Tow'rds the mountains beyond; his back was turn'd to his mother.
Softly creeping up, she lightly tapp'd on his shoulder;
And he hastily turn'd; she saw that his eyes full of tears were.

"Mother," he said in confusion:--"You greatly surprise me!" and quickly
Wiped he away his tears, the noble and sensitive youngster.
"What! You are weeping, my son?" the startled mother continued
"That is indeed unlike you! I never before saw you crying!
Say, what has sadden'd your heart? What drives you to sit here all lonely
Under the shade of the pear-tree? What is it that makes you unhappy?"

Then the excellent youth collected himself, and made answer
"Truly that man can have no heart, but a bosom of iron,
Who no sympathy feels for the wants of unfortunate exiles;
He has no sense in his head who, in times of such deep tribulation,
Has no concern for himself or for his country's well-being.
What I to-day have seen and heard, has stirr'd up my feelings;
Well, I have come up here, and seen the beautiful, spreading
Landscape, which in fruitful hills to our sight is presented,
Seen the golden fruit of the sheaves all nodding together,
And a plentiful crop of fruit, full garners foreboding.
But, alas, how near is the foe! By the Rhine's flowing waters
We are protected indeed; but what are rivers and mountains
To such a terrible nation, which hurries along like a tempest!
For they summon together the young and the old from all quarters,
Rushing wildly along, while the multitude little is caring
Even for death; when one falls, his place is straight fill'd by another,
Ah! and can Germans dare to remain at home in their dwellings,
Thinking perchance to escape from the widely-threat'ning disaster?
Dearest mother, I tell you that I to-day am quite sorry
That I was lately excused, when they selected the fighters
Out of the townfolk. 'Tis true I'm an only son, and more-over
Large is our inn, and our business also is very important;
Were it not better however for me to fight in the vanguard
On the frontier, than here to await disaster and bondage?
Yes, my spirit has told me, and in my innermost bosom
Feel I courage and longing to live and die for my country,
And to others to set an example worthy to follow.
Oh, of a truth, if the strength of the German youths was collected
On the frontier, all bound by a vow not to yield to the stranger,
He on our noble soil should never set foot, or be able
Under our eyes to consume the fruits of the land, or to issue
Orders unto our men, or despoil our women and maidens!
See, good mother, within my inmost heart I've determined
Soon and straightway to do what seems to me right and becoming;
For the man who thinks long, not always chooses what best is.
See, I will not return to the house, but will go from here straightway
Into the town, and there will place at the fighters' disposal
This stout arm and this heart, to serve, as I best can, my country.
Then let my father say whether feelings of honour are stirring
In my bosom or not, and whether I yearn to mount upwards."

Then with significance answer'd his good and sensible mother,
Shedding tears in silence, which easily rose in her eyelids:--

"Son, what has wrought so strange a change in your temper and feelings,
That you freely and openly speak to your mother no longer,
As you till yesterday did, nor tell her truly your wishes?
If another had heard you speaking, he doubtless would praise you
Highly, and deem your new resolution as worthy of honour,
Being deceived by your words, and by your manner of speaking.
I however can only blame you. I know you much better.
You are concealing your heart, and very diff'rent your thoughts are;
For I am sure you care not at all for drum and for trumpet,
Nor, to please the maidens, care you to wear regimentals.
For, though brave you may be, and gallant, your proper vocation
Is to remain at home, the property quietly watching.
Therefore tell me truly: What means this sudden decision?"

Earnestly answer'd the son:--"You are wrong, dear-mother, one day is
Unlike another. The youth soon ripens into his manhood.
Ofttimes he ripens better to action in silence than living
That tumultuous noisy life which ruins so many.
And though silent I have been, and am, a heart has been fashion'd
Inside my bosom, which hates whatever unfair and unjust is,
And I am able right well to discriminate secular matters.
Work moreover my arms and my feet has mightily strengthen'd.
All that I tell you is true; I boldly venture to say so.
And yet, mother, you blame me with reason; you've caught me employing
Words that are only half true, and that serve to conceal my true feelings.
For I must need confess, it is not the advent of danger
Calls me away from my father's house, nor a resolute purpose
Useful to be to my country, and dreaded to be by the foeman.
Words alone it was that I utter'd,--words only intended
Those deep feelings to hide, which within my breast are contending.
And now leave me, my mother! For as in my bosom I cherish
Wishes that are but vain, my life will be to no purpose.
For I know that the Unit who makes a self-sacrifice, only
Injures himself, unless all endeavour the Whole to accomplish."

"Now continue," replied forthwith his sensible mother:--
"Tell me all that has happen'd, the least as w'ell as the greatest
Men are always hasty, and only remember the last thing,
And the hasty are easily forced from the road by obstructions.
But a woman is skillful, and full of resources, and scorns not
Bye-roads to traverse when needed, well-skill'd to accomplish her purpose.
Tell me then all, and why you are stirr'd by such violent feelings
More than I ever have seen, while the blood is boiling within you,
And from your eyes the tears against your will fain would fall now."

Then the youth gave way to his sorrow, and burst into weeping,
Weeping aloud on the breast of his mother, and softly replying
"Truly, my father's words to-day have wounded me sadly,
Never have I deserved at his hands such treatment,--no, never!
For to honour my parents was always my wish from my childhood,
No one ever appear'd so prudent and wise as my parents,
Who in the darker days of childhood carefully watch'd me.
Much indeed it has been my lot to endure from my playmates,
When with their knavish pranks they used to embitter my temper.
Often I little suspected the tricks they were playing upon me:
But if they happen'd to ridicule Father, whenever on Sundays
Out of church he came with his slow deliberate footsteps,
If they laugh'd at the strings of his cap, and his dressing-gown's flowers,
Which he in stately wise wore, and to-day at length has discarded,
Then in a fury I clench'd my fist, and, storming and raging,
Fell upon them and hit and struck with terrible onslaught,
Heedless where my blows fell. With bleeding noses they hallooed,
And could scarcely escape from the force of my blows and my kicking.
Then, as in years I advanced, I had much to endure from my father,
Who, in default of others to blame, would often abuse me,
When at the Council's last sitting his anger perchance was excited,
And I the penalty paid of the squabbles and strife of his colleagues.
You yourself have oft pitied me; I endured it with patience,
Always rememb'ring the much-to-be-honour'd kindness of parents,
Whose only thought is to swell for our sakes their goods and possessions,
And who deprive themselves of much, to save for their children.
But, alas, not saving alone, for enjoyment hereafter,
Constitutes happiness, no, not heaps of gold or of silver,
Neither field upon field, however compact the estate be.
For the father grows old, and his son at the same time grows older,
Feeling no joy in To-day, and full of care for To-morrow.
Now look down from this height, and see how beauteous before us
Lies the fair rich expanse, with vineyard and gardens at bottom;
There are the stables and barns, and the rest of the property likewise;
There I also descry the back of our house, in the gables
Of the roof may be seen the window of my small apartment.
When I remember the time when I used to look out for the moon there
Half through the night, or perchance at morning awaited the sunrise,
When with but few hours of healthy sleep I was fully contented,
Ah, how lonely do all things appear! My chamber, the court, and
Garden, the beautiful field which spreads itself over the hillside;
All appears but a desert to me: I still am unmarried!"
Then his good mother answer'd his speech in a sensible manner

"Son, your wish to be able to lead your bride to her chamber,
Turning the night to the dearest and happiest half of your lifetime,
Making your work by day more truly free and unfetter'd,
Cannot be greater than that of your father and mother. We always
Urged you,--commanded, I even might say,--to choose some fair maiden.
But I know full well, and my heart has told me already
If the right hour arrives not, or if the right maiden appears not
Instantly when they are sought for, man's choice is thrown in confusion,
And he is driven by fear to seize what is counterfeit only.
If I may tell you, my son, your choice already is taken,
For your heart is smitten, and sensitive more than is usual.
Answer me plainly, then, for my spirit already has told me:
She whom now you have chosen is that poor emigrant maiden!"

"Yes, dear mother, you're right!" the son with vivacity answer'd
Yes, it is she! And unless this very day I conduct her
Home as my bride, she will go on her way and escape me for ever,
In the confusion of war, and in moving backwards and forwards.
Mother, then before my eyes will in vain he unfolded
All our rich estate, and each year henceforward be fruitful.
Yes, the familiar house and the garden will be my aversion.
Ah, and the love of my mother no comfort will give to my sorrow,
For I feel that by Love each former bond must be loosen'd,
When her own bonds she knits; 'tis not the maiden alone who
Leaves her father and mother behind, when she follows her husband.
So it is with the youth; no more he knows mother and father.
When he beholds the maiden, the only beloved one, approaching.
Therefore let me go hence, to where desperation may lead me,
For my father already has spoken in words of decision,
And his house no longer is mine, if he shuts out the maiden
Whom alone I would fain take home as my bride from henceforward."

Then the excellent sensible mother answer'd with quickness
"Men are precisely like rocks when they stand opposed to each other!
Proud and unyielding, the one will never draw near to the other.
Neither will suffer his tongue to utter the first friendly accent.
Therefore I tell you, my son, a hope still exists in my bosom,
If she is worthy and good, he will give his consent to your marriage,
Poor though she be, and although with disdain he refused you the poor thing.
For in his hot-beaded fashion he utters many expressions
Which he never intends; and so will accept the Refused One.
But he requires kind words, and has a right to require them,
For your father he is; his anger is all after dinner,
When he more eagerly speaks, and questions the reasons of others,

Meaning but little thereby; the wine then excites all the vigour
Of his impetuous will, and prevents him from giving due weight to
Other people's opinions; he hears and he feels his own only.
But when evening arrives, the tone of the many discourses
Which his friends and himself hold together, is very much alter'd.
Milder becomes he, as soon as his liquor's effects have passed over
And he feels the injustice his eagerness did unto others.
Come, we will venture at once! Success the reward is of boldness,
And we have need of the friends who now have assembled around him.--
Most of all we shall want the help of our excellent pastor."
Thus she eagerly spoke, and leaving the stone that she sat on,
Also lifted her son from his seat. He willingly follow'd,
And they descended in silence, revolving the weighty proposal.

V. POLYHYMNIA.

THE COSMOPOLITE.

BUT the Three, as before, were still sitting and talking together,
With the landlord, the worthy divine, and also the druggist,
And the conversation still concern'd the same subject,
Which in every form they had long been discussing together.
Full of noble thoughts, the excellent pastor continued
"I can't contradict you. I know 'tis the duty of mortals
Ever to strive for improvement; and, as we may see, they strive also
Ever for that which is higher, at least what is new they seek after,
But don't hurry too fast! For combined with these feelings, kind Nature
Also has given us pleasure in dwelling on that which is ancient,
And in clinging to that to which we have long been accustom'd.
Each situation is good that's accordant to nature and reason.
Many things man desires, and yet he has need of but little;
For but short are the days, and confined is the lot of a mortal.
I can never blame the man who, active and restless,
Hurries along, and explores each corner of earth and the ocean
Boldly and carefully, while he rejoices at seeing the profits
Which round him and his family gather themselves in abundance.
But I also duly esteem the peaceable burgher,
Who with silent steps his paternal inheritance paces,
And watches over the earth, the seasons carefully noting.
'Tis not every year that he finds his property alter'd;
Newly-planted trees cannot stretch out their arms tow'rds the heavens
All in a moment, adorn'd with beautiful buds in abundance.
No, a man has need of patience, he also has need of
Pure unruffled tranquil thoughts and an intellect honest;

For to the nourishing earth few seeds at a time he entrusteth,
Few are the creatures he keeps at a time, with a view to their breeding,
For what is Useful alone remains the first thought of his lifetime.
Happy the man to whom Nature a mind thus attuned may have given!
'Tis by him that we all are fed. And happy the townsman
Of the small town who unites the vocations of town and of country.
He is exempt from the pressure by which the poor farmer is worried,
Is not perplex'd by the citizens' cares and soaring ambition,
Who, with limited means,--especially women and maidens,--
Think of nothing but aping the ways of the great and the wealthy,
You should therefore bless your son's disposition so peaceful,
And the like-minded wife whom we soon may expect him to marry.

Thus he spoke. At that moment the mother and son stood before them.
By the hand she led him and placed him in front of her husband
"Father," she said, "how often have we, when talking together,
Thought of that joyful day in the future, when Hermann, selecting
After long waiting his bride at length would make us both happy!
All kinds of projects we form'd. designing first one, then another
Girl as his wife, as we talk'd in the manner that parents delight in.
Now the day has arrived; and now has his bride been conducted
Hither and shown him by Heaven; his heart at length has decided.
Were we not always saying that he should choose for himself, and
Were you not lately wishing that he might feel for a maiden
Warm and heart-felt emotions? And now has arrived the right moment!
Yes, he has felt and has chosen, and like a man has decided.
That fair maiden it is, the Stranger whom he encounter'd.
Give her him; else he'll remain--he has sworn it--unmarried for ever."

And the son added himself:--"My father, O give her! My heart has
Chosen purely and truly: she'll make you an excellent daughter."

But the father was silent. Then suddenly rose the good pastor,
And address'd him as follows:--" One single moment's decisive
Both of the life of a man, and of the whole of his Future.
After lengthen'd reflection, each resolution made by him
Is but the work of a moment; the prudent alone seize the right one.
Nothing more dangerous is, in making a choice, than revolving
First this point and then that, and so confusing the feelings.
Pure is Hermann's mind; from his youth I have known him; he never,
Even in boyhood, was wont to extend his hand hither and thither.
What he desired, was suitable to him; he held to it firmly.
Be not astonish'd and scared, because there appears on a sudden
What you so long have desired. 'Tis true the appearance at present

Bears not the shape of the wish, as you in your mind had conceived it.
For our wishes conceal the thing that we wish for; our gifts too
Come from above upon us, each clad in its own proper figure.
Do not now mistake the maiden who has succeeded
First in touching the heart of your good wise son, whom you love so.
Happy is he who is able to clasp the hand of his first love,
And whose dearest wish is not doom'd to pine in his bosom!
Yes, I can see by his face, already his fate is decided;
True affection converts the youth to a man in a moment.
He little changeable is; I fear me, if this you deny him,
All the fairest years of his life will be changed into sorrow."

Then in prudent fashion the druggist, who long had been wanting
His opinion to give, rejoin'd in the following manner
"This is Just a case when the middle course is the wisest!
'Hasten slowly,' you know, was the motto of Caesar Augustus.
I am always ready to be of use to my neighbours,
And to turn to their profit what little wits I can boast of.
Youth especially needs the guidance of those who are older.
Let me then depart; I fain would prove her, that maiden,
And will examine the people 'mongst whom she lives, and who know her.
I am not soon deceived; I know how to rate their opinions."

Then forthwith replied the son, with eagerness speaking:--
"Do so, neighbour, and go, make your inquiries. However,
I should greatly prefer that our friend, the pastor, went with you;
Two such excellent men are witnesses none can find fault with.
O, my father! the maiden no vagabond is, I assure you,
No mere adventurer, wand'ring about all over the country,
And deceiving the inexperienced youths with her cunning;
No! the harsh destiny link'd with this war, so destructive of all things,
Which is destroying the world, and already has wholly uprooted
Many a time-honour'd fabric, has driven the poor thing to exile.
Are not brave men of noble birth now wand'ring in mis'ry?
Princes are fleeing disguised, and monarchs in banishment living.
Ah, and she also herself, the best of her sisters, is driven
Out of her native land; but her own misfortunes forgetting,
Others she seeks to console, and, though helpless, is also most helpful.
Great are the woes and distress which over the earth's face are brooding,
But may happiness not be evoked from out of this sorrow?
May not I, in the arms of my bride, the wife I have chosen,
Even rejoice at the war, as you at the great conflagration?"

Then replied the father, and open'd his mouth with importance:--

"Strangely indeed, my son, has your tongue been suddenly loosen'd,
Which for years has stuck in your mouth, and moved there but rarely
I to-day must experience that which threatens each father:
How the ardent will of a son a too-gentle mother
Willingly favours, whilst each neighbour is ready to back him,
Only provided it be at the cost of a father or husband!
But what use would it be to resist so many together?
For I see that defiance and tears will otherwise greet me.
Go and prove her, and in God's name then hasten to bring her
Home as my daughter; if not, he must think no more of the maiden."

Thus spake the father. The son exclaim'd with jubilant gesture
"Ere the ev'ning arrives, you shall have the dearest of daughters,
Such as the man desires whose bosom is govern'd by prudence
And I venture to think the good creature is fortunate also.
Yes, she will ever be grateful that I her father and mother
Have restored her in you, as sensible children would wish it.
But I will loiter no longer; I'll straightway harness the horses,
And conduct our friends on the traces of her whom I love so,
Leave the men to themselves and their own intuitive wisdom,
And be guided alone by their decision--I swear it,--
And not see the maiden again, until she my own is."
Then he left the house; meanwhile the others were eagerly
Settling many a point, and the weighty matter debating.

Hermann sped to the stable forthwith, where the spirited stallions
Tranquilly stood and with eagerness swallow'd the pure oats before them,
And the well-dried hay, which was cut from the best of their meadows.
Then in eager haste in their mouths the shining bits placed he,
Quickly drew the harness through the well-plated buckles,
And then fastend the long broad reins in proper position,
Led the horses out in the yard, where already the carriage,
Easily moved along by its pole, had been push'd by the servant.
Then they restrain'd the impetuous strength of the fast-moving horses,
Fastening both with neat-looking ropes to the bar of the carriage.
Hermann seized his whip, took his seat, and drove to the gateway.
When in the roomy carriage his friends had taken their places,
Swiftly he drove away, and left the pavement behind them,
Left behind the walls of the town and the clean-looking towers,
Thus sped Hermann along, till he reach'd the familiar highway,
Not delaying a moment, and galloping uphill and downhill.
When however at length the village steeple descried he,
And not far away lay the houses surrounded by gardens,
He began to think it was time to hold in the horses.

By the time-honour'd gloom of noble lime-trees o'er shadow'd,
Which for many a century past on the spot had been rooted,
Stood there a green and spreading grass-plot in front of the village,
Cover'd with turf, for the peasants and neighbouring townsmen a playground.
Scooped out under the trees, to no great depth, stood a fountain.
On descending the steps, some benches of stone might be seen there,
Ranged all around the spring, which ceaselessly well'd forth its waters,
Cleanly, enclosed by a low wall all round, and convenient to draw from.
Hermann then determined beneath the shadow his horses
With the carriage to stop. He did so, and spoke then as follows
"Now, my friends, get down, and go by yourselves to discover
Whether the maiden is worthy to have the hand which I offer.
I am convinced that she is; and you'll bring me no new or strange story:
Had I to manage alone, I would straightway go off to the village,
And in few words should my fate by the charming creature be settled.

Her you will easily recognize 'mongst all the rest of the people,
For her appearance is altogether unlike that of others.
But I will now describe the modest dress she is wearing:--
First a bodice red her well-arch'd bosom upraises,
Prettily tied, while black are the stays fitting closely around her.
Then the seams of the ruff she has carefully plaited and folded,
Which with modest grace, her chin so round is encircling.
Free and joyously rises her head with its elegant oval,
Strongly round bodkins of silver her back-hair is many times twisted
Her blue well-plaited gown begins from under her bodice.
And as she walks envelopes her well-turn'd ankles completely.
But I have one thing to say, and this must expressly entreat you:
Do not speak to the maiden, and let not your scheme be discover'd.
But inquire of others, and hearken to all that they tell you,
When you have learnt enough to satisfy father and mother,
Then return to me straight, and we'll settle future proceedings.
This is the plan which I have matured, while driving you hither."

Thus he spoke, and the friends forthwith went on to the village,
Where, in gardens and barns and houses, the multitude crowded;
All along the broad road the numberless carts were collected,
Men were feeding the lowing cattle and feeding the horses.
Women on every hedge the linen were carefully drying,
Whilst the children in glee were splashing about in the streamlet.
Forcing their way through the waggons, and past the men and the cattle,
Walk'd the ambassador spies, looking well to the righthand and lefthand,
Hoping somewhere to see the form of the well-described maiden;

But wherever they look'd, no trace of the girl they discover'd.

Presently denser became the crowd. Round some of the waggons.
Men in a passion were quarrelling, women also were screaming.
Then of a sudden approach'd an aged man with firm footstep
Marching straight up to the fighters; and forthwith was hush'd the contention,
When he bade them be still, and with fatherly earnestness threaten'd.
"Are we not yet," he exclaim'd, "by misfortune so knitted together,
As to have learnt at length the art of reciprocal patience
And toleration, though each cannot measure the actions of others?
Prosperous men indeed may quarrel! Will sorrow not teach you
How no longer as formerly you should quarrel with brethren?
Each should give way to each other, when treading the soil of the stranger,
And, as you hope for mercy yourselves, you should share your possessions."

Thus the man address'd them, and all were silent. In peaceful
Humour the reconciled men look'd after their cattle and waggons.
When the pastor heard the man discourse in this fashion,
And the foreign magistrate's peaceful nature discovered,
He approach'd him in turn, and used this significant language
"Truly, Father, when nations are living in days of good fortune,
Drawing their food from the earth, which gladly opens its treasures,
And its wish'd-for gifts each year and each month is renewing,
Then all matters go smoothly; each thinks himself far the wisest,
And the best, and so they exist by the side of each other,
And the most sensible man no better than others is reckon'd
For the world moves on, as if by itself and in silence.
But when distress unsettles our usual manner of living,
Pulls down each time-honour'd fabric, and roots up the seed in our gardens,
Drives the man and his wife far away from the home they delight in,
Hurries them off in confusion through days and nights full of anguish,
Ah! then look we around in search of the man who is wisest,
And no longer in vain he utters his words full of wisdom.
Tell me whether you be these fugitives' magistrate, Father,
Over whose minds you appear to possess such an influence soothing?
Aye, to-day I could deem you one of the leaders of old time,
Who through wastes and through deserts conducted the wandering people;
I could imagine 'twas Joshua I am addressing, or Moses."

Then with solemn looks the magistrate answer'd as follows
"Truly the present times resemble the strangest of old times,
Which are preserved in the pages of history, sacred or common.
He in these days who has lived to-day and yesterday only,
Many a year has lived, events so crowd on each other.

When I reflect back a little, a grey old age I could fancy
On my head to be lying, and yet my strength is still active.
Yes, we people in truth may liken ourselves to those others
Unto whom in a fiery bush appear'd, in a solemn
Moment, the Lord our God; in fire and clouds we behold him."

When the pastor would fain continue to speak on this subject,
And was anxious to learn the fate of the man and his party,
Quickly into his ear his companion secretly whisper'd
"Speak for a time with the magistrate, turning your talk on the maiden,
Whilst I wander about, endeav'ring to find her. Directly
I am successful, I'll join you again." Then nodded the pastor,
And the spy went to seek her, in barns and through hedges and gardens.

VI. KLIO.

THE AGE.

WHEN the pastor ask'd the foreign magistrate questions,
What the people had suffer'd, how long from their homes they had wander'd,
Then the man replied:--"By no means short are our sorrows,
For we have drunk the bitters of many a long year together,
All the more dreadful, because our fairest hopes have been blighted.
Who can deny that his heart beat wildly and high in his bosom
And that with purer pulses his breast more freely was throbbing,
When the newborn sun first rose in the whole of its glory,
When we heard of the right of man, to have all things in common,
Heard of noble Equality, and of inspiriting Freedom!
Each man then hoped to attain new life for himself, and the fetters
Which had encircled many a land appear'd to be broken,
Fetters held by the hands of sloth and selfish indulgence.
Did not all nations turn their gaze, in those days of emotion,
Tow'rds the world's capital, which so many a long year had been so,
And then more than ever deserved a name so distinguish'd?
Were not the men, who first proclaim'd so noble a message,
Names that are worthy to rank with the highest the sun ever shone on,
Did not each give to mankind his courage and genius and language?

"And we also, as neighbours, at first were warmly excited.
Presently after began the war, and the train of arm'd Frenchmen
Nearer approach'd; at first they appear'd to bring with them friendship,
And they brought it in fact; for all their souls were exalted.
And the gay trees of liberty ev'rywhere gladly they planted,
Promising unto each his own, and the government long'd for.

Greatly at this was youth, and greatly old age was delighted,
And the joyous dance began round the newly-raised standards.
In this manner the overpowering Frenchmen soon conquer'd
First the minds of the men, with their fiery lively proceedings,
Then the hearts of the women, with irresistible graces.
Even the strain of the war, with its many demands, seem'd but trifling,
For before our eyes the distance by hope was illumined,
Luring our gaze far ahead into paths now first open'd before us.
"O how joyful the time, when with his bride the glad bridegroom
Whirls in the dance, awaiting the day that will join them for ever
But more glorious far was the time when the Highest of all things
Which man's mind can conceive, close by and attainable seemed.
Then were the tongues of all loosen'd, and words of wisdom and feeling
Not by greybeards alone, but by men and by striplings were utter'd.

"But the heavens soon clouded became. For the sake of the mast'ry
Strove a contemptible crew, unfit to accomplish good actions.
Then they murder'd each other, and took to oppressing their new-found
Neighbours and brothers, and sent on missions whole herds of selfÄseekers
And the superiors took to carousing and robbing by wholesale,
And the inferiors down to the lowest caroused and robb'd also.
Nobody thought of aught else than having enough for tomorrow.
Terrible was the distress, and daily increased the oppression.
None the cry understood, that they of the day were the masters.
Then even temperate minds were attack'd by sorrow and fury;
Each one reflected, and swore to avenge all the injuries suffer'd,
And to atone for the hitter loss of hopes twice defrauded.
Presently Fortune declared herself on the side of the Germans,
And the French were compell'd to retreat by forced marches before them.
Ah! the sad fate of the war we then for the first time experienced.
For the victor is kind and humane, at least he appears so,
And he spares the man he has vanquish'd, as if he his own were,
When he employs him daily, and with his property helps him.
But the fugitive knows no law; he wards off death only,
And both quickly and recklessly all that he meets with, consumes he.
Then his mind becomes heated apace; and soon desperation
Fills his heart, and impels him to all kinds of criminal actions.
Nothing then holds he respected, he steals It. With furious longing
On the woman he rushes; his lust becomes awful to think of.
Death all around him he sees, his last minutes in cruelty spends he,
Wildly exulting in blood, and exulting in howls and in anguish.

"Then in the minds of our men arose a terrible yearning
That which was lost to avenge, and that which remain'd to defend still.

All of them seized upon arms, lured on by the fugitives' hurry,
By their pale faces, and by their shy, uncertain demeanour.
There was heard the sound of alarm-bells unceasingly ringing,
And the approach of danger restrain'd not their violent fury.
Soon into weapons were turn'd the implements peaceful of tillage,
And with dripping blood the scythe and the pitchfork were cover'd.
Every foeman without distinction was ruthlessly slaughter'd,
Fury was ev'rywhere raging, and artful, cowardly weakness.
May I never again see men in such wretched confusion!
Even the raging wild beast is a better object to gaze on.
Ne'er let them speak of freedom, as if themselves they could govern!
All the evil which Law has driven farback in the corner
Seems to escape, as soon as the fetters which bound it are loosen'd."

"Excellent man," replied the pastor, with emphasis speaking
"If you're mistaken in man, 'tis not for me to reprove you.
Evil enough have you suffer'd indeed from his cruel proceedings!
Would you but look back, however, on days so laden with sorrow,
You would yourself confess how much that is good you have witness'd,
Much that is excellent, which remains conceald in the bossom
Till by danger 'tis stirr'd, and till necessity makes man
Show himself as an angel, a tutelar God unto others."

Then with a smile replied the worthy old magistrate, saying
"Your reminder is wise, like that which they give to the suff'rer
Who has had his dwelling burnt down, that under the ruins,
Gold and silver are lying, though melted and cover'd with ashes.
Little, indeed, it may be, and yet that little is precious,
And the poor man digs it up, and rejoices at finding the treasure.
Gladly, therefore, I turn my thoughts to those few worthy actions
Which my memory still is able to dwell on with pleasure.
Yes, I will not deny it, I saw late foemen uniting
So as to save the town from harm; I saw with devotion
Parents, children and friends impossible actions attempting,
Saw how the youth of a sudden became a man, how the greybeard
Once more was young, how the child as a stripling appear'd in a moment.
Aye, and the weaker sex, as people commonly call it,
Show'd itself brave and daring, with presence of mind all-unwonted.
Let me now, in the first place, describe a deed of rare merit
By a high-spirited girl accomplish'd, an excellent maiden,
Who in the great farmhouse remain'd behind with the servants,
When the whole of the men had departed, to fight with the strangers.
Well, there fell on the court a troop of vagabond scoundrels,
Plund'ring and forcing their way inside the rooms of the women.

Soon they cast their eyes on the forms of the grown-up fair maiden
And of the other dear girls, in age little more than mere children.
Hurried away by raging desire, unfeelingly rush'd they
On the trembling band, and on the high-spirited maiden.
But she instantly seized the sword from the side of a ruffian,
Hew'd him down to the ground; at her feet straight fell he, all bleeding,
Then with doughty strokes the maidens she bravely deliver'd.
Wounded four more of the robbers; with life, however, escaped they.
Then she lock'd up the court, and, arm'd still, waited for succour.

When the pastor heard the praise of the maiden thus utter'd
Feelings of hope for his friend forthwith arose in his bosom,
And he prepared to ask what had been the fate of the damsel,
Whether she, in the sorrowful flight, form'd one of the people?
At this moment, however, the druggist nimbly approach'd them,
Pull'd the sleeve of the pastor, and whisper'd to him as follows
"I have at last pick'd out the maiden from many a hundred
By her description! Pray come and judge for yourself with your own eyes;
Bring the magistrate with you, that we may learn the whole story."

So they turn'd themselves round; but the magistrate found himself summon'd
By his own followers, who had need of his presence and counsel.
But the pastor forthwith the druggist accompanied, till they
Came to a gap in the hedge, when the latter pointed with slyness,
"See you," exclaim'd he, "the maiden? The child's clothes she has been changing.
And I recognise well the old calico--also the cushion--
Cover of blue, which Hermann took in the bundle and gave her.
Quickly and well, of a truth, she has used the presents left with her.
These are evident proofs; and all the rest coincide too;
For a bodice red her well-arch'd bosom upraises,
Prettily tied, while black are the stays fitting close around her.
Then the seams of the ruff she has carefully plaited and folded,
Which, with modest grace, her chin so round is encircling;
Free and joyously rises her head, with its elegant oval,
Strongly round bodkins of silver her back-hair is many times twisted.
When she is sitting, we plainly see her noble proportions,
And the blue well-plaited gown which begins from close to her bosom,
And in rich folds descending, her well-turn'd ankles envelops.
'Tis she, beyond all doubt. So come, that we may examine
Whether she be both a good and a frugal and virtuous maiden."
Then the pastor rejoin'd, the sitting damsel inspecting
"That she enchanted the youth, I confess is no matter of wonder,
For she stands the test of the gaze of a man of experience.
Happy the person to whom Mother Nature the right face has given!

She recommends him at all times, he never appears as a stranger,
Each one gladly approaches, and each one beside him would linger,
If with his face is combined a pleasant and courteous demeanour.
Yes, I assure you the youth has indeed discover'd a maiden
Who the whole of the days of his life will enliven with gladness,
And with her womanly strength assist him at all times and truly.
Thus a perfect body preserves the soul also in pureness,
And a vigorous youth of a happy old age gives assurance.

After reflecting a little, the druggist made answer as follows:--
"Yet appearances oft are deceitful. I trust not the outside.
Often, indeed, have I found the truth of the proverb which tells us
Ere you share a bushel of salt with a new-found acquaintance,
Do not trust him too readily; time will make you more certain
How you and he will get on, and whether your friendship is lasting.
Let us then, in the first place, inquire amongst the good people
Unto whom the maiden is known, who can tell us about her."

"Well, of a truth I commend your prudence," the pastor continued
"Not for ourselves are we wooing! To woo for others is serious."
So they started to meet the worthy magistrate seeing
How in the course of his business he was ascending the main street.
And the wise pastor straightway address'd him with foresight as follows
"We, by-the-bye, have just seen a girl in the neighbouring garden
Under an apple-tree sitting, and clothes for the children preparing,
Made of worn calico, which for the purpose was doubtless presented.
We were pleased by her face; she appears to be one of the right sort.
Tell us, what know you about her? We ask from a laudable motive."

When the magistrate came to the garden and peep'd in, exclaimed he
"Well do I know her, in truth; for when I told you the story
Of that noble deed which was done by the maiden I spoke of,
How she seized on the sword, and defended herself, and the servants,
She the heroine was! You can see how active her nature.
But she's as good as she's strong; for her aged kinsman she tended
Until the time of his death, for he died overwhelm'd by affliction
At the distress of his town, and the danger his goods were exposed to.
Also with mute resignation she bore the grievous affliction
Of her betroth'd's sad death, a noble young man who, incited
By the first fire of noble thoughts to struggle for freedom,
Went himself to Paris, and soon found a terrible death there.
For, as at home, so there, he fought 'gainst intrigue and oppression."

Thus the magistrate spoke. The others departed and thanked him,

And the pastor produced a gold piece (the silver his purse held
He some hours before had with genuine kindness expended
When he saw the fugitives passing in sorrowful masses).

And to the magistrate handed it, saying:--" Divide it, I pray you,
'Mongst those who need it the most. May God give it prosperous increase."

But the man refused to accept it, and said:--"I assure you,
Many a dollar we've saved, and plenty of clothing and such things,
And I trust we may reach our homes before they are finish'd."

Then continued the pastor, the gold in his hand once more placing
"None should delay to give in days like the present, and no one
Ought to refuse to receive what is offer'd with liberal kindness.
No one can tell how long he will keep what in peace he possesses,
No one, how long he is doom'd in foreign countries to wander,
While he's deprived of the field and the garden by which he is nurtured."

"Bravo!" added in turn the druggist, with eagerness speaking
"Had I but money to spare in my pocket, you surely should have it,
Silver and gold alike; for your followers certainly need it.
Yet I'll not leave you without a present, if only to show you
My good will, and I hope you will take the will for the action."
Thus he spoke, and pull'd out by the strings the leather embroider'd
Pouch, in which he was wont his stock of tobacco to carry,
Daintily open'd and shared its contents--some two or three pipes' full.
"Small in truth is the gift," he added. The magistrate answered:
"Good tobacco is always a welcome present to trav'llers."
Then the druggist began his canister to praise very highly.
But the pastor drew him away, and the magistrate left them.
"Come, let us hasten!" exclaimed the sensible man, "for our young friend
Anxiously waits; without further delay let him hear the good tidings."

So they hasten'd and came, and found that the youngster was leaning
'Gainst his carriage under the lime-trees. The horses were pawing
Wildly the turf; he held them in check and stood there all pensive,
Silently gazing in front, and saw not his friends coming near him,
Till, as they came, they called him and gave him signals of triumph.
Some way off the druggist already began to address him,
But they approach'd the youth still nearer, and then the good pastor
Seized his hand and spoke and took the word from his comrade
"Friend, I wish you joy! Your eye so true and your true heart
Rightly have chosen! May you and the wife of your young days be happy!
She is full worthy of you; so come and turn around the carriage,

That we may reach without delay the end of the village,
So as to woo her, and shortly escort the dear creature home with us."
But the youth stood still, and without any token of pleasure
Heard the words of the envoy, though sounding consoling and heav'nly,
Deeply sigh'd and said:--"We came full speed in the carriage
And shall probably go back home ashamed and but slowly;
For, since I have been waiting care has fallen upon me,
Doubt and suspicion and all that a heart full of love is exposed to.
Do you suppose we have only to come, for the maiden to follow,
Just because we are rich, and she poor and wandering in exile?
Poverty, when undeserved, itself makes proud. The fair maiden
Seems to be active and frugal; the world she may claim as her portion.
Do you suppose that a woman of such great beauty and manners
Can have grown up without exciting love in man's bosom?
Do you suppose that her heart until now has to love been fast closed?
Do not drive thither in haste, for perchance to our shame and confusion
We shall have slowly to turn towards home the heads of our horses.
Yes, some youth, I fear me, possesses her heart, and already
She has doubtless promised her hand and her solemn troth plighted,
And I shall stand all ashamed before her, When making my offer."

Then the pastor proceeded to cheer him with words of good comfort,
But his companion broke in, in his usual talkative manner
"As things used to be, this embarrassment would not have happened,
When each matter was brought to a close in an orthodox fashion.
Then for their son themselves the bride the parents selected,
And a friend of the house was secretly call'd in the first place.
He was then quietly sent as a suitor to visit the parents
Of the selected bride; and, dress'd in his gayest apparel,
Went after dinner some Sunday to visit the excellent burgher,
And began by exchanging polite remarks on all subjects,
Cleverly turning and bending the talk in the proper direction.
After long beating about the bush, he flatter'd the daughter,
And spoke well of the man and the house that gave his commission.
Sensible people soon saw his drift, and the sensible envoy
Watch'd how the notion was taken, and then could explain himself farther.
If they declined the proposal, why then the refusal cost nothing,
But if all prosper'd, why then the suitor for ever thereafter
Play'd the first fiddle at every family feast and rejoicing.
For the married couple remember'd the whole of their lifetime
Whose was the skilful hand by which the marriage knot tied was.
All this now is chang'd, and with many an excellent custom
Has gone quite out of fashion. Each person woos for himself now.
Everyone now must bear the weight of a maiden's refusal

On his own shoulders, and stand all ashamed before her, if needs be."

"Let that be as it may," then answered the young man who scarcely
Heard what was said, and his mind had made up already in silence
"I will go myself, and out of the mouth of the maiden
Learn my own fate, for towards her I cherish the most trustful feelings
That any man ever cherish'd towards any woman whatever.
That which she says will be good and sensible,--this I am sure of.
If I am never to see her again, I must once more behold her,
And the ingenuous gaze of her black eyes must meet for the last time.
If to my heart I may clasp her never, her bosom and shoulders
I would once more see, which my arm so longs to encircle:
Once more the mouth I would see, from which one kiss and a Yes will
Make me happy for ever, a No for ever undo me.
But now leave me alone! Wait here no longer. Return you
Straight to my father and mother, in order to tell them in person
That their son was right, and that the maiden is worthy.
And so leave me alone! I myself shall return by the footpath
Over the hill by the pear-tree and then descend through the vineyard,
Which is the shortest way back. Oh may I soon with rejoicing
Take the beloved one home! But perchance all alone I must slink back
By that path to our house and tread it no more with a light heart."
Thus he spoke, and then placed the reins in the hands of the pastor,
Who, in a knowing way both the foaming horses restraining,
Nimbly mounted the carriage, and took the seat of the driver.

But you still delay'd, good cautious neighbour, and spoke thus
Friend, I will gladly entrust to you soul, and spirit, and mind too,
But my body and bones are not preserved in the best way
When the hand of a parson such worldly matters as reins grasps!"

But you smiled in return, you sensible pastor, replying
"Pray jump in, nor fear with both body and spirit to trust me,
For this hand to hold the reins has long been accustom'd,
And these eyes are train'd to turn the corner with prudence.
For we were wont to drive the carriage, when living at Strasburg,
At the time when with the young baron I went there, for daily,
Driven by me, through the echoing gateway thunder'd the carriage
By the dusty roads to distant meadows and lindens,
Through the crowds of the people who spend their lifetime in walking."

Partially comforted, then his neighbour mounted the carriage,
Sitting like one prepared to make a wise jump, if needs be,
And the stallions, eager to reach their stables, coursed homewards,

While beneath their powerful hoofs the dust rose in thick clouds.
Long there stood the youth, and saw the dust rise before him,
Saw the dust disperse; but still he stood there, unthinking.

VII. ERATO.

DOROTHEA.

As the man on a journey, who, just at the moment of sunset,
Fixes his gaze once more on the rapidly vanishing planet,
Then on the side of the rocks and in the dark thicket still sees he
Hov'ring its image; wherever he turns his looks, on in front still
Runs it, and glitters and wavers before him in colours all splendid,
So before Hermanns eyes did the beautiful form of the maiden
Softly move, and appear'd to follow the path through the cornfields.

But he roused himself up from his startling dream, and then slowly
Turn'd tow'rd the village his steps, and once more started,--for once more
Saw he the noble maiden's stately figure approaching.
Fixedly gazed he; it was no phantom in truth; she herself 'twas
In her hands by the handle she carried two pitchers,--one larger,
One of a smaller size, and nimbly walk'd to the fountain.
And he joyfully went to meet her; the sight of her gave him
Courage and strength, and so he address'd the surprised one as follows:--
"Do I find you again, brave maiden, engaged in assisting
Others so soon, and in giving refreshment to those who may need it?
Tell me why you have come all alone to the spring so far distant,
Whilst the rest are content with the water that's found in the village?
This one, indeed, special virtue possesses, and pleasant to drink is.
Is't for the sake of that sick one you come, whom you saved with such courage?"

Then the good maiden the youth in friendly fashion saluted,
Saying:--"Already my walk to the fountain is fully rewarded,
Since I have found the kind person who gave us so many good presents;
For the sight of a giver, like that of a gift, is refreshing.
Come and see for yourself the persons who tasted your kindness,
And receive the tranquil thanks of all you have aided.
But that you may know the reason why I have come here,
Water to draw at a spot where the spring is both pure and unceasing,
I must inform you that thoughtless men have disturb'd all the water
Found in the village, by carelessly letting the horses and oxen
Wade about in the spring which give the inhabitants water.
In the same manner, with all their washing and cleaning they've dirtied
All the troughs of the village, and all the fountains have sullied.

For each one of them only thinks how quickly and soon he
May supply his own wants, and cares not for those who come after."

Thus she spoke, and soon she arrived at the foot of the broad steps
With her companion, and both of them sat themselves down on the low wall
Round the spring. She bent herself over, to draw out the water,
He the other pitcher took up, and bent himself over,
And in the blue of the heavens they saw their figures reflected,
Waving, and nodding, and in the mirror their greetings exchanging.
"Now let me drink," exclaim'd the youth in accents of gladness.
And she gave him the pitcher. They then, like old friends, sat together,
Leaning against the vessels, when she address'd him as follows
"Say, why find I you here without your carriage and horses,
Far from the place where first I saw you. Pray how came you hither?"

Hermann thoughtfully gazed on the ground, but presently lifted
Calmly towards her his glances, and gazed on her face in kind fashion,
Feeling quite calm and composed. And yet with love to address her
Found he quite out of the question; for love from her eyes was not beaming,
But an intellect clear, which bade him use sensible language.
Soon he collected his thoughts, and quietly said to the maiden:--
"Let me speak, my child, and let me answer your questions.
"'Tis for your sake alone I have come,--why seek to conceal it?
For I happily live with two affectionate parents,
Whom I faithfully help to look after our house and possessions,
Being an only son, while numerous are our employments.
I look after the field work; the house is carefully managed
By my father; my mother the hostelry cheers and enlivens.
But you also have doubtless found out how greatly the servants,
Sometimes by fraud, and sometimes by levity, worry their mistress,
Constantly making her change them, and barter one fault for another.
Long has my mother, therefore, been wanting a girl in the household,
Who, not only with hand, but also with heart might assist her,
In the place of the daughter she lost, alas, prematurely.
Now when I saw you to-day near the carriage, so active and sprightly,
Saw the strength of your arm and the perfect health of your members,
When I heard your sensible words, I was struck with amazement,
And I hasten'd back home, deservedly praising the stranger
Both to my parents and friends. And now I come to inform you
What they desire, as I do. Forgive my stammering language!"

"Do not hesitate," said she, "to tell me the rest of your story
I have with gratitude felt that you have not sought to insult me.
Speak on boldly, I pray; your words shall never alarm me;

You would fain hire me now as maid to your father and mother,
To look after the house, which now is in excellent order.
And you think that in me you have found a qualified maiden,
One that is able to work, and not of a quarrelsome nature.
Your proposal was short, and short shall my answer be also
Yes! with you I will go, and the voice of my destiny follow.
I have fulfill'd my duty, and brought the lying-in woman
Back to her friends again, who all rejoice at her rescue.
Most of them now are together, the rest will presently join them.
All expect that they, in a few short days, will be able
Homewards to go; 'tis thus that exiles themselves love to flatter.
But I cannot deceive myself with hopes so delusive
In these sad days which promise still sadder days in the future
For all the bonds of the world are loosen'd, and nought can rejoin them,
Save that supreme necessity over our future impending.
If in the house of so worthy a man I can earn my own living,
Serving under the eye of his excellent wife, I will do so;
For a wandering girl bears not the best reputation.
Yes! with you I will go, as soon as I've taken the pitcher
Back to my friends, and received the blessing of those worthy people.
Come! you needs must see them, and from their hands shall receive me."

Joyfully heard the youth the willing maiden's decision,
Doubting whether he now had not better tell her the whole truth;
But it appear'd to him best to let her remain in her error,
First to take her home, and then for her love to entreat her.
Ah! but now he espied a golden ring on her finger,
And so let her speak, while he attentively listen'd:--

"Let us now return," she continued, "the custom is always
To admonish the maidens who tarry too long at the fountain,
Yet how delightful it is by the fast-flowing water to chatter!"
Then they both arose, and once more directed their glances
Into the fountain, and then a blissful longing came o'er them.

So from the ground by the handles she silently lifted the pitchers,
Mounted the steps of the well, and Hermann follow'd the loved one.
One of the pitchers he ask'd her to give him, thus sharing the burden.
"Leave it," she said, "the weight feels less when thus they are balanced;
And the master I've soon to obey, should not be my servant.
Gaze not so earnestly at me, as if my fate were still doubtfull!
Women should learn betimes to serve, according to station,
For by serving alone she attains at last to the mast'ry,
To the due influence which she ought to possess in the household.

Early the sister must learn to serve her brothers and parents,
And her life is ever a ceaseless going and coming,
Or a lifting and carrying, working and doing for others.
Well for her, if she finds no manner of life too offensive,
And if to her the hours of night and of day all the same are,
So that her work never seems too mean, her needle too pointed,
So that herself she forgets, and liveth only for others!
For as a mother in truth she needs the whole of the virtues,
When the suckling awakens the sick one, and nourishment calls for
From the exhausted parent, heaping cares upon suff'ring.
Twenty men together could not endure such a burden,
And they ought not,--and yet they gratefully ought to behold it."

Thus she spoke, and with her silent companion advanced she
Through the garden, until the floor of the granary reach'd they,
Where the sick woman lay, whom she left by her daughters attended,
Those dear rescued maidens, the types of innocent beauty.
Both of them enter'd the room, and from the other direction,
Holding a child in each hand, her friend, the magistrate, enter'd.
These had lately been lost for some time by the sorrowing mother,
But the old man had now found them out in the crowd of the people.
And they sprang in with joy, to greet their dearly-loved mother,
To rejoice in a brother, the playmate now seen for the first time!

Then on Dorothea they sprang, and greeted her warmly,
Asking for bread and fruit, but asking for drink before all things.
And they handed the water all round. The children first drank some,
Then the sick woman drank, with her daughters, the magistrate also.
All were refresh'd, and sounded the praise of the excellent water;
Mineral was it, and very reviving, and wholesome for drinking.

Then with a serious look continued the maiden, and spoke thus
Friends, to your mouths for the last time in truth I have lifted the pitcher,
And for the last time, alas, have moisten'd your lips with pure water.
But whenever in scorching heat your drink may refresh you,
And in the shade you enjoy repose and a fountain unsullied,
Then remember me, and all my friendly assistance,
Which I from love, and not from relationship merely have render'd.
All your kindness to me, as long as life lasts, I'll remember,
I unwillingly leave you; but each one is now to each other
Rather a burden than comfort. We all must shortly be scatter'd
Over a foreign land, unless to return we are able.
See, here stands the youth to whom for those gifts we're indebted,
All those clothes for the child, and all those acceptable viands.

Well, he has come, and is anxious that I to his house should go with him,
There as a servant to act to his rich and excellent parents,
And I have not refused him, for serving appears my vocation,
And to be served by others at home would seem like a burden.
So I'll go willingly with him; the youth appears to be prudent,
Thus will his parents be properly cared for, as rich people should be.
Therefore, now, farewell, my much-loved friend, and be joyful
In your living infant, who looks so healthily at you.
When you press him against your bosom, wrapp'd up in those colour'd
Swaddling-clothes, then remember the youth who so kindly bestow'd them,
And who in future will feed and clothe me also, your loved friend.
You too, excellent man," to the magistrate turning, she added
"Warmly I thank for so often acting the part of a father."

Then she knelt herself down before the lying-in patient,
Kiss'd the weeping woman, her whisper'd blessing receiving.
Meanwhile the worthy magistrate spoke to Hermann as follows
"You deserve, my friend to be counted amongst the good landlords
Who are anxious to manage their house through qualified people.
For I have often observed how cautiously men are accustom'd
Sheep and cattle and horses to watch, when buying or bart'ring
But a man, who's so useful, provided he's good and efficient,
And who does so much harm and mischief by treacherous dealings,
Him will people admit to their houses by chance and haphazard,
And too late find reason to rue an o'erhasty decision.
This you appear to understand, for a girl you have chosen
As your servant, and that of your parents, who thoroughly good is.
Treat her well, and as long as she finds the business suit her,
You will not miss your sister, your parents will miss not their daughter."

Other persons now enter'd, the patient's nearest relations,
Many articles bringing, and better lodgings announcing.
All were inform'd of the maiden's decision, and warmly bless'd Hermann,
Both with significant looks, and also with grateful expressions,
And one secretly whispered into the ear of another
"If the master should turn to a bridegroom, her home is provided."
Hermann then presently took her hand, and address'd her as follows
"Let us be going; the day is declining, and far off the village."
Then the women, with lively expressions, embraced Dorothea;
Hermann drew her away; they still continued to greet her.
Next the children, with screams and terrible crying attack'd her,
Pulling her clothes, their second mother refusing to part from.
But first one of the women, and then another rebuked them
"Children, hush! to the town she is going, intending to bring you

Plenty of gingerbread back, which your brother already had order'd,
From the confectioner, when the stork was passing there lately,
And she'll soon return, with papers prettily gilded."

So at length the children released her; but scarcely could Hermann
Tear her from their embraces and distant-signalling kerchiefs.

VIII. MELPOMENE.

HERMANN AND DOROTHEA.

So tow'rd the sun, now fast sinking to rest, the two walk'd together,
Whilst he veil'd himself deep in clouds which thunder portended.
Out-of his veil now here, now there, with fiery glances
Beaming over the plain with rays foreboding and lurid.
"May this threatening weather," said Hermann, "not bring to us shortly
Hail and violent rain, for well does the harvest now promise."
And they both rejoiced in the corn so lofty and waving,
Well nigh reaching the heads of the two tall figures that walk'd there.
Then the maiden spoke to her friendly leader as follows
"Generous youth, to whom I shall owe a kind destiny shortly,
Shelter and home, when so many poor exiles must weather the tempest,
In the first place tell me all about your good parents,
Whom I intend to serve with all my soul from hence-forward;
Knowing one's master, 'tis easier far to give satisfaction,
By rememb'ring the things which he deems of the highest importance,
And on which he has set his heart with the greatest decision.
Tell me, then, how best I can win your father and mother."

Then the good and sensible youth made answer as follows
"You are indeed quite right, my kind and excellent maiden,
To begin by asking about the tastes of my parents!
For I have hitherto striven in vain to satisfy Father,
When I look'd after the inn, as well as my regular duty,
Working early and late in the field, and tending the vineyard.
Mother indeed was contented; she knew how to value my efforts;
And she will certainly hold you to be an excellent maiden,
If you take care of the house, as though the dwelling your own were.
But my father's unlike her; he's fond of outward appearance.
Gentle maiden, deem me not cold and void of all feeling,
If I disclose my father's nature to you, who're a stranger.
Yes, such words have never before escaped, I assure von
Out of my mouth, which is little accustom'd to babble and chatter;
But you have managed to worm all my secrets from out of my bosom.

Well, my worthy father the graces of life holds in honour,
Wishes for outward signs of love, as well as of rev'rence,
And would doubtless be satisfied with an inferior servant
Who understood this fancy, and hate a better, who did not."

Cheerfully she replied, with gentle movement increasing
Through the darkening path the speed at which she was walking:
I in truth shall hope to satisfy both of your parents,
For your mother's character my own nature resembles,
And to external graces have I from my youth been accustom'd.
Our old neighbours, the French, in their earlier days laid much stress on
Courteous demeanour; 'twas common alike to nobles and burghers,
And to peasants, and each enjoin'd it on all his acquaintance.
in the same way, on the side of the Germans, the children were train'd up
Every morning, with plenty of kissing of hands and of curtsies,
To salute their parents, and always to act with politeness.
All that I have learnt, and all I have practised since childhood,
All that comes from my heart,--I will practise it all with the old man.
But on what terms shall I--I scarcely dare ask such a question,--
Be with yourself, the only son, and hereafter my master?"

Thus she spoke, and at that moment they came to the peartree.
Down from the skies the moon at her full was shining in glory;
Night had arrived, and the last pale gleam of the sunset had vanish'd.
So before them were lying, in masses all heap'd up together,
Lights as clear as the day, and shadows of night and of darkness.
And the friendly question was heard by Hermann with pleasure,
Under the shade of the noble tree at the spot which he loved so
Which that day had witness'd his tears at the fate of the exile.
And whilst they sat themselves down, to take a little repose there,
Thus the loving youth spoke, whilst he seized the hand of the maiden
"Let your heart give the answer, and always obey what it tells you!"
But he ventured to say no more, however propitious
Was the moment; he feard that a No would be her sole answer,
Ah! and he felt the ring on her finger, that sorrowful token.
So by the side of each other they quietly sat and in silence,
But the maiden began to speak, and said, "How delightful
Is the light of the moon! The clearness of day it resembles.
Yonder I see in the town the houses and courtyards quite plainly,
In the gable a window; methinks all the panes I can reckon."

"That which you see," replied the youth, who spoke with an effort,
"That is our house down to which I now am about to conduct you,
And that window yonder belongs to my room in the attic,

Which will probably soon be yours, as we're making great changes.
All these fields are ours, and ripe for the harvest to-morrow;
Here in the shade we are wont to rest, enjoying our meal-time.
But let us now descend across the vineyard and garden,
For observe how the threatening storm is hitherward rolling,
Lightening first, and then eclipsing the beautiful full moon."
So the pair arose, and wauder'd down by the corn-field,

Through the powerful corn, in the nightly clearness rejoicing;
And they reach'd the vineyard, and through its dark shadows proceeded.
So he guided her down the numerous tiers of the flat stones
Which, in an unhewn state, served as steps to the walk through the foliage.
Slowly she descended, and placed her hands on his shoulders;
And, with a quivering light, the moon through the foliage o'erlook'd them,
Till by storm-clouds envelop'd, she left the couple in darkness.
Then the strong youth supported the maiden, who on him was leaning;
She, however, not knowing the path, or observing the rough steps,
Slipp'd as she walk'd, her foot gave way, and she well nigh was falling.
Hastily held out his arm the youth with nimbleness thoughtful,
And held up his beloved one; she gently sank on his shoulders,
Breast was press'd against breast, and cheek against cheek, and so stood he
Fix'd like a marble statue, restrained by a firm resolution;
He embraced her no closer, thoughall her weight he supported;
So he felt his noble burden, the warmth of her bosom,
And her balmy breath, against his warm lips exhaling,
Bearing with manly feelings the woman's heroical greatness.

But she conceal'd the pain which she felt, and jestingly spoke thus
"It betokens misfortune,--so scrupulous people inform us,--
For the foot to give way on entering a house, near the threshold.
I should have wish'd, in truth, for a sign of some happier omen!
Let us tarry a little, for fear your parents should blame you
For their limping servant, and you should be thought a bad landlord."

IX. URANIA.

CONCLUSION.

O YE Muses, who gladly favour a love that is heartfelt,
Who on his way the excellent youth have hitherto guided,
Who have press'd the maid to his bosom before their betrothal,
Help still further to perfect the bonds of a couple so loving,
Drive away the clouds which over their happiness hover!
But begin by saying what now in the house has been passing.

For the third time the mother impatiently enter'd the chamber
Where the men were sitting, which she had anxiously quitted,
Speaking of the approaching storm, and the loss of the moon's light,
Then of her son's long absence, and all the perils that night brings.
Strongly she censured their friends for having so soon left the youngster,
For not even addressing the maiden, or seeking to woo her.

"Make not the worst of the mischief," the father peevishly answer'd;
"For you see we are waiting ourselves, expecting the issue."

But the neighbour sat still, and calmly address'd them as follows:--
"In uneasy moments like these, I always feel grateful
To my late father, who when I was young all seeds of impatience
In my mind uprooted, and left no fragment remaining,
And I learnt how to wait, as well as the best of the wise men.
"Tell us what legerdemain he employ'd," the pastor made answer.
"I will gladly inform you, and each one may gain by the lesson,"
Answer'd the neighbour. "When I was a boy, I was standing one Sunday
In a state of impatience, eagerly waiting the carriage
Which was to carry us out to the fountain under the lime-trees;
But it came not; I ran like a weasel now hither, now thither,
Up and down the stairs, and from the door to the window;
Both my hands were prickling, I scratch'd away at the tables,
Stamping and trotting about, and scarcely refrain'd I from crying.
All this the calm man composedly saw; but finally when I
Carried my folly too far, by the arm he quietly took me,
Led me up to the window, and used this significant language
'See you up yonder the joiner's workshop, now closed for the Sunday?
'Twill be re-open'd to-morrow, and plane and saw will be working.
Thus will the busy hours be pass'd from morning till evening.
But remember this: the rimming will soon be arriving,
When the master, together with all his men, will be busy
In preparing and finishing quickly and deftly your coffin,
And they will carefully bring over here that house made of boards, which
Will at length receive the patient as well as impatient,
And which is destined to carry a roof that's unpleasantly heavy.
All that he mention'd I forthwith saw taking place in my mind's eye,
Saw the boards join'd together, and saw the black cover made ready,
Patiently then I sat, and meekly awaited the carriage.
And I always think of the coffin whenever I see men
Running about in a state of doubtful and wild expectation."

Smilingly answered the pastor:--"Death's stirring image is neither

Unto the wise a cause of alarm,--or an end to the pious.
Back into life it urges the former, and teaches him action,
And, for the weal of the latter, it strengthens his hope in affliction.
Death is a giver of life unto both. Your father did wrongly
When to the sensitive boy he pointed out death in its own form.
Unto the youth should be shown the worth of a noble and ripen'd
Age, and unto the old man, youth, that both may rejoice in
The eternal circle, and life may in life be made perfect!"

Here the door was open'd. The handsome couple appear'd there,
And the friends were amazed, the loving parents astonish'd
At the form of the bride, the form of the bridegroom resembling.
Yes! the door appear'd too small to admit the tall figures
Which now cross'd the threshold, in company walking together.
To his parents Hermann presented her, hastily saying:--
"Here is a maiden just of the sort you are wishing to have here,
Welcome her kindly, dear father! she fully deserves it, and you too,
Mother dear, ask her questions as to her housekeeping knowledge,
That you may see how well she deserves to form one of our party."
Then he hastily took on one side the excellent pastor,
Saying:--" Kind sir, I entreat you to help me out of this trouble
Quickly, and loosen the knot, whose unravelling I am so dreading;
For I have not ventured to woo as my bride the fair maiden,
But she believes she's to be a maid in the house, and I fear me
She will in anger depart, as soon as we talk about marriage.
But it must be decided at once! no longer in error
Shall she remain, and I no longer this doubt can put up with.
Hasten and once more exhibit that wisdom we all hold in honour."
So the pastor forthwith turn'd round to the rest of the party,
But the maiden's soul was, unhappily, troubled already
By the talk of the father, who just had address'd her as follows,
Speaking good humour'dly, and in accents pleasant and lively
"Yes, I'm well satisfied, child! I joyfully see that my son has
Just as good taste as his father, who in his younger days show'd it,
Always leading the fairest one out in the dance, and then lastly
Taking the fairest one home as his wife--'twas your dear little mother!
For by the bride whom a man selects, we may easily gather
What kind of spirit his is, and whether he knows his own value.
But you will surely need but a short time to form your decision,
For I verily think he will find it full easy to follow."
Hermann but partially heard the words; the whole of his members
Inwardly quivered, and all the circle were suddenly silent.

But the excellent maiden, by words of such irony wounded,

(As she esteem'd them to be) and deeply distress'd in her spirit,
Stood, while a passing flush from her cheeks as far as her neck was
Spreading, but she restrain'd herself, and collected her thoughts soon;
Then to the old man she said, not fully concealing her sorrow
"Truly I was not prepared by your son for such a reception,
When he described his father's nature,--that excellent burgher,
And I know I am standing before you, a person of culture,
Who behaves himself wisely to all, in a suitable manner.
But it would seem that you feel not pity enough for the poor thing
Who has just cross'd your threshold, prepared to enter your service
Else you would not seek to point out, with ridicule bitter,
How far removed my lot from your son's and that of yourself is.
True, with a little bundle, and poor, I have enter'd your dwelling,
Which it is the owner's delight to furnish with all things.
But I know myself well, and feel the whole situation.
Is it generous thus to greet me with language so jeering,
Which was well nigh expelled me the house, when just on the threshold?"

Hermann uneasily moved about, and signed to the pastor
To interpose without delay, and clear up the error.
Quickly the wise man advanced to the spot, and witness'd the maiden's
Silent vexation and tearful eyes and scarce-restrain'd sorrow.
Then his spirit advised him to solve not at once the confusion,
But, on the contrary, prove the excited mind of the maiden.
So, in words framed to try her, the pastor address'd her as follows:--
"Surely, my foreign maiden, you did not fully consider,
When you made up your mind to serve a stranger so quickly,
What it really is to enter the house of a master;
For a shake of the hand decides your fate for a twelvemonth,
And a single word Yes to much endurance will bind you.
But the worst part of the service is not the wearisome habits,
Nor the bitter toil of the work, which seems never-ending;
For the active freeman works hard as well as the servant.
But to suffer the whims of the master, who blames you unjustly,
Or who calls for this and for that, not knowing his own mind,
And the mistress's violence, always so easily kindled,
With the children's rough and supercilious bad manners,--
This is indeed hard to bear, whilst still fulfilling your duties
Promptly and actively, never becoming morose or ill-natured;
Yet for such work you appear little fit, for already the father's
Jokes have offended you deeply; yet nothing more commonly happens
Than to tease a maiden about her liking a youngster."
Thus he spoke, and the maiden felt the weight of his language,
And no more restrain'd herself; mightily all her emotions

Show'd themselves, her bosom heaved, and a deep sigh escaped her,
And whilst shedding burning tears, she answer'd as follows:--
"Ne'er does the clever man, who seeks to advise us in sorrow,
Think how little his chilling words our hearts can deliver
From the pangs which an unseen destiny fastens upon us.
You are happy and merry. How then should a jest ever wound you?
But the slightest touch gives torture to those who are suff'ring.
Even dissimulation would nothing avail me at present.
Let me at once disclose what later would deepen my sorrow,
And consign me perchance to agony mute and consuming.
Let me depart forthwith! No more in this house dare I linger;
I must hence and away, and look once more for my poor friends
Whom I left in distress, when seeking to better my fortunes.
This is my firm resolve; and now I may properly tell you
That which had else been buried for many a year in my bosom.
Yes, the father's jest has wounded me deeply, I own it,
Not that I'm proud and touchy, as ill becometh a servant,
But because in truth in my heart a feeling has risen
For the youth, who to-day has fill'd the part of my Saviour.
For when first in the road he left me, his image remain'd still
Firmly fix'd in my mind; and I thought of the fortunate maiden
Whom, as his betroth'd one, he cherish'd perchance in his bosom.
And when I found him again at the well, the sight of him charm'd me
Just as if I had-seen an angel descending from heaven.
And I follow'd him willingly, when as a servant he sought me,
But by my heart in truth I was flatter'd (I need must confess it),
As I hitherward came, that I might possibly win him,
If I became in the house an indispensable pillar.
But, alas, I now see the dangers I well nigh fell into,
When I bethought me of living so near a silently-loved one.
Now for the first time I feel how far removed a poor maiden
Is from a richer youth, however clever she may be.
I have told you all this, that you my heart may mistake not,
Which an event that in thought I foreshadow has wounded already.
For I must have expected, my secret wishes concealing,
That, ere much time had elapsed, I should see him bringing his bride home.
And how then could I have endured my hidden affliction!
Happily I am warn'd in time, and out of my bosom
Has my secret escaped, whilst curable still is the evil.
But no more of the subject! I now must tarry no longer
In this house, where I now am standing in pain and confusion,
All my foolish hopes and my feelings freely confessing.
Not the night which, with sinking clouds, is spreading around us,
Not the rolling thunder (I hear it already) shall stop me,

Not the falling rain, which outside is descending in torrents,
Not the blustering storm. All this I had to encounter
In that sorrowful flight, while the enemy follow'd behind Us.
And once more I go on my way, as I long have been wont to,
Seized by the whirlpool of time, and parted from all that I care for.
So farewell! I'll tarry no longer. My fate is accomplish'd!"

Thus she spoke, and towards the door she hastily turn'd her,
Holding under her arm the bundle she brought when arriving.
But the mother seized by both of her arms the fair maiden,
Clasping her round the body, and cried with surprise and amazement
"Say, what signifies this? These fruitless tears, what denote they?
No, I'll not leave you alone! You're surely my dear son's betroth'd one!"
But the father stood still, and show'd a great deal of reluctance,
Stared at the weeping girl, and peevishly spoke then as follows
"This, then, is all the indulgence my friends are willing to give me,
That at the close of the day the most unpleasant thing happens!
For there is nothing I hate so much as the tears of a woman,
And their passionate cries, set up with such heat and excitement,
Which a little plain sense would show to be utterly needless.
Truly, I find the sight of these whimsical doings a nuisance.
Matters must shift for themselves; as for me, I think it is bed-time."
So he quickly turn'd round, and hasten'd to go to the chamber
Where the marriage-bed stood, in which he slept for the most part.
But his son held him back, and spoke in words of entreaty
"Father, don't go in a hurry, and be not amniote with the maiden!
I alone have to bear the blame of all this confusion,
Which our friend has increased by his unexpected dissembling.
Speak then, honour'd Sir! for to you the affair I confided;
Heap not up pain and annoyance, but rather complete the whole matter;
For I surely in future should not respect you so highly,
If you play practical jokes, instead of displaying true wisdom."

Thereupon the worthy pastor smilingly answer'd
"What kind of wisdom could have extracted the charming confession
Of this good maiden, and so have reveal'd all her character to us?
Is not your care converted at once to pleasure and rapture?
Speak out, then, for yourself! Why need explanations from others
Hermann then stepped forward, and gently address'd her as follows
"Do not repent of your tears, nor yet of your passing affliction;
For they perfect my happiness; yours too, I fain would consider.
I came not to the fountain, to hire so noble a maiden
As a servant, I came to seek to win you affections.
But, alas! my timid gaze had not strength to discover

Your heart's leanings; it saw in your eye but a friendly expression,
When you greeted it out of the tranquil fountain's bright mirror.
Merely to bring you home, made half of my happiness certain
But you now make it complete! May every blessing be yours, then!"
Then the maiden look'd on the youth with heartfelt emotion,
And avoided not kiss or embrace, the summit of rapture,
When they also are to the loving the long-wish'd-for pledges
Of approaching bliss in a life which now seems to them endless.
Then the pastor told the others the whole of the story;
But the maiden came and gracefully bent o'er the father,
Kissing the while his hand, which he to draw back attempted.
And she said:--" I am sure that you will forgive the surprised one,
First for her tears of sorrow, and then for her tears of true rapture.
O forgive the emotions by which they both have been prompted,
And let me fully enjoy the bliss that has now been vouchsafed me!
Let the first vexation, which my confusion gave rise to,
Also be the last! The loving service which lately
Was by the servant promised, shall now by the daughter be render'd."

And the father, his tears concealing, straightway embraced her;
Lovingly came the mother in turn, and heartily kiss'd her,
Warmly shaking her hand; and silently wept they together.
Then in a hasty manner, the good and sensible pastor
Seized the hand of the father, his wedding-ring off from his finger
Drawing (not easily though; so plump was the member that held it)
Then he took the mother's ring, and betroth'd the two children,
Saying:--"Once more may it be these golden hoops' destination
Firmly to fasten a bond altogether resembling the old one!
For this youth is deeply imbued with love for the maiden,
And the maiden confesses that she for the youth has a liking.
Therefore, I now betroth you, and wish you all blessings hereafter,
With the parents' consent, and with our friend here as a witness."

And the neighbour bent forward, and added his own benediction;
But when the clergyman placed the gold ring on the hand of the maiden,
He with astonishment saw the one which already was on it,
And which Hermann before at the fountain had anxiously noticed.
Whereupon he spoke in words at once friendly and jesting
"What! You are twice engaging yourself? I hope that the first one
May not appear at the altar, unkindly forbidding the banns there!"

But she said in reply:--"O let me devote but one moment
To this mournful remembrance! For well did the good youth deserve it,
Who, when departing, presented the ring, but never return'd home.

All was by him foreseen, when freedom's love of a sudden,
And a desire to play his part in the new-found Existence,
Drove him to go to Paris, where prison and death were his portion.
'Farewell,' said he, 'I go; for all things on earth are in motion
At this moment, and all things appear in a state of disunion.
Fundamental laws in the steadiest countries are loosen'd,
And possessions are parted from those who used to possess them,
Friends are parted from friends, and love is parted from love too.
I now leave you here, and whether I ever shall see you
Here again,--who can tell? Perchance these words will our last be.
Man is a stranger here upon earth, the proverb informs us;
Every person has now become more a stranger than ever.
Ours the soil is no longer; our treasures are fast flying from us;
All the sacred old vessels of gold and silver are melted,
All is moving, as though the old-fashion'd world would roll backwards
Into chaos and night, in order anew to be fashion'd.
You of my heart have possession, and if we shall ever here-after
Meet again over the wreck of the world, it will be as new creatures,
All remodell'd and free and independent of fortune;
For what fetters can bind down those who survive such a period!
But if we are destined not to escape from these dangers,
If we are never again to embrace each other with raptures
O then fondly keep in your thoughts my hovering image,
That you may be prepared with like courage for good and ill fortune!
If a new home or a new alliance should chance to allure you,
Then enjoy with thanks whatever your destiny offers,
Purely loving the loving, and grateful to him who thus loves you.
But remember always to tread with a circumspect footstep,
For the fresh pangs of a second loss will behind you be lurking.
Deem each day as sacred; but value not life any higher
Than any other possession, for all possessions are fleeting.'
Thus he spoke; and the noble youth and I parted for ever:
Meanwhile I ev'rything lost, and a thousand times thought of his warning.
Once more I think of his words, now that love is sweetly preparing
Happiness for me anew, and the brightest of hopes is unfolding.
Pardon me, dearest friend, for trembling e'en at the moment
When I am clasping your arm! For thus, on first landing, the sailor
Fancies that even the solid ground is shaking beneath him."

Thus she spoke, and she placed the rings by the side of each other.
But the bridegroom answer'd, with noble and manly emotion
"All the firmer, amidst the universal disruption,
Be, Dorothea, our union! We'll show ourselves bold and enduring,
Firmly hold our own, and firmly retain our possessions.

For the man who in wav'ring times is inclined to be wav'ring
Only increases the evil, and spreads it wider and wider;
But the man of firm decision the universe fashions.
'Tis not becoming the Germans to further this fearful commotion,
And in addition to waver uncertainly hither and thither.
'This is our own!' we ought to say, and so to maintain it!
For the world will ever applaud those resolute nations
Who for God and the Law, their wives, and parents, and children
Struggle, and fall when contending against the foeman together.
You are mine; and now what is mine, is mine more than ever.
Not with anxiety will I preserve it, or timidly use it,
But with courage and strength. And if the enemy threaten
Now or hereafter, I'll hold myself ready, and reach down my weapons.
If I know that the house and my parents by you are protected,
I shall expose my breast to the enemy, void of all terror;
And if all others thought thus, then might against might should be measured,
And in the early prospect of peace we should all be rejoicing."

       1796Ä7.

WEST-EASTERN DIVAN.

Who the song would understand,
Needs must seek the song's own land.
Who the minstrel understand,
Needs must seek the minstrel's land.

THE Poems comprised in this collection are written in the
Persian style, and are greatly admired by Oriental scholars, for
the truthfulness with which the Eastern spirit of poetry is
reproduced by the Western minstrel. They were chiefly composed
between the years 1814 and 1819, and first given to the world in
the latter year. Of the twelve books into which they are divided,
that of Suleika will probably be considered the best, from the
many graceful love-songs which it contains. The following is
Hanoi's account of the Divan, and may well serve as a substitute
for anything I could say respecting it:--

It contains opinions and sentiments on the East, expressed in a
series of rich cantos and stanzas full of sweetness and spirit,
and all this as enchanting as a harem emitting the most delicious

and rare perfumes, and blooming with exquisitely-lovely nymphs with eyebrows painted black, eyes piercing as those of the antelope, arms white as alabaster, and of the most graceful and perfectly-formed shapes, while the heart of the reader beats and grows faint, as did that of the happy Gaspard Debaran, the clown, who, when on the highest step of his ladder, was enabled to peep into the Seraglio of Constantinople--that recess concealed from the inspection of man. Sometimes also the reader may imagine himself indolently stretched on a carpet of Persian softness, luxuriously smoking the yellow tobacco of Turkistan through a long tube of jessamine and amber, while a black slave fans him with a fan of peacock's feathers, and a little boy presents him with a cup of genuine Mocha. Goethe has put these enchanting and voluptuous customs into poetry, and his verses are so perfect, so harmonious, so tasteful, so soft, that it seems really surprising that he should ever have been able to have brought the German language to this state of suppleness. The charm of the book is inexplicable; it is a votive nosegay sent from the West to the East, composed of the most precious and curious plants: red roses, hortensias like the breast of a spotless maiden, purple digitalis like the long finger of a man, fantastically formed ranunculi, and in the midst of all, silent and tastefully concealed, a tuft of German violets. This nosegay signifies that the West is tired of thin and icy-cold spirituality, and seeks warmth in the strong and healthy bosom of the East."

Translations are here given of upwards of sixty of the best Poems embraced in the Divan, the number in the original exceeding two hundred.

I. MORGAGNI NAME.

BOOK OF THE MINSTREL.

TALISMANS.

GOD is of the east possess'd,
God is ruler of the west;
North and south alike, each land
Rests within His gentle hand.

HE, the only righteous one,
Wills that right to each be done.

'Mongst His hundred titles, then,
Highest praised be this!--Amen.

ERROR seeketh to deceive me,
Thou art able to retrieve me;
Both in action and in song
Keep my course from going wrong.

   1819.*

THE FOUR FAVOURS.

THAT Arabs through the realms of space

May wander on, light-hearted,
Great Allah hath, to all their race,

Four favours meet imparted.

The turban first--that ornament

All regal crowns excelling;
A light and ever-shifting tent,

Wherein to make our dwelling;

A sword, which, more than rocks and walls

Doth shield us, brightly glistening;
A song that profits and enthrall,

For which the maids are list'ning!

   1814.

DISCORD.

WHEN by the brook his strain

Cupid is fluting,
And on the neighboring plain

Mayors disputing,
There turns the ear ere long,

Loving and tender,
Yet to the noise a song

Soon must surrender.
Loud then the flute-notes glad

Sound 'mid war's thunder;
If I grow raving mad,

Is it a wonder?
Flutes sing and trumpets bray,

Waxing yet stronger;
If, then, my senses stray,

Wonder no longer.

1814.

SONG AND STRUCTURE.

LET the Greek his plastic clay

Mould in human fashion,
While his own creation may

Wake his glowing passion;

But it is our joy to court

Great Euphrates' torrent,
Here and there at will to sport

In the Wat'ry current.

Quench'd I thus my spirit's flame,

Songs had soon resounded;
Water drawn by bards whose fame

Pure is, may be rounded.+

1819.*

(+ This oriental belief in the power of the pure to roll-up water into a crystal hail is made the foundation of the Interesting Pariah Legend, that will be found elsewhere amongst the Ballads.)

II. HAFIS NAME.

BOOK OF HAFIS.

SPIRIT let us bridegroom call,

And the word the bride;
Known this wedding is to all

Who have Hafis tried.

THE UNLIMITED.

THAT thou can't never end, doth make thee great,
And that thou ne'er beginnest, is thy fate.
Thy song is changeful as yon starry frame,
End and beginning evermore the same;
And what the middle bringeth, but contains
What was at first, and what at last remains.
Thou art of joy the true and minstrel-source,
From thee pours wave on wave with ceaseless force.
A mouth that's aye prepared to kiss,

A breast whence flows a loving song,
A throat that finds no draught amiss,

An open heart that knows no wrong.

And what though all the world should sink!

Hafis, with thee, alone with thee

Will I contend! joy, misery,

The portion of us twain shall be;
Like thee to love, like thee to drink,--

This be my pride,--this, life to me!

Now, Song, with thine own fire be sung,--
For thou art older, thou more young!

          1817.*

TO HAFIS.

HAFIS, straight to equal thee,

One would strive in vain;
Though a ship with majesty

Cleaves the foaming main,
Feels its sails swell haughtily

As it onward hies
Crush'd by ocean's stern decree,

Wrecked it straightway lies.
Tow'rd thee, songs, light, graceful, free,

Mount with cooling gush;
Then their glow consumeth me,

As like fire they rush.
Yet a thought with ecstasy

Hath my courage moved;
In the land of melody

I have lived and loved.

          1815.

III. USCHK NAME.

BOOK OF LOVE.

THE TYPES.

LIST, and in memory bear
These six fond loving pair.
Love, when aroused, kept true
Rustan and Rad!
Strangers approach from far
Joseph and Suleika;
Love, void of hope, is in
Ferhad and Schirin.
Born for each other are
Medschnun and Lily;
Loving, though old and grey,
Dschemil saw Boteinah.
Love's sweet caprice anon,
Brown maid + and Solomon!
If thou dost mark them well,
Stronger thy love will swell.

   1817.*
(+ Brown maid is the Queen of Sheba.)

ONE PAIR MORE.

LOVE is indeed a glorious prize!
What fairer guerdon meets our eyes?--
Though neither wealth nor power are thine,
A very hero thou dost shine.
As of the prophet, they will tell,
Wamik and Asia's tale as well.--
They'll tell not of them,--they'll but give
Their names, which now are all that live.
The deeds they did, the toils they proved
No mortal knows! But that they loved
This know we. Here's the story true
Of Wamik and of Asia too.

1827.*

LOVE's torments sought a place of rest,

Where all might drear and lonely be;
They found ere long my desert breast,

And nestled in its vacancy.

1827.*

IV. TEFKIR NAME.

BOOK OF CONTEMPLATION.

FIVE THINGS.

WHAT makes time short to me?

Activity!
What makes it long and spiritless?

'Tis idleness!
What brings us to debt?

To delay and forget!
What makes us succeed?

Decision with speed
How to fame to ascend?

Oneself to defend!

1814

FOR woman due allowance make!

Form'd of a crooked rib was she,--

By Heaven she could not straightened be.
Attempt to bend her, and she'll break;
If left alone, more crooked grows madam;
What well could be worse, my good friend, Adam?--
For woman due allowance make;

'Twere grievous, if thy rib should break!

    1819.*

FIRDUSI (Speaks).

OH world, with what baseness and guilt thou art rife!

Thou nurtures, trainest, and illest the while.

He only whom Allah doth bless with his smile
Is train'd and is nurtured with riches and life.

    1819.*

SULEIKA (Speaks).

THE mirror tells me, I am fair!

Thou sayest, to grow old my fate will be.
Nought in God's presence changeth e'er,--

Love him, for this one moment, then, in me.

    1819.*

V. RENDSCH NAME

BOOK OF GLOOM.

IT is a fault oneself to praise,

And yet 'tis done by each whose deeds are kind;
And if there's no deceit in what he says,

The good we still as good shall find.

Let, then, ye fools, that wise man taste

Of joy, who fancies that he s wise,
That he, a fool like you, may waste

Th' insipid thanks the world supplies.

1816.

VI. HIKMET NAME.

BOOK OF PROVERBS.

CALL on the present day and night for nought,
Save what by yesterday was brought.

THE sea is flowing ever,
The land retains it never.

BE stirring, man, while yet the day is clear;
The night when none can work fast Draweth near.

WHEN the heavy-laden sigh,
Deeming help and hope gone by,
Oft, with healing power is heard,
Comfort-fraught, a kindly word.

How vast is mine inheritance, how glorious and sublime!
For time mine own possession is, the land I till is time!

UNWARY saith,--ne'er lived a man more true;
The deepest heart, the highest head he knew,--
"In ev'ry place and time thou'lt find availing
Uprightness, judgment, kindliness unfailing."

THOUGH the bards whom the Orient sun bath bless'd
Are greater than we who dwell in the west,
Yet in hatred of those whom our equals we find.
In this we're not in the least behind.

WOULD we let our envy burst,

Feed its hunger fully first!
To keep our proper place,

  We'll show our bristles more;
With hawks men all things chase,

  Except the savage boar.

BY those who themselves more bravely have fought
A hero's praise will be joyfully told.
The worth of man can only be taught
By those who have suffer'd both heat and cold.

"WHEREFORE is truth so far from our eyes,
Buried as though in a distant land?"
None at the proper moment are wise!

Could they properly understand,

Truth would appear in her own sweet guise,
Beauteous, gentle, and close at hand.

WHY these inquiries make,

Where charity may flow?
Cast in the flood thy cake,--

Its eater, who will know?

ONCE when I a spider had kill'd,

Then methought: wast right or wrong?

That we both to these times should belong,
This had God in His goodness willed.

MOTLEY this congregation is, for, lo!
At the communion kneel both friend and foe.

IF the country I'm to show,
Thou must on the housetop go.

A MAN with households twain

Ne'er finds attention meet,
A house wherein two women reign

Is ne'er kept clean and neat.

BLESS, thou dread Creator,

Bless this humble fane;

Man may build them greater,--

More they'll not contain.

LET this house's glory rise,

Handed to far ages down,

And the son his honour prize.
As the father his renown.

O'ER the Mediterranean sea

Proudly hath the Orient sprung;
Who loves Hafis and knows him, he

Knows what Caldron hath sung.

IF the ass that bore the Saviour

Were to Mecca driven, he

Would not alter, but would be
Still an ass in his behavior.

THE flood of passion storms with fruitless strife

'Gainst the unvanquished solid land.--

It throws poetic pearls upon the strand,
And thus is gain'd the prize of life.

WHEN so many minstrels there are,

How it pains me, alas, to know it!
Who from the earth drives poetry far?

Who but the poet!

VII. TIMUR NAME.

BOOK OF TIMUR.

THE WINTER AND TIMUR.

So the winter now closed round them
With resistless fury. Scattering
Over all his breath so icy,
He inflamed each wind that blithe
To assail them angrily.
Over them he gave dominion
To his frost-unsharpened tempests;
Down to Timur's council went he,
And with threat'ning voice address'd him:--
"Softly, slowly, wretched being!
Live, the tyrant of injustice;
But shall hearts be scorch'd much longer
By thy flames,--consume before them?
If amongst the evil spirits
Thou art one,--good! I'm another.
Thou a greybeard art--so I am;
Land and men we make to stiffen.
Thou art Mars! And I Saturnus,--
Both are evil-working planets,
When united, horror-fraught.
Thou dost kill the soul, thou freezes
E'en the atmosphere; still colder
Is my breath than thine was ever.
Thy wild armies vex the faithful
With a thousand varying torments;
Well! God grant that I discover
Even worse, before I perish!
And by God, I'll give thee none.
Let God hear what now I tell thee!
Yes, by God! from Death's cold clutches
Nought, O greybeard, shall protect thee,
Not the hearth's broad coalfire's ardour,
Not December's brightest flame."

1814.

TO SULEIKA.

FITTING perfumes to prepare,

And to raise thy rapture high,
Must a thousand rosebuds fair

First in fiery torments die.

One small flask's contents to glean,

Whose sweet fragrance aye may live,
Slender as thy finger e'en,

Must a world its treasures give;

Yes, a world where life is moving,

Which, with impulse full and strong,
Could forbode the Bulbul's loving,

Sweet, and spirit-stirring song.

Since they thus have swell'd our joy,

Should such torments grieve us, then?
Doth not Timur's rule destroy

Myriad souls of living men?

    1815.*

VIII. SULEIKA NAME.

BOOK OF SULEIKA.

ONCE, methought, in the night hours cold,

That I saw the moon in my sleep;
But as soon as I waken'd, behold

Unawares rose the sun from the deep.

THAT Suleika's love was so strong

For Joseph, need cause no surprise;

He was young, youth pleaseth the eyes,--

He was fair, they say, beyond measure

Fair was she, and so great was their pleasure.
But that thou, who awaitedst me long,
Youthful glances of fire dost throw me,
Soon wilt bless me, thy love now dost show me,
This shall my joyous numbers proclaim,
Thee I for ever Suleika shall name.

1815.

HATEM.

NOT occasion makes the thief;

She's the greatest of the whole;
For Love's relics, to my grief,

From my aching heart she stole.

She hath given it to thee,--

All the joy my life had known,
So that, in my poverty,

Life I seek from thee alone.

Yet compassion greets me straight

In the lustre of thine eye,
And I bless my newborn fate,

As within thine arms I lie.

1815.

SULEIKA.

THE sun appears! A glorious sight!

The crescent-moon clings round him now.
What could this wondrous pair unite?

How to explain this riddle? How?

HATEM.

May this our joy's foreboder prove!

In it I view myself and thee;
Thou calmest me thy sun, my love,--

Come, my sweet moon, cling thou round me!

           1815.

LOVE for love, and moments sweet,

Lips returning kiss for kiss,
Word for word, and eyes that meet;

Breath for breath, and bliss for bliss.
Thus at eve, and thus the morrow!

Yet thou feeblest, at my lay,
Ever some half-hidden sorrow;
Could I Joseph's graces borrow,

All thy beauty I'd repay!

           1815.

HATEM.

O, SAY, 'neath what celestial sign

The day doth lie,
When ne'er again this heart of mine

Away will fly?
And e'en though fled (what thought divine!)

Would near me lie?--
On the soft couch, on whose sweet shrine

My heart near hers will lie!

           1816.

HATEM.

HOLD me, locks, securely caught

In the circle of her face!
Dear brown serpents, I have nought

To repay this act of grace,

Save a heart whose love ne'er dies,

Throbbing with aye-youthful glow;
For a raging ETA lies

'Neath its veil of mist and snow.

Yonder mountain's stately brow

Thou, like morning beams, dost shame;
Once again feels Hatem now

Spring's soft breath and summer's flame.

One more bumper! Fill the glass;

This last cup I pledge to thee!--
By mine ashes if she pass,

"He consumed," she'll say, "for me."

   1815.

THE LOVING ONE SPEAKS.

AND wherefore sends not
The horseman-captain
His heralds hither

Each day, unfailing?
Yet hath he horses,
He writes well.

He waiteth Tali,
And Neski knows he
To write with beauty

On silken tablets.
I'd deem him present,
Had I his words.

The sick One will not,
Will not recover
From her sweet sorrow;
She, when she heareth
That her true lover
Grows well, falls sick.

1819.*

THE LOVING ONE AGAIN.

WRITES he in Neski,
Faithfully speaks he;
Writes he in Tali,
Joy to give, seeks he:
Writes he in either,
Good!--for he loves!

1819.*

THESE tufted branches fair

Observe, my loved one, well!
And see the fruits they bear

In green and prickly shell!

They've hung roll'd up, till now,

Unconsciously and still;
A loosely-waving bough

Doth rock them at its will.

Yet, ripening from within.

The kernel brown swells fast;
It seeks the air to win,

It seeks the sun at last.

With joy it bursts its thrall,

The shell must needs give way.
'Tis thus my numbers fall

Before thy feet, each day.

                    1815.

SULEIKA.

WHAT is by this stir reveal'd?

Doth the East glad tidings bring?
For my heart's deep wounds are heal'd

By his mild and cooling wing.

He the dust with sports doth meet,

And in gentle cloudlets chase;
To the vineleaf's safe retreat

Drives the insects' happy race,

Cools these burning cheeks of mine,

Checks the sun's fierce glow Adam,
Kisses, as he flies, the vine,

Flaunting over hill and plain.

And his whispers soft convey

Thousand greetings from my friend;
Ere these hills own night's dark sway,

Kisses greet me, without end.

Thus canst thou still onward go,

Serving friend and mourner too!
There, where lofty ramparts glow,

Soon the loved one shall I view.

Ah, what makes the heart's truth known,--

Love's sweet breath,--a newborn life,--
Learn I from his mouth alone,

In his breath alone is rife!

                    1815.

THE SUBLIME TYPE.

THE sun, whom Grecians Helms call,

His heavenly path with pride doth tread,
And, to subdue the world's wide all,

Looks round, beneath him, high o'er head.

He sees the fairest goddess pine,

Heaven's child, the daughter of the clouds,--
For her alone he seems to shine;

In trembling grief his form he shrouds,

Careless for all the realms of bliss,--

Her streaming tears more swiftly flow:
For every pearl he gives a kiss,

And changeth into joy her woe.

She gazeth upward fixedly,

And deeply feels his glance of might,
While, stamped with his own effigy,

Each pearl would range itself aright.

Thus wreath'd with bows, with hues thus grac'd,

With gladness beams her face so fair,
While he, to meet her, maketh haste,

And yet, alas! can reach her ne'er.

So, by the harsh decree of Fate,

Thou modest from me, dearest one;
And were I Helms e'en, the Great,

What would avail his chariot-throne?

    1815.

SULEIKA.

ZEPHYR, for thy humid wing,

Oh, how much I envy thee!
Thou to him canst tidings bring

How our parting saddens me!

In my breast, a yearning still

As thy pinions wave, appears;
Flow'rs and eyes, and wood, and hill

At thy breath are steeped in tears.

Yet thy mild wing gives relief,

Soothes the aching eyelid's pain;
Ah, I else had died for grief,

Him ne'er hoped to see again.

To my love, then, quick repair,

Whisper softly to his heart;
Yet, to give him pain, beware,

Nor my bosom's pangs impart.

Tell him, but in accents coy,

That his love must be my life;
Both, with feelings fraught with joy,

In his presence will be rife.

1815.

THE REUNION.

CAN it be! of stars the star,

Do I press thee to my heart?
In the night of distance far,

What deep gulf, what bitter smart!
Yes, 'tis thou, indeed, at last,

Of my joys the partner dear!
Mindful, though, of sorrows past,

I the present needs must fear.

When the still-unfashion'd earth

Lay on God's eternal breast,
He ordain'd its hour of birth,

With creative joy possess'd.
Then a heavy sigh arose,

When He spake the sentence:--"Be!"
And the All, with mighty throes,

Burst into reality.

And when thus was born the light,

Darkness near it fear'd to stay,
And the elements with might

Fled on every side away;
Each on some far-distant trace,

Each with visions wild employ,
Numb, in boundless realm of space,

Harmony and feeling-void.

Dumb was all, all still and dead,

For the first time, God alone!
Then He form'd the morning-red,

Which soon made its kindness known:
It unravelled from the waste,

Bright and glowing harmony,
And once more with love was grac'd

What contended formerly.

And with earnest, noble strife,

Each its own Peculiar sought;
Back to full, unbounded life

Sight and feeling soon were brought.
Wherefore, if 'tis done, explore

How? why give the manner, name?
Allah need create no more,

We his world ourselves can frame.

So, with morning pinions bright,

To thy mouth was I impell'd;
Stamped with thousand seals by night,

Star-clear is the bond fast held.
Paragons on earth are we

Both of grief and joy sublime,
And a second sentence:--"Be!"

Parts us not a second time.

1815.

SULEIKA.

WITH what inward joy, sweet lay,

I thy meaning have descried!
Lovingly thou seem'st to say

That I'm ever by his side;

That he ever thinks of me,

That he to the absent gives
All his love's sweet ecstasy,

While for him alone she lives.

Yes, the mirror which reveals

Thee, my loved one, is my breast;
This the bosom, where thy seals

Endless kisses have impress'd.

Numbers sweet, unsullied truth,

Chain me down in sympathy!
Love's embodied radiant youth,

In the garb of poesy!

1819.*

IN thousand forms mayst thou attempt surprise,

Yet, all-beloved-one, straight know I thee;
Thou mayst with magic veils thy face disguise,

And yet, all-present-one, straight know I thee.

Upon the cypress' purest, youthful bud,

All-beauteous-growing-one, straight know I thee;
In the canal's unsullied, living flood,

All-captivating-one, well know I thee.

When spreads the water-column, rising proud,

All-sportive one, how gladly know I thee;
When, e'en in forming, is transform'd the cloud,

All-figure-changing-one, there know I thee.

Veil in the meadow-carpet's flowery charms,

All-checkered-starry-fair-one, know I thee;
And if a plant extend its thousand arms,

O, all-embracing-one, there know I thee.

When on the mount is kindled morn's sweet light,

Straightway, all-gladdening-one, salute I thee,
The arch of heaven o'er head grows pure and bright,--

All-heart-expanding-one, then breathe I thee.

That which my inward, outward sense proclaims,

Thou all-instructing-one, I know through thee;
And if I utter Allah's hundred names,

A name with each one echoes, meant for thee.

    1819.*

IX. SAKE NAME.

THE CONVIVIAL BOOK.

CAN the Koran from Eternity be?

'Tis worth not a thought!
Can the Koran a creation, then, be?

Of that, I know nought!
Yet that the book of all books it must be,

I believe, as a Mussulman ought.
That from Eternity wine, though, must be,

I ever have thought;
That 'twas ordain'd, ere the Angels, to be,

As a truth may be taught.
Drinkers, however these matters may be,

Gaze on God's face, fearing nought.

1815.

YE'VE often, for our drunkenness,

Blamed us in ev'ry way,
And, in abuse of drunkenness,

Enough can never say.
Men, overcome by drunkenness,

Are wont to lie till day;
And yet I find my drunkenness

All night-time make me stray;
For, oh! 'tis Love's sweet drunkenness

That maketh me its prey,
Which night and day, and day and night,

My heart must needs obey,--
A heart that, in its drunkenness,

Pours forth full many a lay,
So that no trifling drunkenness

Can dare assert its sway.
Love, song, and wine's sweet drunkenness,

By night-time and by day,--
How god-like is the drunkenness

That maketh me its prey!

                1815.

X. MATHAL NAME.

BOOK OF PARABLES.

FROM heaven there fell upon the foaming wave

A timid drop; the flood with anger roared,--

But God, its modest boldness to reward,
Strength to the drop and firm endurance gave.
Its form the mussel captive took,

And to its lasting glory and renown,

The pearl now glistens in our monarch's crown,
With gentle gleam and loving look.

                1819.*

BULBUL'S song, through night hours cold,

Rose to Allah's throne on high;

To reward her melody,
Giveth he a cage of gold.
Such a cage are limbs of men,--

Though at first she feels confin'd,

Yet when all she brings to mind,
Straight the spirit sings again.

                1819.*

IN the Koran with strange delight
A peacock's feather met my sight:
Thou'rt welcome in this holy place,
The highest prize on earth's wide face!
As in the stars of heaven, in thee,

God's greatness in the small we see;
For he whose gaze whole worlds bath bless'd
His eye hath even here impress'd,
And the light down in beauty dress'd,
So that e'en monarchs cannot hope
In splendour with the bird to cope.
Meekly enjoy thy happy lot,
And so deserve that holy spot!

   1815.

ALL kinds of men, both small and great,
A fine-spun web delight to create,
And in the middle they take their place,
And wield their scissors with wondrous grace.
But if a besom should sweep that way:
"What a most shameful thing," they say,--
"They've crush'd a mighty palace to-day."

   1815.

IT IS GOOD.

IN Paradise while moonbeams play'd,

Jehovah found, in slumber deep,
Adam fast sunk; He gently laid

Eve near him,--she, too, fell asleep.
There lay they now, on earth's fair shrine,
God's two most beauteous thoughts divine.--
When this He saw, He cried:--'Tis Good!!!
And scarce could move from where He stood.

No wonder, that our joy's complete
While eye and eye responsive meet,
When this blest thought of rapture moves us--
That we're with Him who truly loves us,
And if He cries:--Good, let it be!
'Tis so for both, it seems to me.
Thou'rt clasp'd within these arms of mine,
Dearest of all God's thoughts divine!

   1815.

XI. PARIS NAME.

BOOK OF THE PARSEES.

THE BEQUEST OF THE ANCIENT PERSIAN FAITH.

BRETHREN, what bequest to you should come
From the lowly poor man, going home,
Whom ye younger ones with patience tended,
Whose last days ye honour'd and defended?

When we oft have seen the monarch ride,
Gold upon him, gold on ev'ry side;
Jewels on him, on his courtiers all,
Thickly strewed as hailstones when they fall,

Have ye e'er known envy at the sight?
And not felt your gaze become more bright,
When the sun was, on the wings of morning,
Darnawend's unnumber'd peaks adorning,

As he, bow-like, rose? How each eye dwelt
On the glorious scene! I felt, I felt,
Thousand times, as life's days fleeted by,
Borne with him, the coming one, on high.

God upon His throne then to proclaim,
Him, the life-fount's mighty Lord, to name,
Worthily to prize that glorious sight,
And to wander on beneath His light.

When the fiery orb was all defined,
There I stood, as though in darkness, blind,
Beat my breast, my quicken'd members threw
On the earth, brow-foremost, at the view.

Let this holy, great bequest reward
Brotherly good-will and kind regard:
SOLEMN DUTY'S DAILY observation.--
More than this, it needs no revelation.

If its gentle hands a new-born one
Move, then straightway turn it tow'rd the sun,--

Soul and body dip in bath of fire!
Then each morning's favour 'twill acquire.

To the living one, commit the dead,
O'er the beast let earth and dust be spread,
And, so far as may extend your might,
What ye deem impure, conceal from sight.

Till your plains to graceful purity,
That the sun with joy your labours see;
When ye plant, your trees in rows contrive,
For he makes the Regular to thrive.

E'en the floods that through the channel rush
Must not fail in fulness or in gush;
And as Senderud, from mountain high,
Rises pure, in pureness must it die.

Not to weaken water's gentle fall,
Carefully cleanse out the channels all;
Salamander, snake, and rush, and reed,--
All destroy,--each monster and each weed.

If thus pure ye earth and water keep,
Through the air the sun will gladly peep,
Where he, worthily enshrined in space,
Worketh life, to life gives holy grace.

Ye, by toil on toil so sorely tried,
Comfort take, the All is purified;
And now man, as priest, may boldly dare
From the stone God's image to prepare.

When the flame burns joyously and bright,
Limbs are supple, radiant is the night;
On the hearth when fire with ardour glows,
Ripe the sap of plants and creatures grows.

Dragging wood, with rapture be it done,
'Tis the seed of many an earthly sun;
Plucking Pambeh, gladly may ye say:--
This, as wick, the Holy will convey.

If ye meekly, in each burning lamp,

See the nobler light's resplendent stamp,
Ne'er will Fate prevent you, void of feeling,
At God's throne at morningtide from kneeling.

This is Being's mighty signet, then,
God's pure glass to angels and to men;
Each word lisped the Highest's praise to sound,
Ring in ring, united there is found.

From the shore of Senderud ascendeth,
Up to Darnawend its pinions bendeth,
As He dawns, with joy to greet His light,
You with endless blessings to requite.

   1819.*

XII. CHULD NAME.

BOOK OF PARADISE.

THE PRIVILEGED MEN.

AFTER THE BATTLE OF BADE, BENEATH THE CANOPY OF HEAVEN.

[This battle was fought in the second year of the Hegira (A.A. 623), between the followers of Mahomet, who numbered three hundred and thirteen, possessing two horses and seventy camels, and the 'idolaters,' or Meccans, whose forces amounted to nine hundred and fifty, including two hundred cavalry. The victory remained with Mahomet, who lost fourteen men, while seventy of the enemy were slain. A great accession of strength ensued in consequence to the Prophet, who pretended that miracles were wrought in his behalf in the battle, God having sent angels to fight on his side, and having also made his army to appear larger to the enemy than it really was.--See the Koran, chapter viii., and ABULFEDA'S Life of Mahomet.]

MAHOMET (Speaks).

LET the foeman sorrow o'er his dead,

Ne'er will they return again to light;
O'er our brethren let no tear be shed,

For they dwell above yon spheres so bright.

All the seven planets open throw

All their metal doors with mighty shock,
And the forms of those we loved below

At the gates of Eden boldly knock.

There they find, with bliss ne'er dream'd before,

Glories that my flight first show'd to eye,
When the wondrous steed my person bore

In one second through the realms on high.

Wisdom's trees, in cypress-order growing,

High uphold the golden apples sweet;
Trees of life, their spreading shadows throwing,

Shade each blossoming plant, each flow'ry seat.

Now a balmy zephyr from the East

Brings the heavenly maidens to thy view;
With the eye thou now dost taste the feast,

Soon the sight pervades thee through and through.

There they stand, to ask thee thy career:

Mighty plans? or dangerous bloody rout?
Thou'rt a hero, know they,--for Thou'rt here,

What a hero?--This they'll fathom out.

By thy wounds soon clearly this is shown,

Wounds that write thy fame's undying story;
Wounds the true believer mark alone,

When have perish'd joy and earthly glory.

To chiosks and arbors thou art brought,

Fill'd with checkered marble columns bright;
To the noble grape-juice, solace-fraught,

They the guest with kindly sips invite.

Youth! Thou'rt welcome more than e'er was youth

All alike are radiant and serene;
When thou tak'st one to thine heart with truth,

Of thy band she'll be the friend and queen.

So prepare thee for this place of rest,

Never can it now be changed again;
Maids like these will ever make thee blest,

Wines like these will never harm thy brain.

    1819.

THE FAVOURED BEASTS.

Or beasts there have been chosen four

To come to Paradise,
And there with saints for evermore

They dwell in happy wise.

Amongst them all the Ass stands first;

He comes with joyous stride,
For to the Prophet-City erst

Did Jesus on him ride.

Half timid next a Wolf doth creep,

To whom Mahomet spake
"Spoil not the poor man of his sheep,

The rich man's thou mayst take."

And then the brave and faithful Hound,

Who by his master kept,
And slept with him the slumbers sound

The seven sleepers slept.

Abuherrira's Cat, too, here,

Purrs round his master blest,
For holy must the beast appear

The Prophet hath caress'd.

    1815.

THE SEVEN SLEEPERS.

Six among the courtiers favour'd
Fly before the Caesar's fury,
Who would as a god be worshipp'd,
Though in truth no god appearing,
For a fly prevents him ever
From enjoying food at table.
Though with fans his servants scare it,
They the fly can never banish.
It torments him, stings, and troubles,
And the festal board perplexes,
Then returning like the herald
Of the olden crafty Fly-God.
"What!"--the striplings say together--
"Shall a fly a god embarrass?

Shall a god drink, eat at table,
Like us mortals? No, the Only,
Who the sun and moon created,
And the glowing stars arch'd o'er us,
He is God,--we'll fly!"--The gentle,
Lightly shod, and dainty striplings
Did a shepherd meet, and hide them,
With himself, within a cavern.

And the sheep-dog will not leave them,--
Scared away, his foot all-mangled,
To his master still he presses,
And he joins the hidden party,
Joins the favorites of slumber.

And the prince, whom they had fled from,
Fondly-furious, thinks of vengeance,
And, discarding sword and fire,
Has them walled-up in the cavern,
Walled-up fast with bricks and mortar.

But the others slumber ever,
And the Angel, their protector,
Gives before God's throne this notice
"To the right and left alternate
Have I ever cared to turn them,
That their fair and youthful members
Be not by the mould-damp injured;
Clefts within the rocks I open'd,
That the sun may, rising, setting,
Keep their cheeks in youthful freshness."
So they lie there, bless'd by Heaven.
And, with forepaws sound and scatheless,
Sleeps the dog in gentle slumber.

Years come round, and years fly onward,
And the youths at length awaken,
And the wall, which now had moldered,
From its very age has fallen.
And Jamblika says,--whose beauty
Far exceedeth all the others,--
When the fearful shepherd lingers:--
"I will run, and food procure you,
Life and piece of gold I'll wager!"--
Ephebus had many a year now
Own'd the teaching of the Prophet
Jesus (Peace be with the Good One!)

And he ran, and at the gateway
Were the warders and the others.
Yet he to the nearest baker's,
Seeking bread, went swiftly onwards.--
"Rogue!" thus cried the baker--"hast thou,

Youth, a treasure, then, discover'd?
Give me,--for the gold betrays thee,--
Give me half, to keep thy secret!"--

And they quarrel.--To the monarch
Comes the matter; and the monarch
Fain would halve it, like the baker.

Now the miracle is proven
Slowly by a hundred tokens.
He can e'en his right establish
To the palace he erected,
For a pillar, when pierced open.

Leads to wealth he said 'twould lead to.
Soon are gather'd there whole races,
Their relationship to show him.
And as great-grandfather, nobly
Stands Jamblika's youthful figure.

As of ancestors, he hears them,
Speaking of his son and grandsons.
His great-grandsons stand around him,
Like a race of valiant mortals,
Him to honour,--him, the youngest.
And one token on another
Rises up, the proof completing;
The identity is proven
Of himself, and of his comrades.

Now returns he to the cavern,
With him go both king and people.--
Neither to the king nor people
E'er returns that chosen mortal;
For the Seven, who for ages--
Eight was, with the dog, their number--
Had from all the world been sunder'd,
Gabriel's mysterious power,
To the will of God obedient,
Hath to Paradise conducted,--
And the cave was closed for ever.

1814-15.

SONGS FROM VARIOUS PLAYS, ETC

FROM FAUST.

I.
DEDICATION.

YE shadowy forms, again ye're drawing near,

So wont of yore to meet my troubled gaze!
Were it in vain to seek to keep you here?

Loves still my heart that dream of olden days?
Oh, come then! and in pristine force appear,

Parting the vapor mist that round me plays!
My bosom finds its youthful strength again,
Feeling the magic breeze that marks your train.

Ye bring the forms of happy days of yore,

And many a shadow loved attends you too;
Like some old lay, whose dream was well nigh o'er,

First-love appears again, and friendship true;
Upon life's labyrinthine path once more

Is heard the sigh, and grief revives anew;
The friends are told, who, in their hour of pride,
Deceived by fortune, vanish'd from my side.

No longer do they hear my plaintive song,

The souls to whom I sang in life's young day;
Scatter'd for ever now the friendly throng,

And mute, alas! each sweet responsive lay.
My strains but to the careless crowd belong,

Their smiles but sorrow to my heart convey;
And all who heard my numbers erst with gladness,
If living yet, roam o'er the earth in sadness.

Long buried yearnings in my breast arise,

Yon calm and solemn spirit-realm to gain;
Like the AEONIAN harp's sweet melodies,

My murmuring song breathes forth its changeful strain.
A trembling seizes me, tears fill mine eyes,

And softer grows my rugged heart amain.
All I possess far distant seems to be,
The vanish'd only seems reality.

II.
PROLOGUE IN HEAVEN.

THE ARCHANGELS' SONG.

RAPHAEL.

THE sun still chaunts, as in old time,

With brother-spheres in choral song,
And with his thunder-march sublime

Moves his predestined course along.
Strength find the angels in his sight,

Though he by none may fathomed be;
Still glorious is each work of might

As when first form'd in majesty.

GABRIEL.

And swift and swift, in wondrous guise,

Revolves the earth in splendour bright,
The radiant hues of Paradise

Alternating with deepest night.
From out the gulf against the rock,

In spreading billows foams the ocean,--

And cliff and sea with mighty shock,

The spheres whirl round in endless motion.

MICHAEL.

And storms in emulation growl

From land to sea, from sea to land,
And fashion, as they wildly howl,

A circling, wonder-working band.
Destructive flames in mad career

Precede Thy thunders on their way;
Yet, Lord, Thy messengers revere

The soft mutations of Thy day.

THE THREE.

Strength find the angels in Thy sight,

Though none may hope to fathom Thee;
Still glorious are Thy works of might,

As when first form'd in majesty.

III.
CHORUS OF ANGELS.

CHRIST is arisen!

Mortal, all hail!
Thou, of Earth's prison

Dreary and frail,
Bursting the veil,

Proudly hast risen!

CHORUS OF WOMEN.

Rich spices and myrrh,

To embalm Him we brought;
His corpse to inter

His true followers sought.
In pure cerements shrin'd,

'Twas placed in the bier
But, alas! we now find

That Christ is not here.

CHORUS OF ANGELS.

Christ is arisen!

Speechless His love.
Who to Earth's prison

Came from above,
Trials to prove.

Now is He risen!

CHORUS OF YOUTHS.

Death's gloomy portal

Now hath He rended,--
Living, immortal,

Heavenward ascended;
Freed from His anguish,

Sees He God's throne;
We still must languish,

Earthbound, alone.
Now that He's reft us,

Heart-sad we pine;
Why hast Thou left us,

Master divine?

CHORUS OF ANGELS.

Christ is arisen,

  Death hath He slain;

Burst ye your prison,

  Rend ye each chain!

Songs of praise lead ye,--

Love to show, heed ye,--

Hungry ones feed ye,--

Preaching, on speed ye,--

Coming joys plead ye,--
Then is the Master near,
Then is He here!

IV.
CHORUS OF SPIRITS.

VANISH, dark clouds on high,

Offspring of night!
Let a more radiant beam
Through the blue ether gleam,

Charming the sight!
Would the dark clouds on high

Melt into air!
Stars glimmer tenderly,

Planets more fair

Shed their soft light.
Spirits of heav'nly birth,
Fairer than sons of earth,

Quivering emotions true

Hover above;
Yearning affections, too,

In their train move.
See how the spirit-band,
By the soft breezes fann'd,
Covers the smiling land,--
Covers the leafy grove,
Where happy lovers rove,
Deep in a dream of love,
True love that never dies!
Bowers on bowers rise,

Soft tendrils twine;
While from the press escapes,
Born of the juicy grapes,

Foaming, the wine;
And as the current flows
O'er the bright stones it goes,--
Leaving the hilly lands

Far, far behind,--
Into a sea expands,

Loving to wind
Round the green mountain's base;
And the glad-winged race,

Rapture sip in,
As they the sunny light,
And the fair islands bright,

Hasten to win,
That on the billows play
With sweet deceptive ray,
Where in glad choral song
Shout the exulting throng;
Where on the verdant plain

Dancers we see,
Spreading themselves amain

Over the lea.
Some boldly climbing are

O'er the steep brake,
Others are floating far

O'er the smooth lake.
All for a purpose move,

All with life teem,
While the sweet stars above

Blissfully gleam.

V.
MARGARET AT HER SPINNING-WHEEL.

MY heart is sad,

My peace is o'er;
I find it never

And nevermore.

When gone is he,
The grave I see;
The world's wide all
Is turned to gall.

Alas, my head

Is well-nigh crazed;
My feeble mind

Is sore amazed.

My heart is sad,

My peace is o'er;
I find it never

And nevermore.

For him from the window

Alone I spy;
For him alone

From home go I.

His lofty step,

His noble form,
His mouth's sweet smile,

His glances warm,

His voice so fraught

With magic bliss,
His hand's soft pressure,

And, ah, his kiss!

My heart is sad,

My peace is o'er;
I find it never

And nevermore.

My bosom yearns

For his form so fair;
Ah, could I clasp him

And hold him there!

My kisses sweet

Should stop his breath,
And 'neath his kisses

I'd sink in death!

VI.
SCENE--A GARDEN,

Margaret. Faust.

MARGARET.

DOST thou believe in God?

FAUST.

          Doth mortal live

Who dares to say that he believes in God?
Go, bid the priest a truthful answer give,

Go, ask the wisest who on earth e'er trod,--
Their answer will appear to be
Given alone in mockery.

MARGARET.

Then thou dost not believe? This sayest thou?

FAUST.

Sweet love, mistake not what I utter now!
Who knows His name?
Who dares proclaim:--
Him I believe?
Who so can feel
His heart to steel
To sari believe Him not?
The All-Embracer,
The All-Sustained,
Holds and sustains He not
Thee, me, Himself?

Hang not the heavens their arch overhead?
Lies not the earth beneath us, firm?
Gleam not with kindly glances
Eternal stars on high?
Looks not mine eye deep into thine?
And do not all things
Crowd on thy head and heart,

And round thee twine, in mystery eterne,
Invisible, yet visible?
Fill, then, thy heart, however vast, with this,
And when the feeling perfecteth thy bliss,
O, call it what thou wilt,
Call it joy! heart! love! God!
No name for it I know!
'Tis feeling all--nought else;
Name is but sound and smoke,
Obscuring heaven's bright glow.

VII.
MARGARET, Placing fresh flowers in the flower-pots.

O THOU well-tried in grief,

Grant to thy child relief,
And view with mercy this unhappy one!

The sword within thy heart,

Speechless with bitter smart,
Thou Lookest up towards thy dying son.

Thou look'st to God on high,

And breathest many a sigh
O'er his and thy distress, thou holy One!

  Who e'er can know

  The depth of woe

Piercing my very bone?
The sorrows that my bosom fill,
Its trembling, its aye-yearning will,

Are known to thee, to thee alone!

Wherever I may go,

With woe, with woe, with woe,
My bosom sad is aching!

I scarce alone can creep,

I weep, I weep, I weep,
My very heart is breaking.

The flowers at my window

My falling tears bedewed,
When I, at dawn of morning,

For thee these flow'rets strewed.

When early to my chamber

The cheerful sunbeams stole,
I sat upon my pallet,

In agony of soul.

Help! rescue me from death and misery!

Oh, thou well-tried in grief,

Grant to thy child relief,
And view with mercy my deep agony!

FROM FAUST--SECOND PART.

I.

ARIEL.

WHEN in spring the gentle rain

Breathes into the flower new birth,
When the green and happy plain

Smiles upon the sons of earth,

Haste to give what help we may,

Little elves of wondrous might!
Whether good or evil they,

Pity for them feels the sprite.

II.
CHORUS OF SPIRITS.

WHEN the moist and balmy gale

Round the verdant meadow sighs,
Odors sweet in misty veil

At the twilight-hour arise.
Murmurings soft of calm repose

Rock the heart to child-like rest,
And the day's bright portals close

On the eyes with toil oppress'd.

Night already reigns o'er all,

Strangely star is link'd to star;
Planets mighty, sparkling small,

Glitter near and gleam afar.
Gleam above in clearer night,

Glitter in the glassy sea;
Pledging pure and calm delight,

Rules the moon in majesty.

Now each well-known hour is over,

Joy and grief have pass'd away;
Feel betimes! thoult then recover:

Trust the newborn eye of day.
Vales grow verdant, hillocks teem,

Shady nooks the bushes yield,
And with waving, silvery gleam,

Rocks the harvest in the field.

Wouldst thou wish for wish obtain,

Look upon yon glittering ray!
Lightly on thee lies the chain,

Cast the shell of sleep away!
Tarry not, but be thou bold,

When the many loiter still;
All with ease may be controll'd

By the man of daring will.

III.
ARIEL.

HARK! the storm of hours draws near,
Loudly to the spirit-ear
Signs of coming day appear.
Rocky gates are wildly crashing,
Phoebus' wheels are onward dashing;

(A wonderful noise proclaims the approach of the sun.)

Light doth mighty sounds beget!
Pealing loud as rolling thunder,
Eye and ear it fills with wonder,

Though itself unconscious yet.
Downward steals it,'mongst the flowers
Seeking deeper, stiller bowers,
'Mongst the foliage, 'neath the rock;
Thou'lt be deafened by the shock!

FROM FAUST--SECOND PART.

SCENE THE LAST.

ANGELS.
[Hovering in the higher regions of air, and hearing the immortal part of Faust.]

THE spirit-region's noble limb

Hath 'scaled the Archfiend's power;
For we have strength to rescue him

Who labours ev'ry hour.
And if he feels within his breast

A ray of love from heaven.
He's met by all the squadron blest

With welcome gladly given.

THE YOUNGER ANGELS.

Yonder roses, from the holy
Hands of penitents so lowly,
Help'd to render us victorious,
And to do the deed all-glorious;
For they gain'd us this soul-treasure.

Evil ones those roses banish'd,

Devils, when we met them, vanish'd.
Spirits felt love's pangs with pleasure,
Where hell's torments used to dwell;
E'en the hoary king of hell
Felt sharp torments through him run.
Shout for joy! the prize is won.

THE MORE PERFECT ANGELS.

Strains of mortality

Long have oppress'd us;
Pure could they ever be,

If of asbestos.
If mighty spirit-strength

Elements ever
Knew how to seize at length,

Angels could never
Link'd twofold natures move,

Where single-hearted;
By nought but deathless love

Can they be parted.

THE YOUNGER ANGELS.

See where a spirit-race

Bursts on the sight!
Dimly their forms I trace

Round the far height.
Each cloud becometh clear,
While the bright troops appear

Of the blest boys,

From the Earth's burden free,
In a glad company

Drinking in joys,
Born of the world above,

Springtime and bliss.
May they forerunners prove
Of a more perfect love,

Link'd on to this!

THE BEATIFIED CHILDREN.

Thus as a chrysalis

Gladly we gain him,
And as a pledge of bliss

Safely retain him;

When from the shell he's free

Whereby he's tainted,
Perfect and fair he'll be,

Holy and sainted.

DOCTOR MARINAS.
(In the highest, purest cell.)

Wide is the prospect here,

Raised is the soul;
Women on high appear,

Seeking their goal.

'Mongst them the radiant one,

Queen of the skies,
In her bright starry crown

Greets my glad eyes.

    (With ecstasy.)

Thou who art of earth the queen.

Let me, 'neath the blue
Heav'nly canopy serene

Thy sweet mystery view!
Grant the gentle solemn force

Which the breast can move.
And direct our onward course

Tow'rd thy perfect love.
Dauntless let our courage be,

At thy bright behest;
Mild our ardour suddenly,

When thou bidd'st us rest.
Virgin, type of holiness,

Mother, honour-crown'd,
Thou whom we as queen confess,

Godlike and renowned.

Round her, in gentle play,

Light clouds are stealing;
Penitents fair are they,

Who, humbly kneeling,
Sip in the ether sweet,
 As they for grace entreat.

Thou, who art from passions free,

Kindly art inclin'd,
When the sons of frailty

Seek thee, meek in mind.

Borne by weakness' stream along,

Hard it is to save them;
Who can burst lust's chains so strong,

That, alas, enslave them?
O how soon the foot may slip,

When the smooth ground pressing!
O, how false are eye and lip,

False a breath caressing!

    MATER GLORLOSA hovers past.

CHORUS OF PENITENT WOMEN.

To bring realms on high

In majesty soaring,
O, hark to our cry

Thy pity imploring,
Thou help to the cheerless,
In glory so peerless!

MAGNA PECCATRIX (St. Luke vii. 36).

By the love, which o'er the feet

Of thy God-transfigur'd Son
Dropp'd the team, like balsam sweet,

Spite of ev'ry scornful one;
By the box of ointment rare,

Whence the drops so fragrant fell;
By the locks, whose gentle care

Dried His holy members well--

muller SAMARITANA (St, John iv.).

By the well where Abram erst

Drove his flocks to drink their fill;
By the bucket which the thirst

Of the Saviour served to still;
By the fountain, balm-exhaling,

That from yon bright region flows,
Ever clear and never failing.

As round ev'ry world it goes--

MARIA AEGYPTIACA (Acta Sanctorum).

By the sacred spot immortal,

Where the Lord's remains they plac'd;
By the arm, that from the portal

Drove me back with warning haste;
By my forty years of lowly

Penance in a desert land;
By the farewell greetings holy

That I wrote upon the sand--

THE THREE.

Thou who ne'er thy radiant face

From the greatest sinners hides,
Thou who Thine atoning grace

Through eternity provident,

Let this soul, by virtue stirr'd,

Self-forgetful though when living,
That perceived not that it err'd,

Feel thy mercy, sin forgiving!

UNA POENITENTIUM.
(Once named Margaret, pressing near them.)

Oh radiance-spreading One,

Who equall'd art by none,
In mercy view mine ecstasy!

For he whom erst I loved,

No more by sorrow proved,
Returns at length to me!

BEATIFIED CHILDREN.
(Approaching as they hover round.)

He now in strength of limb

Far doth outweigh us,

And, as we tended him,

So will repay us.
Early removed were we

Far from life's story;
Train'd now himself, will he

Train us in glory.

THE PENITENT, once named Margaret.

Link'd with the noble band of spirits,

Scarce can the new one feel or see
The radiant life he now inherits,

So like that holy band is he.
See how he bursts each bond material,

And parts the olden veil at length,--
In vesture clad of grace ethereal,

Comes in the glow of youthful strength.
Oh, let me guide his steps victorious,

While dazzled by the new-born light.

MATER GLORIOSA.

Come! raise thyself to spheres more glorious,
He'll follow when thou matzoth his sight.

DOCTOR MARINAS.
(Prostrated in adoration.)

O repentant sinful ones,

On that bright face gaze ye,
And, in grateful orisons,

Your blest fortune praise ye!
Be each virtue of the mind

To thy service given!
Virgin, mother, be thou kind!

Goddess, queen of heaven!

CHORUS MYSTICS.

Each thing of mortal birth

Is but a type
What was of feeble worth

Here becomes ripe.
What was a mystery

Here meets the eye;
The ever-womanly

Draws us on high.

     (Finis.)

FROM IPHIGENIA IN TAURIS.

ACT IV. SCENE 5.

SONG OF THE FATES.

YE children of mortals
The deities dread!
The mastery hold they
In hands all-eternal,
And use them, unquestioned,
What manner they like.

Let him fear them doubly,
Whom they have uplifted!
On cliffs and on clouds, oh,
Round tables all-golden,
he seats are made ready.

When rises contention,
The guests are humid downwards
With shame and dishonor

To deep depths of midnight,
And vainly await they,
Bound fast in the darkness,
A just condemnation.

But they remain ever
In firmness unshaken
Round tables all-golden.
On stride they from mountain
To mountain far distant:
From out the abysses'
Dark jaws, the breath rises
Of torment-choked Titans
Up tow'rds them, like incense
In light clouds ascending.

The rulers immortal
Avert from whole peoples
Their blessing-fraught glances,
And shun, in the children,
To trace the once cherish'd,
Still, eloquent features
Their ancestors wore.

Thus chanted the Parae;
The old man, the banish'd,
In gloomy vault lying,
Their song overheareth,
Sons, grandsons remembereth,
And shaketh his head.

FROM GOTZ VON BERLICHINGEN.

ACT II.

LIEBETRAUT plays and sings.

HIS bow and dart bearing,
And torch brightly flaring,

  Dan Cupid on flies;
With victory laden,
To vanquish each maiden

He roguishly tries.

Up! up!

On! on!
His arms rattle loudly,
His wings rustle proudly,
And flames fill his eyes.

Then finds he each bosom

Defenseless and bare;
They gladly receive him

And welcome him there.
The point of his arrows

He lights in the glow;
They clasp him and kiss him

And fondle him so.
He e o! Pap!

FROM EGMONT.

ACT I.

CLARA winds a skein, and sings with Brackenburg.

THE drum gives the signal!

Loud rings the shrill fife!
My love leads his troops on

Full arm'd for the strife,
While his hand grasps his lance
As they proudly advance.

My bosom pants wildly!
My blood hotly flows!
Oh had I a doublet,
A helmet, and hose!

Through the gate with bold footstep

I after him hied,--
Each province, each country

Explored by his side.
The coward foe trembled
 Then rattled our shot:
What bliss e'er resembled

A soldier's glad lot!

ACT III.

CLARA sings.

  Gladness

  And sadness
And pensiveness blending

  Yearning

  And burning
In torment ne'er ending;

Sad unto death,
Proudly soaring above;

Happy alone
Is the soul that doth love!

FROM "WILHELM MEISTER'S APPRENTICESHIP."

BOOK II., CHAP. XIII.

WHO never eat with tears his bread,

Who never through night's heavy hours
Sat weeping on his lonely bed,--

He knows you not, ye heavenly powers!

Through you the paths of life we gain,

Ye let poor mortals go astray,
And then abandon them to pain,--

E'en here the penalty we pay,

WHO gives himself to solitude,

Soon lonely will remain;
Each lives, each loves in joyous mood,

And leaves him to his pain.

Yes! leave me to my grief!
Were solitude's relief

E'er granted me,

Alone I should not be.

A lover steals, on footstep light,

To learn if his love's alone;
Thus o'er me steals, by day and night,

Anguish before unknown,
Thus o'er me steals deep grief.
Ah, when I find relief

Within the tomb so lonely,

Will rest be met with only!

BOOK IV., CHAP. XI.

My grief no mortals know,

Except the yearning!
Alone, a prey to woe,

All pleasure spurning,
Up tow'rds the sky I throw

A gaze discerning.

He who my love can know

Seems ne'er returning;
With strange and fiery glow

My heart is burning.
My grief no mortals know,

Except the yearning!

BOOK V., CHAP. X.

SING no more in mournful tones

Of the loneliness of night;
For 'tis made, ye beauteous ones,

For all social pleasures bright.

As of old to man a wife

As his better half was given,
So the night is half our life,

And the fairest under heaven.

How can ye enjoy the day,

Which obstructs our rapture's tide?
Let it waste itself away;

Worthless 'tis for aught beside.

But when in the darkling hours

From the lamp soft rays are glowing,
And from mouth to mouth sweet showers,

Now of jest, now love, are flowing,--

When the nimble, wanton boy,

Who so wildly spends his days,

Oft amid light sports with joy

O'er some trifling gift delays,Ä

When the nightingale is singing

Strains the lover holds so dear,
Though like sighs and wailings ringing

In the mournful captive's ear,--

With what heart-emotion blest

Do ye hearken to the bell,
Wont of safety and of rest

With twelve solemn strokes to tell!

Therefore in each heavy hour,

Let this precept fill your heart:
O'er each day will sorrow loud,

Rapture ev'ry night impart.

EPILOGUE TO SCHILLER'S "SONG OF THE BELL."

[This fine piece, written originally in 1805, on Schiller's death, was altered and recast by Goethe in 1815, on the occasion of the performance on the stage of the Song of the Bell. Hence the allusion in the last verse.]

> To this city joy reveal it!
>
> Peace as its first signal peal it!
>
> (Song of the Bell--concluding lines.)

AND so it proved! The nation felt, ere long,

That peaceful signal, and, with blessings fraught,
A new-born joy appear'd; in gladsome song

To hail the youthful princely pair we sought;

While in a living, ever-swelling throng

Mingled the crowds from ev'ry region brought,
And on the stage, in festal pomp array'd
The HOMAGE OF THE ARTS * we saw displayed.

(* The title of a lyric piece composed by Schiller in honour of
the marriage of the hereditary Prince of Weimar to the Princess
Maria of Russia, and performed in 1804.)

When, lo! a fearful midnight sound I hear,

That with a dull and mournful echo rings.
And can it be that of our friend so dear

It tells, to whom each wish so fondly clings?
Shall death overcome a life that all revere?

How such a loss to all confusion brings!
How such a parting we must ever rue!
The world is weeping,--shall not we weep too?

He was our own! How social, yet how great

Seem'd in the light of day his noble mind!
How was his nature, pleasing yet sedate,

Now for glad converse joyously incline,
Then swiftly changing, spirit-fraught, elate,

Life's plan with deep-felt meaning it design'd,
Fruitful alike in counsel and in deed!
This have we proved, this tasted, in our need.

He was our own! O may that thought so blest

Overcome the voice of wailing and of woe
He might have sought the Lasting, safe at rest

In harbour, when the tempest ceased to blow.
Meanwhile his mighty spirit onward press'd

Where goodness, beauty, truth, for ever grow;
And in his rear, in shadowy outline, lay

The vulgar, which we all, alas, obey!

Now doth he deck the garden-turret fair

Where the stars' language first illuded his soul,
As secretly yet clearly through the air

On the eterne, the living sense it stole;
And to his own, and our great profit, there

Exchangeth he the seasons as they roll;
Thus nobly doth he vanquish, with renown,
The twilight and the night that weigh us down.

Brighter now glow'd his cheek, and still more bright.

With that unchanging, ever-youthful glow,--
That courage which overcomes, in hard-fought fight,

Sooner or later, ev'ry earthly foe--
That faith which, soaring to the realms of light,

Now boldly Presseth on, now bendeth low,
So that the good may work, wax, thrive amain,
So that the day the noble may attain.

Yet, though so skill'd, of such transcendent worth,

This boarded scaffold doth he not despise;
The fate that on its axis turns the earth

From day to night, here shows he to our eyes,
Raising, through many a work of glorious birth,

Art and the artist's fame up tow'rd the skies.
He fills with blossoms of the noblest strife,
With life itself, this effigy of life.

His giant-step, as ye full surely knew,

Measured the circle of the will and deed,
Each country's changing thoughts and morals too,

The darksome book with clearness could he read;

Yet how he, breathless 'midst his friends so true,

Despaired in sorrow, scarce from pain was freed,--
All this have we, in sadly happy years,
For he was ours, bewailed with feeling tears.

When from the agonizing weight of grief

He raised his eyes upon the world again,
We show'd him how his thoughts might find relief

From the uncertain present's heavy chain,
Gave his fresh-kindled mind a respite brief,

With kindly skill beguiling ev'ry pain,
And e'en at eve, when setting was his sun,
From his wan cheeks a gentle smile we won.

Full early had he read the stern decree,

Sorrow and death to him, alas, were known;
Ofttimes recovering, now departed he,--

Dread tidings, that our hearts had fear'd to own!
Yet his transfigured being now can see

Itself, e'en here on earth, transfigured grown.
What his own age reproved, and deem'd a crime,
Hath been ennobled now by death and time.

And many a soul that with him strove in fight,

And his great merit grudged to recognise,
Now feels the impress of his wondrous might,

And in his magic fetters gladly lies;
E'en to the highest bath he winged his flight,

In close communion link'd with all we prize.
Extol him then! What mortals while they live
But half receive, posterity shall give.

Thus is he left us, who so long ago,--

Ten years, alas, already!--turn'd from earth;
We all, to our great joy, his precepts know,

Oh may the world confess their priceless worth!
In swelling tide tow'rd every region flow

The thoughts that were his own peculiar birth;
He gleams like some departing meteor bright,
Combining, with his own, eternal light.

L'ENVOl.

Now, gentle reader, is our journey ended,

Mute is our minstrel, silent is our song;
Sweet the bard's voice whose strains our course attended,

Pleasant the paths he guided us along.
Now must we part,--Oh word all full of sadness,
Changing to pensive retrospect our gladness!

Reader, farewell! we part perchance for ever,

Scarce may I hope to meet with thee again;
But e'en though fate our fellowship may sever,

Reader, will aught to mark that tie remain?
Yes! there is left one sad sweet bond of union,--
Sorrow at parting links us in communion.

But of the twain, the greater is my sorrow,--

Reader, and why?--Bethink thee of the sun,
How, when he sets, he waiteth for the morrow,

Proudly once more his giant-race to run,--
Yet, e'en when set, a glow behind him leaving,
Gladdening the spirit, which had else been grieving.

Thus mayst thou feel, for thou to GOETHE only

Baldest farewell, nor camest aught for me.

Twofold my parting, leaving me all lonely,--

I now must part from GOETHE and from thee,
Parting at once from comrade and from leader,--
Farewell, great minstrel! farewell, gentle reader!

Hush'd is the harp, its music sunk in slumbers,
Memory alone can waken now its numbers.

www.bookjungle.com *email: sales@bookjungle.com fax: 630-214-0564 mail: Book Jungle PO Box 2226 Champaign, IL 61825*

The Codes Of Hammurabi And Moses
W. W. Davies

QTY

The discovery of the Hammurabi Code is one of the greatest achievements of archaeology, and is of paramount interest, not only to the student of the Bible, but also to all those interested in ancient history...

Religion   **ISBN:** *1-59462-338-4*   **Pages:132**
MSRP $12.95

The Theory of Moral Sentiments
Adam Smith

QTY

This work from 1749. contains original theories of conscience amd moral judgment and it is the foundation for systemof morals.

Philosophy   **ISBN:** *1-59462-777-0*   **Pages:536**
MSRP $19.95

Jessica's First Prayer
Hesba Stretton

QTY

In a screened and secluded corner of one of the many railway-bridges which span the streets of London there could be seen a few years ago, from five o'clock every morning until half past eight, a tidily set-out coffee-stall, consisting of a trestle and board, upon which stood two large tin cans, with a small fire of charcoal burning under each so as to keep the coffee boiling during the early hours of the morning when the work-people were thronging into the city on their way to their daily toil...

Childrens   **ISBN:** *1-59462-373-2*   **Pages:84**
MSRP $9.95

My Life and Work
Henry Ford

QTY

Henry Ford revolutionized the world with his implementation of mass production for the Model T automobile. Gain valuable business insight into his life and work with his own auto-biography... "We have only started on our development of our country we have not as yet, with all our talk of wonderful progress, done more than scratch the surface. The progress has been wonderful enough but..."

Biographies/   **ISBN:** *1-59462-198-5*   **Pages:300**
MSRP $21.95

www.bookjungle.com *email: sales@bookjungle.com fax: 630-214-0564 mail: Book Jungle PO Box 2226 Champaign, IL 61825*

The Art of Cross-Examination
Francis Wellman

QTY

I presume it is the experience of every author, after his first book is published upon an important subject, to be almost overwhelmed with a wealth of ideas and illustrations which could readily have been included in his book, and which to his own mind, at least, seem to make a second edition inevitable. Such certainly was the case with me; and when the first edition had reached its sixth impression in five months, I rejoiced to learn that it seemed to my publishers that the book had met with a sufficiently favorable reception to justify a second and considerably enlarged edition. ..

Reference   ISBN: *1-59462-647-2*   Pages:412   MSRP $19.95

On the Duty of Civil Disobedience
Henry David Thoreau

QTY

Thoreau wrote his famous essay, On the Duty of Civil Disobedience, as a protest against an unjust but popular war and the immoral but popular institution of slave-owning. He did more than write—he declined to pay his taxes, and was hauled off to gaol in consequence. Who can say how much this refusal of his hastened the end of the war and of slavery?

Law   ISBN: *1-59462-747-9*   Pages:48   MSRP $7.45

Dream Psychology Psychoanalysis for Beginners
Sigmund Freud

QTY

Sigmund Freud, born Sigismund Schlomo Freud (May 6, 1856 - September 23, 1939), was a Jewish-Austrian neurologist and psychiatrist who co-founded the psychoanalytic school of psychology. Freud is best known for his theories of the unconscious mind, especially involving the mechanism of repression; his redefinition of sexual desire as mobile and directed towards a wide variety of objects; and his therapeutic techniques, especially his understanding of transference in the therapeutic relationship and the presumed value of dreams as sources of insight into unconscious desires.

Psychology   ISBN: *1-59462-905-6*   Pages:196   MSRP $15.45

The Miracle of Right Thought
Orison Swett Marden

QTY

Believe with all of your heart that you will do what you were made to do. When the mind has once formed the habit of holding cheerful, happy, prosperous pictures, it will not be easy to form the opposite habit. It does not matter how improbable or how far away this realization may see, or how dark the prospects may be, if we visualize them as best we can, as vividly as possible, hold tenaciously to them and vigorously struggle to attain them, they will gradually become actualized, realized in the life. But a desire, a longing without endeavor, a yearning abandoned or held indifferently will vanish without realization.

Self Help   ISBN: *1-59462-644-8*   Pages:360   MSRP $25.45

www.bookjungle.com *email: sales@bookjungle.com fax: 630-214-0564 mail: Book Jungle PO Box 2226 Champaign, IL 61825*

QTY

	Title	ISBN	Price
☐	**The Rosicrucian Cosmo-Conception Mystic Christianity** by *Max Heindel*	ISBN: 1-59462-188-8	$38.95

The Rosicrucian Cosmo-conception is not dogmatic, neither does it appeal to any other authority than the reason of the student. It is: not controversial, but is: sent forth in the, hope that it may help to clear...   New Age/Religion Pages 646

☐	**Abandonment To Divine Providence** by *Jean-Pierre de Caussade*	ISBN: 1-59462-228-0	$25.95

"The Rev. Jean Pierre de Caussade was one of the most remarkable spiritual writers of the Society of Jesus in France in the 18th Century. His death took place at Toulouse in 1751. His works have gone through many editions and have been republished..."   Inspirational/Religion Pages 400

☐	**Mental Chemistry** by *Charles Haanel*	ISBN: 1-59462-192-6	$23.95

Mental Chemistry allows the change of material conditions by combining and appropriately utilizing the power of the mind. Much like applied chemistry creates something new and unique out of careful combinations of chemicals the mastery of mental chemistry...   New Age Pages 354

☐	**The Letters of Robert Browning and Elizabeth Barret Barrett 1845-1846 vol II** by *Robert Browning* and *Elizabeth Barrett*	ISBN: 1-59462-193-4	$35.95

Biographies Pages 596

☐	**Gleanings In Genesis (volume I)** by *Arthur W. Pink*	ISBN: 1-59462-130-6	$27.45

Appropriately has Genesis been termed "the seed plot of the Bible" for in it we have, in germ form, almost all of the great doctrines which are afterwards fully developed in the books of Scripture which follow...   Religion/Inspirational Pages 420

☐	**The Master Key** by *L. W. de Laurence*	ISBN: 1-59462-001-6	$30.95

In no branch of human knowledge has there been a more lively increase of the spirit of research during the past few years than in the study of Psychology, Concentration and Mental Discipline. The requests for authentic lessons in Thought Control, Mental Discipline and...   New Age/Business Pages 422

☐	**The Lesser Key Of Solomon Goetia** by *L. W. de Laurence*	ISBN: 1-59462-092-X	$9.95

This translation of the first book of the "Lemegton" which is now for the first time made accessible to students of Talismanic Magic was done, after careful collation and edition, from numerous Ancient Manuscripts in Hebrew, Latin, and French...   New Age/Occult Pages 92

☐	**Rubaiyat Of Omar Khayyam** by *Edward Fitzgerald*	ISBN: 1-59462-332-5	$13.95

Edward Fitzgerald, whom the world has already learned, in spite of his own efforts to remain within the shadow of anonymity, to look upon as one of the rarest poets of the century, was born at Bredfield, in Suffolk, on the 31st of March, 1809. He was the third son of John Purcell...   Music Pages 172

☐	**Ancient Law** by *Henry Maine*	ISBN: 1-59462-128-4	$29.95

The chief object of the following pages is to indicate some of the earliest ideas of mankind, as they are reflected in Ancient Law, and to point out the relation of those ideas to modern thought.   Religion/History Pages 452

☐	**Far-Away Stories** by *William J. Locke*	ISBN: 1-59462-129-2	$19.45

"Good wine needs no bush, but a collection of mixed vintages does. And this book is just such a collection. Some of the stories I do not want to remain buried for ever in the museum files of dead magazine-numbers an author's not unpardonable vanity..."   Fiction Pages 272

☐	**Life of David Crockett** by *David Crockett*	ISBN: 1-59462-250-7	$27.45

"Colonel David Crockett was one of the most remarkable men of the times in which he lived. Born in humble life, but gifted with a strong will, an indomitable courage, and unremitting perseverance...   Biographies/New Age Pages 424

☐	**Lip-Reading** by *Edward Nitchie*	ISBN: 1-59462-206-X	$25.95

Edward B. Nitchie, founder of the New York School for the Hand of Hearing, now the Nitchie School of Lip-Reading, Inc, wrote "LIP-READING Principles and Practice". The development and perfecting of this meritorious work on lip-reading was an undertaking...   How-to Pages 400

☐	**A Handbook of Suggestive Therapeutics, Applied Hypnotism, Psychic Science** by *Henry Munro*	ISBN: 1-59462-214-0	$24.95

Health/New Age/Health/Self-help Pages 376

☐	**A Doll's House: and Two Other Plays** by *Henrik Ibsen*	ISBN: 1-59462-112-8	$19.95

Henrik Ibsen created this classic when in revolutionary 1848 Rome. Introducing some striking concepts in playwriting for the realist genre, this play has been studied the world over.   Fiction/Classics/Plays 308

☐	**The Light of Asia** by *sir Edwin Arnold*	ISBN: 1-59462-204-3	$13.95

In this poetic masterpiece, Edwin Arnold describes the life and teachings of Buddha. The man who was to become known as Buddha to the world was born as Prince Gautama of India but he rejected the worldly riches and abandoned the reigns of power when...   Religion/History/Biographies Pages 170

☐	**The Complete Works of Guy de Maupassant** by *Guy de Maupassant*	ISBN: 1-59462-157-8	$16.95

"For days and days, nights and nights, I had dreamed of that first kiss which was to consecrate our engagement, and I knew not on what spot I should put my lips..."   Fiction/Classics Pages 240

☐	**The Art of Cross-Examination** by *Francis L. Wellman*	ISBN: 1-59462-309-0	$26.95

Written by a renowned trial lawyer, Wellman imparts his experience and uses case studies to explain how to use psychology to extract desired information through questioning.   How-to/Science/Reference Pages 408

☐	**Answered or Unanswered?** by *Louisa Vaughan*	ISBN: 1-59462-248-5	$10.95

Miracles of Faith in China   Religion Pages 112

☐	**The Edinburgh Lectures on Mental Science (1909)** by *Thomas*	ISBN: 1-59462-008-3	$11.95

This book contains the substance of a course of lectures recently given by the writer in the Queen Street Hall, Edinburgh. Its purpose is to indicate the Natural Principles governing the relation between Mental Action and Material Conditions...   New Age/Psychology Pages 148

☐	**Ayesha** by *H. Rider Haggard*	ISBN: 1-59462-301-5	$24.95

Verily and indeed it is the unexpected that happens! Probably if there was one person upon the earth from whom the Editor of this, and of a certain previous history, did not expect to hear again...   Classics Pages 380

☐	**Ayala's Angel** by *Anthony Trollope*	ISBN: 1-59462-352-X	$29.95

The two girls were both pretty, but Lucy who was twenty-one who supposed to be simple and comparatively unattractive, whereas Ayala was credited, as her Bomb what romantic name might show, with poetic charm and a taste for romance. Ayala when her father died was nineteen...   Fiction Pages 484

☐	**The American Commonwealth** by *James Bryce*	ISBN: 1-59462-286-8	$34.45

An interpretation of American democratic political theory. It examines political mechanics and society from the perspective of Scotsman James Bryce   Politics Pages 572

☐	**Stories of the Pilgrims** by *Margaret P. Pumphrey*	ISBN: 1-59462-116-0	$17.95

This book explores pilgrims religious oppression in England as well as their escape to Holland and eventual crossing to America on the Mayflower, and their early days in New England...   History Pages 268

www.bookjungle.com email: sales@bookjungle.com fax: 630-214-0564 mail: Book Jungle PO Box 2226 Champaign, IL 61825

			QTY
The Fasting Cure by *Sinclair Upton*	ISBN: *1-59462-222-1*	**$13.95**	
In the Cosmopolitan Magazine for May, 1910, and in the Contemporary Review (London) for April, 1910, I published an article dealing with my experiences in fasting. I have written a great many magazine articles, but never one which attracted so much attention... *New Age/Self Help/Health Pages 164*			
Hebrew Astrology by *Sepharial*	ISBN: *1-59462-308-2*	**$13.45**	
In these days of advanced thinking it is a matter of common observation that we have left many of the old landmarks behind and that we are now pressing forward to greater heights and to a wider horizon than that which represented the mind-content of our progenitors... *Astrology Pages 144*			
Thought Vibration or The Law of Attraction in the Thought World by *William Walker Atkinson*	ISBN: *1-59462-127-6*	**$12.95**	
	Psychology/Religion Pages 144		
Optimism by *Helen Keller*	ISBN: *1-59462-108-X*	**$15.95**	
Helen Keller was blind, deaf, and mute since 19 months old, yet famously learned how to overcome these handicaps, communicate with the world, and spread her lectures promoting optimism. An inspiring read for everyone... *Biographies/Inspirational Pages 84*			
Sara Crewe by *Frances Burnett*	ISBN: *1-59462-360-0*	**$9.45**	
In the first place, Miss Minchin lived in London. Her home was a large, dull, tall one, in a large, dull square, where all the houses were alike, and all the sparrows were alike, and where all the door-knockers made the same heavy sound... *Childrens/Classic Pages 88*			
The Autobiography of Benjamin Franklin by *Benjamin Franklin*	ISBN: *1-59462-135-7*	**$24.95**	
The Autobiography of Benjamin Franklin has probably been more extensively read than any other American historical work, and no other book of its kind has had such ups and downs of fortune. Franklin lived for many years in England, where he was agent... *Biographies/History Pages 332*			

Name	
Email	
Telephone	
Address	
City, State ZIP	

☐ Credit Card   ☐ Check / Money Order

Credit Card Number	
Expiration Date	
Signature	

Please Mail to: Book Jungle
PO Box 2226
Champaign, IL 61825
or Fax to: 630-214-0564

ORDERING INFORMATION

web: www.bookjungle.com
email: sales@bookjungle.com
fax: 630-214-0564
mail: Book Jungle PO Box 2226 Champaign, IL 61825
or PayPal to sales@bookjungle.com

Please contact us for bulk discounts

DIRECT-ORDER TERMS

20% Discount if You Order Two or More Books
Free Domestic Shipping!
Accepted: Master Card, Visa, Discover, American Express

www.ingramcontent.com/pod-product-compliance
Lightning Source LLC
Chambersburg PA
CBHW082143230426
43672CB00015B/2834